The Battle for
NATURAL
RESOURCES

The Battle for
NATURAL
RESOURCES

Congressional Quarterly Inc.
1414 22nd Street N.W.
Washington, D.C. 20037

Congressional Quarterly Inc.

Congressional Quarterly Inc., an editorial research service and publishing company, serves clients in the fields of news, education, business, and government. It combines specific coverage of Congress, government, and politics by Congressional Quarterly with the more general subject range of an affiliated service, Editorial Research Reports.

Congressional Quarterly publishes the *Congressional Quarterly Weekly Report* and a variety of books, including college political science textbooks under the CQ Press imprint and public affairs paperbacks designed as timely reports to keep journalists, scholars, and the public abreast of developing issues and events. CQ also publishes information directories and reference books on the federal government, national elections, and politics, including the *Guide to Congress,* the *Guide to the U.S. Supreme Court,* the *Guide to U.S. Elections,* and *Politics in America.* The *CQ Almanac,* a compendium of legislation for one session of Congress, is published each year. *Congress and the Nation,* a record of government for a presidential term, is published every four years.

CQ publishes *The Congressional Monitor,* a daily report on current and future activities of congressional committees, and several newsletters including *Congressional Insight,* a weekly analysis of congressional action, and *Campaign Practices Reports,* a semimonthly update on campaign laws.

CQ conducts seminars and conferences on Congress, the legislative process, the federal budget, national elections and politics, and other current issues. CQ Direct Research is a consulting service that performs contract research and maintains a reference library and query desk for clients.

Library of Congress Cataloging in Publication Data

Main entry under title:

The Battle for natural resources

    Bibliography: p.
    Includes index.
    1. Natural resources — Government policy — United States. 2. Conservation of natural resources — Government policy — United States. I. Congressional Quarterly, inc.

HC103.7.B325 1983	333.7'0973	83-20939

ISBN 0-87187-263-3

Author: Tom Arrandale
Editor: Nancy Lammers
Bibliographer: Kathy Goodwin
Designer: Mary L. McNeil
Cover and Graphics: Robert Redding
Indexer: Elizabeth Furbush
Photo Credits: Photofile International Ltd. (cover); p. xiv, Library of Congress; p. 14, Library of Congress; p. 36, National Park Service; p. 78, National Coal Association; p. 102, Cities Service Co.; p. 130, U.S. Forest Service; p. 154, U.S. Forest Service; p. 170, American Mining Congress; p. 184, Library of Congress.

Table of Contents

Tables and Maps

PREFACE

Raw and rough-hewn, southern Wyoming's Red Desert is a stern land of brown-gold draws and ridges studded by gray-green sagebrush. Wild stallions still fight for dominion over free-roaming bands of mares and colts. Pronghorn antelope skim gracefully across the treeless plains, and does drop their fawns in late spring under cover of low-growing brush and cactus. Coyotes greet the dawn with piercing cries that break a wild and lonely stillness.

The federally owned desert cannot match the sublime beauty of Yellowstone, Yosemite, the Grand Tetons, or the Grand Canyon; nor can it offer the soothing solitude of towering Douglas fir forests, cool Rocky Mountain meadows, fast-running Sierra Nevada streams, or isolated Appalachian refuges. Yet the Red Desert — like other similar public lands all over the nation — will be a battleground for a growing national struggle over natural resources.

America is still a spacious country. For all its industrial might, the United States never has filled its 2.3 billion-acre expanse with farms and factories and cities. From the Rocky Mountains west to the Pacific Ocean, all across Alaska's vast empty reaches, and in forests from Maine to Florida, the federally owned lands preserve the boundless distance and the abundant promise that always have drawn men and women to the American frontiers.

For four centuries, historian Roderick Nash observes, the North American wilderness has been the basic ingredient from which Americans fashioned their civilization. From the time Spanish colonists first moved up the Rio Grande into New Mexico in 1598, Americans have been torn by conflicting impulses to subdue the land or to revere it for its natural splendor. That historic tension continues, growing more serious as the nation's population approaches 250 million and its natural resources become more precious.

President Ronald Reagan's secretary of the interior, James G. Watt, during two-and-one-half years in charge of the government's principal land managing department, drew attention as never before to the constant conflict in federal resource policy between development and preservation. Watt's aggressive campaign to expand federal coal, offshore oil and gas, and onshore petroleum leasing stirred deep feelings that divide environmentalists from ranchers, miners, loggers, and others who earn their livelihoods by using the public lands.

Watt's October 1983 resignation may calm the acrimony of public land policy debates. But controversy inevitably will continue, as federal land managers out in the field try to balance the conflicting demands. Tough decisions remain to be made on leasing federally owned coal in New Mexico's San Juan Basin and the Powder River Basin of Wyoming and Montana. The Interior Department still must determine whether to open untouched Outer Continental Shelf (OCS) offshore waters to oil and gas drilling platforms. Congress will continue to grapple with requests to expand federally protected wilderness areas, while the U.S. Forest Service will be under continuing pressure to accelerate federal timber harvests. The Interior Department's Bureau of Land Management also must come to grips with the long-term impact of livestock grazing on public rangelands.

Even in places such as the Red Desert that previously had been passed up by the nation's economic development, conflicts over natural resource use are intensifying. Early emigrants on the Oregon Trail skirted north of the Red Desert to follow the Sweetwater River and cross the Continental Divide through South Pass on their way to the Pacific. Modern-day travelers speed through the desert's southern reaches on Interstate 80 that parallels the original transcontinental railroad route. Ranchers in 1983 turn cattle out to graze the Red Desert's sparse brush and grasses, and herders still live in traditional barrel-shaped sheepherders' wagons as they tend their milling bands. Mining-claim stakes now dot the landscape, marking off rich uranium deposits; and energy companies are pressing the government to lease coal there for strip-mining operations. Already power lines, standing etched against the bold blue Wyoming sky, stretch over the desert to reach existing mines. The Interior Department itself has proposed building fences across the wide-open spaces to keep ranchers' cattle inside pastures.

Some argue that coal mining or uranium production is the best use of the Red Desert, providing fuel and jobs to benefit the entire nation. Others contend that preserving the country's remaining landscapes should be an equal, if not priority, objective. The U.S. government, through the Interior Department and the U.S. Forest Service, must try to strike that balance in the Red Desert and other national parks, forests, wildlife refuges, and rangelands. How the government manages its lands — and the coal, oil shale, timber, water, and other resources they hold — may turn out to be one of its most fateful domestic responsibilities.

This book examines crucial federal land management conflicts in the nation's resource battles. It begins by tracing the shift away from the 19th century policy of granting, giving, or selling lands to homesteaders, railroads, and miners toward the modern-day belief in preserving wilderness and conserving public resources through permanent government control. Subsequent chapters outline specific controversies over leasing federal coal, oil and gas, and other energy reserves; selling timber from national forests; controlling grazing by ranchers' livestock on federally owned rangelands; and opening the public lands for prospecting and mining. The book concludes by assessing the building tensions between regions within the United States over federal policies on water, public lands, and their resources.

A newcomer to the West can only stand in awe of the sheer size and diversity of the region's federally owned lands and resources. This book is possible only because long-time Westerners were generous in sharing advice and knowledge. Ranchers, opening their homes to a stranger, expressed a special feeling for the public lands handed down from fathers and grandfathers. Environmentalists and resource management professors provided invaluable insights. Forest Service and Bureau of Land Management officials, both past and present, patiently explained agency policies and objectives. Special thanks are due E. Lavelle Thompson, U.S. Forest Service, retired, a forester from an Idaho ranching family, who taught a tenderfoot the lay of the land and took him to chase wild horses.

This book is dedicated to the memory of Lee J. Thronson (1914-1983), an oilman who explored public lands, not just for their wealth, but also for their adventure and grandeur.

Tom Arrandale
October 1983

The Battle for
NATURAL
RESOURCES

A Rocky Mountain stream cuts through terrain typical of western public lands open for multiple uses; this photograph was taken in Colorado's Ouray County, about half of which is national forest or Bureau of Land Management lands.

Chapter 1

A RICH HERITAGE
OF LAND AND RESOURCES

The lands make a splendid legacy. They sweep across 700 million acres, a third of the entire country. They give all Americans an immeasurable heritage of wilderness and natural resources.

They are public lands, owned by the United States government. Their rugged mountains and deserts preserve some of the last pristine reaches left in North America. Their wide-open spaces guard much of the nation's timber, energy, minerals, water, and other natural wealth. As the United States enters its third century, the federally owned lands offer Americans what may be a final chance to use the country's natural endowment wisely.

For 200 years, the still-young nation has forged its character on the vast public domain that formed its western frontiers. For decades to come, the country will shape its destiny by what it chooses to do with the public lands that still sprawl through most of the West, Alaska, and eastern and southern forests.

"The federal lands always have provided the arena in which we Americans have struggled to fulfill our dreams," D. Michael Harvey, chief Democratic counsel to the Senate Energy and Natural Resources Committee, has commented. "What we do with them tells a great deal about what we are — what we care for — and what is to become of us as a nation." [1]

The frontier closed almost a century ago, after many of the best lands had been claimed and homesteaded. Congress and presidents since then have set aside remaining western lands for continued federal government control as national parks, forests, wilderness, wildlife refuges, and public rangelands. The government since the Depression years has been buying up lands, mainly eastern forests and Great Plains grasslands, that settlers once logged or plowed but eventually abandoned. Thirty years ago, moreover, Congress greatly expanded the federal estate by taking possession of the submerged sea-bed floor three miles beyond the U.S. coastlines.

Americans at the end of 1983 still were weighing what to do with those immense holdings of land and resources. The decisions, when finally made, will influence the nation's economic course and determine where wild lands will be allowed to flourish. The discussions will pose thorny political questions that, in Arizona Gov. Bruce Babbitt's words, "go to the heart of our federalist system." [2] By the turn of the century, Americans will face some fateful — and in some cases irreversible — choices about which public resources to commit to use and which wild lands to save unimpaired for their children.

Taken together, federal lands are large and varied enough to allow for both development and preservation. Some U.S. holdings, notably national parks and congressionally protected wilderness areas, already have been placed off limits to resource projects. Most federal lands, including national forests and public lands in the West and Alaska, generally have been kept open for multiple uses, both economic and aesthetic. Federal land agencies, chiefly the Interior Department and the Agriculture Department's Forest Service, are charged with the difficult task of making federal resources available without ruining fragile lands that would take centuries to recover.

James G. Watt, President Ronald Reagan's combative secretary of the interior, escalated the battle over public lands policy in the early 1980s by pushing all-out resource development. Watt's plans, some stymied by Congress, crystallized historic tensions in federal land management between preserving unspoiled wilderness and making resources available for public use. The Reagan administration's stance favoring development and the responding outcry from environmentalists intensified political conflicts that have produced wide swings in federal land management policy between economic and environmental objectives. As a result of the long-standing conflict, Interior Department economist Robert H. Nelson concluded in a 1981 study, the federal lands "may be producing less commodity output and less environmental 'output' than is possible." [3]

An Abundant and Varied Domain

Federal lands sprawl over the nation's last frontiers. They stretch away, mile after mile, across Alaska and the western mountains, plains,

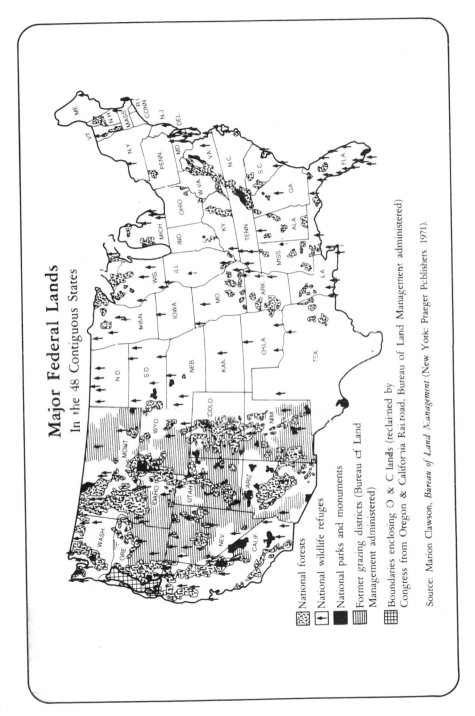

Major Federal Lands
In the 48 Contiguous States

National forests

National wildlife refuges

National parks and monuments

Former grazing districts (Bureau of Land Management administered)

Boundaries enclosing O & C lands (reclaimed by Congress from Oregon & California Railroad, Bureau of Land Management administered)

Source: Marion Clawson, *Bureau of Land Management* (New York: Praeger Publishers, 1971).

and deserts. "No other nation on earth has been graced with so profound a legacy of wilderness," T. H. Watkins, senior editor of *American Heritage* magazine, has written.[4]

In the East and South, federal lands are mostly cutover forests and farmlands that the government bought back from private owners. In the West, too, some U.S. holdings lie in small, scattered tracts, surrounded by state and privately owned lands, even by the neon glitter of Las Vegas and other cities. But taken together, including petroleum-rich offshore lands, the federal domain amounts to a vast national commons open to all Americans.

The Rocky Mountains' lofty ranges and the Sierra Nevada's snow-covered peaks are among the most familiar of federal lands. The Grand Canyon's rock-rimmed gorge also was carved into present-day public lands. Mount Denali, North America's tallest peak, towers from federally owned lands in Alaska. Death Valley, the continent's lowest depression, sinks into federally owned California desert.

Federal lands range from Alaska's frigid Arctic Coast to the tropical Straits of Florida. They preserve a natural cross-section from an expansive continent, a bewildering array of landforms and ecosystems created by climate and geology.

The Great Basin sagebrush plains in Nevada, eastern Oregon, Idaho, and Utah are mostly federal lands, as are many of the boundless shortgrass prairies rolling up to western mountains. Old-growth stands of redwoods and Douglas fir tower from national forests along the Pacific slope. Second-growth pine and hardwood trees cover national forests in the Ozarks, along the Appalachian chain, and on the southeastern Coastal Plain and Piedmont. Federal lands take in dank Deep South swamps and bone-dry southwestern deserts. They include Alaskan tundra and the red and brown canyonlands eroded by wind and water into the Colorado Plateau.

Many of the nation's major river systems — the Mississippi, Ohio, Tennessee, Arkansas, Missouri, Colorado, Columbia, Connecticut, and even the Potomac — rise from headwaters in national forests. In the West virtually all the streamflow into the region's few large rivers comes from federally owned lands that line much of the river routes from mountains to sea.

Most of North America's distinctive wildlife now rely on federally owned lands for survival. Bald eagles soar over Alaska's national parks and wildlife refuges. Grizzly bears roam the Glacier and Yellowstone national parks. Cougars prowl the western mountains and deserts; bighorn sheep scale rocky heights. Prairie falcons swooping over Snake River canyons, caribou migrating across unbroken Alaskan terrain, elk and mule deer browsing Rocky Mountain forests, pronghorn antelope scurrying across unfenced prairies, wild horses and burros roaming the open rangelands — even a few scattered buffalo — find the wild habitat they need mostly on public lands.

For a nation of 200 million people, most living in crowded cities and suburbs, the wild and spacious quality of the federal lands may be their primary value. For Westerners, Babbitt has noted, "the open spaces and scenic beauty preserved in national parks and wilderness areas, open ranges and national forests are an integral part of life...." [5]

A Wealth of Natural Resources

But, as a national storehouse of natural resources, federal lands hold other kinds of wealth. As privately owned reserves become depleted — and foreign supplies less dependable — the United States increasingly is turning to federally owned raw materials to keep its economy running.

The U.S. government owns these resources by accident of history and quirk of geology. As the 19th-century land rush rolled west, the government disposed of the most fertile flatlands, easily cut timber, and richest veins of gold and silver. Settlers passed up the mountain slopes, rangelands, and deserts whose resources at the time were unexplored or held little value.

When the frontier closed the government still held lands that turned out to bear large reserves of raw materials, especially timber and energy minerals, now in demand. In addition the government retained the rights to minerals beneath the 65 million acres of land that it turned over to private owners. These holdings amount to a resources stockpile, which the nation only recently has begun to exploit.

More than any other contemporary event, the 1973 Arab oil embargo confirmed the importance of federally owned resources. Foreign crude oil prices skyrocketed for almost a decade thereafter, and the nation searched for alternative energy sources. The government inevitably turned its attention to the vast energy reserves — coal, oil shale, petroleum, and other forms — in the West, Alaska, and offshore coastal waters.

Federal lands hold roughly one-quarter of the nation's coal, and four-fifths of its huge oil-shale deposits. They contain roughly half of

U.S. uranium deposits and naturally occurring geothermal steam and hot-water pools that can be used to generate electric power. Half of the nation's estimated oil and gas reserves, including the outer continental shelf deposits, lie under federally owned reserves.

Demand for these resources, especially for still-unproved synthetic fuels from coal and oil shale, fell off in the early 1980s as worldwide energy use declined and the Organization of Petroleum Exporting Countries (OPEC) scaled down its crude oil prices. In the long run, however, federal energy reserves will be critical as the nation balances energy supplies with the demands of its industrial economy. As Harvey noted before a Senate committee workshop on federal lands in 1982: "Management of these public resources is arguably the most important energy policy responsibility of the federal government." [6]

Throughout U.S. history, federal lands have provided the bulk of new discoveries that supplied American industry and commerce with gold, silver, copper, lead, and other useful metals. Public lands still are considered by many as the best prospects for further finds of heavily used minerals — possibly including cobalt, titanium, molybdenum, and other "strategic minerals" needed for sophisticated technology and military weaponry. Controversy has been growing over whether the government needs to open federal lands to stepped-up exploration for mineral deposits to head off a potential crisis should foreign supplies be interrupted.

Minerals are the most valuable government-owned resources, because deposits cannot be replenished once mined. But public lands also provide plentiful renewable resources, in timber and rangeland grasses, that if properly managed are continuously productive.

Federal lands have become increasingly important since World War II in supplying timber for housing construction and other uses. National forests already produce one-fifth of the nation's yearly timber cut and hold half of its inventory of softwood sawtimber. Other public lands, while generally less productive, include prime timberland on Oregon's Pacific slope. Federal timber will assume greater importance in upcoming decades as privately held standing timber becomes exhausted.

Most federal lands are rangelands, semiarid country that grows little more than cactus, brush, and tough, scrawny grasses. That vegetation has little value, at least compared with other federally owned commodities, except as livestock forage. In the West, however, public rangelands provide the economic base for a ranching industry that contributes much to the region's distinctive way of life. Western ranchers graze only 4 percent of U.S. beef cattle and 28 percent of domestic sheep on public rangelands. These are slight contributions to total livestock production that now centers on private lands in Texas, the Great Plains states, and the lush pastures of Florida and Louisiana. But ranching still dominates many western regions, and grazing on federal lands still is essential for self-reliant ranching families who have used public ranges for three generations as if the lands were their own.

Battles for Public Resources

Early ranchers fought bloody range wars for dominion on public grasslands. The open range has been divided and fenced for 50 years; but battles continue, all over the West, for control over federal lands and resources. Modern-day range wars are fought in Congress, the courts, and federal land agencies. The conflicts may be less violent, but the stakes have risen as more Americans recognize the many values of lands in which they are part owners.

Congress holds broad constitutional power to manage federal lands for national purposes. That authority enhances the central government's potential control over economic and social development, especially in regions where U.S. holdings are concentrated.

But the government's discretion over public lands has been seriously eroded. Instead of developing public resources itself, the government leases some for private extraction and makes others virtually available for the taking. Over the years ranchers, miners, loggers, outdoorsmen, environmentalists, and state and local governments have staked firm claims — some enforceable in court — for access to the federal domain and its benefits.

The result has been constant skirmishing among competing public land users. The fighting has been most bitter where newly aroused national interests — in preserving federal wilderness, for instance, or in strip mining federal coal — collide with the interests of Westerners who have used public lands all their lives with little government interference.

Demands on federal lands have multiplied since World War II. Americans moved west in growing numbers, seeking economic opportunity and better lives in the Rocky Mountain West and beyond. Timber demand accelerated with the postwar housing boom, and the much-debated energy "crisis" of the 1970s set the stage for vigorous growth in western resource industries. At the same time, conservationist pressures

7

grew as Americans motored west to view the region's scenic wonders and use them for recreational purposes. An awakening environment movement focused national attention on western lands where the nation still had time to head off degradation. These conflicting forces caught federal land managers in the political cross fire.

Congress responded by tightening its grip over public lands and resources. It enlarged the national park system, expanded wildlife refuges, and protected roadless wilderness. It applied new federal environmental laws to public land, including measures that protected endangered species, curbed air and water pollution, and required that federal agencies prepare environmental impact statements before taking major actions. Congress followed up in the mid-1970s with landmark laws that strengthened Interior Department and U.S. Forest Service authority to manage most federal lands for both environmental values and commercial ventures.

Those laws declared, presumably once and for all, that the government would retain ownership of most of its lands and devote them to nationally determined purposes. They directed the Forest Service and Interior Department's Bureau of Land Management (BLM) to draw up long-term plans for multiple-use management of the national forests and public rangelands. They confirmed those agencies' mandates to administer the federal lands by scientific methods to produce lasting benefits for as many Americans as possible. But a decade later it was far from clear that the government could manage its lands either efficiently or fairly.

Congress reserved for itself authority to designate special-purpose federal lands by creating national parks, wildlife refuges, and wilderness preserves, but it refused to set priorities for the multiple-use lands in national forests and BLM-managed holdings. Instead it directed the agencies to draw up comprehensive land-use plans, in consultation with the public. The agencies have responded with costly planning programs that attempt to zone huge land areas for grazing, timber, minerals, recreation, wilderness, wildlife preservation, and other pursuits.

The early results were more confusing than conclusive. Government professionals struggled to come up with ways to balance data on economic demand with aesthetic values that cannot be quantified. The complex planning procedures provided both environmental and commercial public land interests ample grounds for legal challenges to agency decisions. The legal maneuvering has slowed, and at times defeated, efforts to resolve public land conflicts.

Congress already had put basic public land policies into place when President Jimmy Carter took office in 1977. Carter's secretary of the interior, former Idaho Gov. Cecil D. Andrus, and other resource agency officials pursued environmental policies that they contended would correct longstanding abuse of public lands. But those plans, including a controversial hit list of federal water development projects that Carter wanted to cancel, fed mushrooming resentment in the West against changing federal resource policies.

That anger broke out in the heralded "Sagebrush Rebellion" that demanded the government turn most of its western lands over to the states in which they lie. The revolt quickly ebbed, partly because many Westerners supported continued federal management. But its sentiments contributed to Reagan's broad western support in his 1980 landslide electoral college victory over Carter.

Watt's philosophy, which encouraged development, tempered the West's fury, but it outraged environmental groups and powerful members of Congress. His stance sparked controversies over public land management and threatened to produce a backlash that would return U.S. resource policy to a preservationist course.

The political clashes confused federal land agency planning and made resource policy unpredictable. Conflicting congressional mandates for scientific planning and public participation vastly complicated the process by which federal agencies made land-use decisions. Interior Department economist Nelson concluded in a 1981 address that "anyone looking for evidence of the wisdom of American political institutions would do well to look elsewhere than the public lands." [7]

Continuing Public Land Issues

The Interior Department, the government's principal resource management agency, holds far-flung responsibility for national parks, wildlife refuges, rangelands, coal and oil-shale reserves, onshore and offshore oil and gas, other mineral deposits, campgrounds, picnic grounds, historic sites, and Indian reservations. Along with Agriculture's Forest Service, Interior touches the daily lives of Americans more directly than any federal agency except the Internal Revenue Service. The government's land policies, applied by forest and park rangers, wildlife specialists, rangeland conservationists, and other officials who manage public resources throughout the country, determine where, when, and how the American people can use public resources for private enjoyment or profit.

Through the 1970s environmentalists looked to the secretary of the interior as what Rep. Morris K. Udall, D-Ariz., called "the nation's conservationist. This is the guy who's guardian of the resources, this is the man who gets up in the morning and asks what he can do to preserve the wilderness and timber and the water supplies and the watershed and the endangered species and so on." [8] Yet Watt, before the end of the Reagan administration's third year, had shifted drastically the department's objectives away from conservation toward promoting rapid development of federally owned resources for economic use.

"These public lands remain today among our greatest untapped assets," Watt declared in 1982 Senate testimony.[9] He accelerated Interior plans to lease federally owned coal as well as offshore oil and gas, and he also proposed opening the country's western wilderness lands for petroleum and mineral exploration. He slowed land purchases to expand the national park system, and he pushed ahead with plans to sell 2.5 million acres of public lands in small, hard-to-manage tracts. "The secretary's feeling is that the federal government should not be the owner of land and resources," Frank Gregg, who served as BLM director under Andrus, contended in 1983.[10]

Environmental group leaders — and conservation-minded congressional leaders such as Udall — protested Watt's policies. Both the House and Senate voted in 1983 to suspend temporarily Interior coal-lease sales pending a special study commission's review of department procedures. Economists and environmentalists contended that these procedures turned federally owned resources over for private production at far less than their long-term market value.

Influential members of Congress called for Watt's resignation after the secretary joked in public that the coal-leasing commission members included "a black . . . a woman, two Jews, and a cripple." Watt's ill-advised comments and widely criticized policies made him the most visible interior secretary in decades. As the 1984 elections approached Republicans increasingly withdrew their support of him, and on Oct. 9, 1983, Watt submitted his resignation to President Reagan. Reagan nominated William P. Clark, his national security advisor, to the Interior post.

Despite continuous controversy, "most of what this secretary of the interior set out to do . . . has been established in policy," Garrey E.

Carruthers, Watt's assistant secretary for land and water resources, declared in 1983.[11] But those policies will continue to generate heated disputes as federal land managers apply them to specific public resource decisions on federal lands around the country. Former Vice President Walter F. Mondale, a leading candidate for the 1984 Democratic presidential nomination, vowed to "place the issues of conservation and the environment up front as central issues in this campaign." If elected president, Mondale told the National Wildlife Federation's 1983 annual meeting, "I would protect public lands and keep them open to all Americans."[12]

But managing federal lands and resources can only grow more difficult in future years. Watt's policies, by committing federal resources for development, may limit his successors' discretion to dedicate lands to other purposes. Environmental groups, angered by Watt's belligerent stance, were likely to press the department even harder for more restrictive controls on public land activities. And, while the Sagebrush Rebellion has been defused, western governors and members of Congress were certain to continue demanding that Congress and federal land managers grant them a role in setting policies for federally owned lands that make up 60 percent of the region. In the West federal land policy raises "critical concerns that have to be addressed that are not a problem in Rhode Island," U.S. Rep. Larry E. Craig, R-Idaho, observed.[13]

Wise public land policies will be essential. As resource values climbed, public land management became big business for the government. Federal agencies took in $2.2 billion from national forests and public lands in 1981, chiefly by leasing minerals and selling federal timber. Offshore oil and gas revenues added another $12 billion. Resources for the Future economist Marion Clawson, a former BLM director, estimated in 1982 that national forests and BLM-managed lands alone were worth roughly $500 billion.[14] These assets will play important, sometimes critical, roles as the nation confronts serious economic and social problems in the future.

"Although they are rarely recognized as such, many of the most pressing domestic policy issues the nation currently faces are also public lands issues. . . ," Harvey has commented.[15] What the government does with the public lands will determine, at least in part, whether the nation will have sufficient energy supplies. Federal land policy also will determine whether the nation produces sufficient timber to build its houses and key minerals to keep industry running. Public land management, along with federal water policies, will help decide where the nation grows its food and fiber and how it supplies water for homes and factories.

Market forces ultimately will determine when federal resources actually are developed. But under the existing federal lands system, government policy sets the terms for resource development projects, including requirements for protecting the surrounding environment. For some resources, probably timber and possibly coal, federal reserves are large enough that the government's decisions on how much to make available may significantly alter prices for private as well as public resources.

In the process, federal resource policies will steer national economic growth — and alter how wealth is shared among different parts of the country. Regional struggles over resource policy have begun already, notably in a continuing controversy over severance taxes that western states levy on production of federally owned coal. A proposal by midwestern and eastern congressional delegations to limit severance taxes on western coal "is only round one in what is a long-term war," Utah Gov. Scott Matheson, D, commented in 1980.

Federal land policies will have other consequences. They will determine where Americans go for recreation and outdoor solitude, where the open ranges remain, where the American wilderness endures, and where the bald eagle, grizzly bear, and other North American wildlife survive in the 21st century.

"In the future of federal land and resources law," legal scholars George Cameron Coggins and Charles F. Wilkinson wrote, "lies a good part of the nation's future welfare." [16]

Notes

1. D. Michael Harvey, "Public Lands: Ownership — By Whom and for What? A Conservative View," Senate Energy and Natural Resources Committee Workshop on Land Protection and Management, June 1982, 97th Cong., 2d sess., 176.
2. Bruce Babbitt, "Federalism and the Environment: An Intergovernmental Perspective of the Sagebrush Rebellion," *Environmental Law,* 12 (1982): 847.
3. Robert H. Nelson, "The Public Lands," in *Current Issues in Natural Resource Policy,* ed. Paul R. Portney (Washington, D.C.: Resources for the Future, 1982), 57.
4. T. H. Watkins, "Lands of My Youth, Lands of My Heart," *The Living Wilderness,* Summer 1981, 17.
5. Testimony before the Senate Energy and Natural Resources Committee, May 17, 1982, 97th Cong., 2d. sess.
6. Harvey, "Public Lands," 185.

7. Robert H. Nelson, "Making Sense of the Sagebrush Rebellion: A Long Term Strategy for the Public Lands" (Paper prepared for Association for Public Policy Analysis and Management Conference, Washington, D.C., Oct. 23-25, 1981).
8. "Inside Interior: An Abrupt Turn," *Sports Illustrated*, Sept. 26, 1983, 75.
9. Testimony before the Senate Energy and Natural Resources Committee, Subcommittee on Energy and Mineral Resources, June 29, 1983, 98th Cong., 1st sess.
10. Frank Gregg, director of the University of Arizona School of Natural Resources and former director of the Bureau of Land Management, July 8, 1983, telephone interview with author.
11. Garrey E. Carruthers, assistant secretary of the interior for land and water resources, Sept. 7, 1983, interview with author.
12. Walter F. Mondale, D, former vice president of the United States (Speech before the annual meeting of the National Wildlife Federation, Albuquerque, N.M., March 19, 1983).
13. U.S. Rep. Larry E. Craig, R-Idaho, July 28, 1983, telephone interview with author.
14. Marion Clawson, "Alternative Strategies for the Federal Lands," Senate Energy and Natural Resources Committee Workshop on Land Protection and Management, June 1982, 97th Cong., 2d sess., 202.
15. Harvey, "Public Lands," 184.
16. George Cameron Coggins and Charles F. Wilkinson, *Federal Public Land and Resources Law* (Mineola, N.Y.: Foundation Press, 1981), xxviii.

More than 250 million acres of public land were granted to citizens under 19th century homesteading laws designed to turn plots over to settlers who cultivated them. These Nebraskans posed, in about 1887, before their sod house.

Chapter 2

AMERICA'S LAND EMPIRE:
A NATURAL RESOURCE STOREHOUSE

"Ours has been peculiarly the story of man and land, man and the forests, man and the plains, man and water, man and resources."

—John F. Kennedy[1]

Congress took title to the first public lands in 1782, before the American Revolution had ended. In the century that followed, the U.S. government created a mighty nation as it expanded an empire of federal lands that stretched across North America.

The government owned, at one time or another, four-fifths of the 2.3 billion-acre expanse that now makes up the United States. Virtually the whole country, outside the 13 original colonies, Hawaii, and the independent Texas republic, was formed from lands once part of the public domain.

In the process Congress fostered national economic prosperity — and distributed unprecedented wealth among a land-hungry people — by relinquishing two-thirds of its western lands to homesteaders, ranchers, railroads, timber and mining companies, and newly formed state governments. But for 200 years a government based in Washington, D.C., has struggled to mold national policies that could be consistently applied to its diverse and distant dominion.

Almost too late, the government began reserving some leftover public lands for continued federal control to conserve natural resources and save still-wild places as outdoor museums and open-air cathedrals. Not until 1976 did Congress formally conclude that the government should keep most of its remaining public lands in permanent federal ownership.

The U.S. Constitution, in Article IV, Section 3, Clause 2, gives to Congress the authority "to dispose and make all needful Rules and

Regulations respecting the Territory or other Property belonging to the United States." Throughout U.S. history, that power to possess land and resources on the national behalf has served as one of the federal government's most important attributes.

The U. S. Supreme Court has ruled, most recently in 1976, that congressional authority on the public lands can be wielded "without limitation." [2] During the 20th century conservation-minded presidents and Congress have used that power to strengthen federal control over far-flung lands and resources. Since President Theodore Roosevelt directed forester Gifford Pinchot to found the U.S. Forest Service in 1905, federal land agencies have developed a specialized system for managing the government's parks, forests, wildlife refuges, and public rangelands. The general goal, set forth by Pinchot himself, has been "the greatest good of the greatest number in the long run." [3]

The four principal land-holding agencies — Agriculture Department's U.S. Forest Service and the Interior Department's Bureau of Land Management (BLM), National Park Service, and the U.S. Fish and Wildlife Service — now manage more than a million square miles of federally owned lands. Most, but not all, of those lands are the remnants of the remote and rugged western territories the nation acquired in the 19th century.

Expanding the American Empire

The public domain's origins can be traced back to America's colonial past. Similarly, the roots of Americans' fundamental ambivalance toward resource policy can be found in the early colonists' fight to carve new homes from a wild and often frightening country.

When Europeans explored North America, they found a promised land of lush beauty and abundant wealth that appeared to be open for the taking. For nearly 500 years — beginning with Christopher Columbus' accidental discovery of North America in 1492 — the continent's white men have been preoccupied with establishing legal title to lands that Native American Indians revered and occupied in common.

England, France, and Spain each claimed huge North American empires based on early explorers' discoveries. The European powers tried to consolidate their control by planting colonies along the American shores and sending traders and expeditions inland.

The British crown granted vaguely defined lands to court favorites, and companies formed to exploit the New World resources. Those in turn established Atlantic seaboard colonies, eventually 13 in all, by setting up plantations or granting lands to settlers. The prospect of land was a powerful lure for men from countries where aristocratic families beginning in feudal times had controlled most lands, thereby virtually dominating the lives of the landless. Historian and novelist Wallace Stegner noted that, in sharp contrast to Europe, in the colonies ". . . land to settle on and work came to be part of the human expectation." [4]

A powerful social force, that expectation endured well past the colonial period. It drove Americans to subdue the wilderness and defy British attempts to control colonial resource development.

If the New World offered men a promised land, it also posed a formidable challenge. Virtually the entire Atlantic seaboard was covered by virgin forest, composed of trees in variety and size unknown in European woodlands. The North American forests provided colonists with indispensable supplies of fuel, building materials, furniture, fenceposts, and other essential materials. But they also were a dark and strange wilderness, harboring hostile Indian tribes, wild animals, and other hazards. On the frontier, Roderick Nash observed in *Wilderness and the American Mind,* "constant exposure to wilderness gave rise to fear and hatred on the part of those who had to fight it for survival and success." [5]

Forest products, along with furs, fish, and tobacco, gave colonists commercial items to trade with England. For most colonists, the American forests and the lands on which they stood seemed inexhaustible. They cut down trees and cleared the land without regard for future production. If the soil became exhausted by farming, families simply could move along to plow new lands farther west.

In a modern context, colonial land practices seem tragically wasteful. But at the time, when labor and capital both were scarce, intensive use of cheap and plentiful raw materials probably was inevitable. "There was nothing ruthless or reprehensible about this process of resource utilization," Samuel T. Dana and Sally K. Fairfax contended in *Forest and Range Policy.* "It was nothing more or less than a sensible way for the colonists to make the most effective use of the factors at their disposal." [6]

But even in colonial times, forest cutting posed a threat to supplies of oak for ship construction, mulberries for silk production, and pitch pine for naval stores. As early as 1626, six years after the Pilgrims landed, the Plymouth Colony restricted sale of timber outside the colony.

William Penn barred clear-cutting of Pennsylvania's woods in 1681, and colonial assemblies passed numerous laws attempting to control timber cutting, restrict livestock grazing, and reduce fire hazards by limiting burning off of fields.

Beginning in 1691, the British government tried to reserve for itself all trees that could be used for masts in British navy ships. British agents marked trees reserved for masts with the three-blaze "Broad Arrow" symbol of the Royal Navy. But colonists cut them anyway, and their resentment fed the discontent that ultimately threw the colonies into revolt against British policies.

British policy consistently underestimated colonists' determination to acquire lands and use resources themselves. Parliament outraged colonial settlers, traders, and land speculators by adopting the Proclamation of 1763, barring settlement on lands beyond the Appalachian Mountains' crest that the colonies had helped win from the French in the French and Indian War. The measure also gave the crown sole right to dispose of those western lands, ignoring claims by seven colonies to extensive lands beyond the mountains.

Forming the Public Domain

The British attempt to hem in the colonies was but one of the economic grievances that produced the American Revolution. But during the war — and for decades after independence — Americans continued to maneuver for western land control.

By assigning those lands to Congress in the Constitution, and thus creating a national public domain, the Founding Fathers gave a newly formed central government crucial powers that assured its survival and helped bond a tenuous nation together.

The public domain was a product of the 13 colonies' effort to form a united front in their struggle for independence. Led by Maryland, six smaller colonies initially refused to ratify the Articles of Confederation forming a joint government until Virginia, Massachusetts, and five other colonies yielded their overlapping western land claims to the Confederation Congress. In the interest of the union the larger states gave in, beginning with New York and followed by land-rich Virginia on Jan. 2, 1781. The Articles were approved quickly and unanimously in February of that year after those two states' cessions. When Georgia finally complied, in 1802, the states had ceded the national government 236 million acres between the Appalachians and the Mississippi River, which eventually formed Ohio, Indiana, Illinois, Wisconsin, Michigan, Tennessee, and parts of Minnesota, Mississippi, and Alabama.[7]

Those common lands gave Congress a potential revenue base from sales of lands. More important, perhaps, they provided a jointly held empire that checked the centrifugal forces that might well have torn apart 13 semi-autonomous colonies. "The 'public domain' — a new American empire controlled now, not from London, but by 'the united states in Congress assembled' — became a bond among the states," historian Daniel J. Boorstin, the Librarian of Congress, noted in *The Americans, the National Experience.* "Without these lands, and the conflicts with foreign powers which they threatened, could a central government have survived between the peace with Britain in 1783 and the convening of the Constitutional Convention in Philadelphia in 1787?" Boorstin asked.[8]

The Constitution confirmed congressional control of the public domain. The new federal government, founded in 1789, thus assumed the authority to govern the western territories and bring them into the nation. Over the next century, Congress fought formative political battles — on slavery, manifest destiny, banking and tariffs, free lands for homesteaders, and railroads — as the government extended the federal empire across North America and created new states from a spacious and vaguely known continent.

At independence, few of the Founding Fathers imagined that the United States ever would expand beyond the Mississippi River. Thomas Jefferson, known as a strict constitutional constructionist, doubted that Congress or the executive possessed authority to acquire lands outside the existing national boundaries. But as president Jefferson put those misgivings aside in 1803 when his representatives in Paris negotiated the purchase of the Louisiana Territory.

The Louisiana Purchase, ambiguously defined as including all lands west to the Rocky Mountains' crest, doubled the size of the country. Within seven decades, the United States had acquired other vast territories by treaties with Great Britain and Spain, conquest from Mexico, and the Alaskan purchase from Russia. *(Map of U. S. Land Acquisitions, p. 21)*

The U.S. government recognized land titles granted to private owners by former rulers of the western territories. Through most of the 19th century, the government continued to negotiate treaties with Indian tribes in efforts to resolve title to tribal lands. Texas, entering the Union in 1845 as a previously independent republic, retained title to all public lands within its boundaries. But most of the new territories became part of the public domain, owned by the federal government.

From the Republic's beginnings, the prevailing assumption was that the government eventually would turn all its lands over to private owners. During the Revolutionary War, a cash-short Continental Congress offered military land bounties from the public domain to encourage soldiers to enlist. And even before the Constitution was ratified, the Confederation Congress had approved a blueprint conceived of by Jefferson for selling off the government's western lands.

In 1785 Congress adopted his scheme, which called for surveying the unmapped Northwest Territory for sales to the settlers who already were pouring across the Appalachians and down the Ohio River. The Land Ordinance of 1785 provided that the public lands be surveyed into 640-acre rectangles, each one mile square, grouped into townships of 36 sections, or 36 square miles.

The measure reserved one section from each township to be granted to newly formed state governments to finance public schools. It reserved four sections for future disposal by the government but offered the rest at public auction at a minimum price of $1 an acre.

In separate measures, the Northwest Ordinances of 1784 and 1787, Congress approved Jefferson's plans for dividing the territory north and west of the Ohio River into states and admitting them to the Union.

The results of Jefferson's plan are clearly visible today in the great rectangles that roads and fencelines still carve across the farmlands and rangelands from the Midwest to the Pacific that were once part of the public domain.

19th Century Land Disposals

The U.S. government issued the first patent conveying title to public lands in 1788. Over the next two centuries, the government sold or gave away more than 1.1 billion acres of land to settlers, speculators, railroads, homesteaders, ranchers, and others. Until 1934, when the Taylor Grazing Act closed most public rangelands to homesteading, the major objective of federal lands policy was to dispose of the public domain.

Throughout the 19th century, controversies over public land sale policies often dominated congressional debate. Early federal leaders, notably Secretary of the Treasury Alexander Hamilton, viewed public land sales as a badly needed government revenue source. But sales were

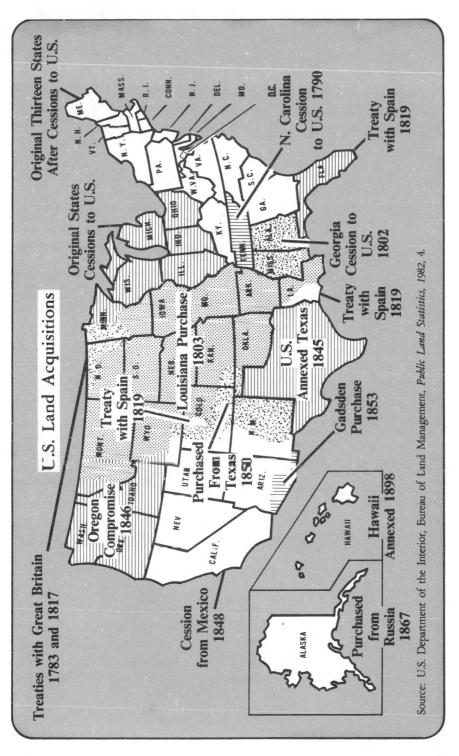

U.S. Land Acquisitions

Treaties with Great Britain 1783 and 1817

Original Thirteen States After Cessions to U.S.

Original States Cessions to U.S.

N. Carolina Cession to U.S. 1790

Treaty with Spain 1819

Georgia Cession to U.S. 1802

Treaty with Spain 1819

Treaty with Spain 1819

Louisiana Purchase 1803

U.S. Annexed Texas 1845

Purchased From Texas 1850

Oregon Compromise 1846

Gadsden Purchase 1853

Cession from Mexico 1848

Hawaii Annexed 1898

Purchased from Russia 1867

ALASKA

HAWAII

N. H.
ME.
MASS.
R. I.
CONN.
VT.
N. Y.
N. J.
DEL.
MD.
D.C.
PA.
W. VA.
VA.
N. C.
S. C.
GA.
FLA.
KY.
TENN.
MISS.
ALA.
MICH.
OHIO
IND.
ILL.
WIS.
MINN.
IOWA
MO.
ARK.
LA.
OKLA.
TEX.
N. D.
S. D.
NEB.
KAN.
N. MEX.
N. D.
MONT.
WYO.
UTAH
IDAHO
WASH.
ORE.
NEV
CALIF.
ARIZ.

Source: U.S. Department of the Interior, Bureau of Land Management, *Public Land Statistics*, 1982, 4.

slow, and revenue expectations never were fulfilled. Speculators bought large blocks, but immigrants who wanted lands to farm simply lacked the money to buy them. Squatters occupied western lands long before government surveyors and sales agents could process them.

The early settlers, Boorstin pointed out, "did not wait for the land to be surveyed or for government to precede them." [9] In Illinois, Boorstin noted, about two-thirds of the residents in 1828 were living on lands that legally still belonged to the federal government. To protect their holdings, Westerners formed "claim clubs" to set their own rules for claiming lands and to discourage outsiders from bidding when the U.S. General Land Office finally put lands up for sale. They also pressed Congress to ease land-sale terms and to recognize the rights of squatters who had been the first to settle the lands.

Congress experimented in the early 1800s with laws that allowed paying by installment, selling land in smaller blocks (eventually as small as 40 acres), and adjusting land prices. In 1841 Congress bowed to western pressure by authorizing U.S. citizens to settle on 160 acres, a quarter section, of public lands and then buy them from the government at $1.25 an acre. Then in 1862, after secession removed southern opposition, Congress passed the famous Homestead Act granting free title to 160 acres to any citizen who settled the land and cultivated it for five years.

During the same period, the government steadily granted public lands to newly formed states as they entered the Union. Congress added a second section per township for public education, beginning when Oregon was organized as a territory in 1848; school land grants later were enlarged to four sections. When Alaska completes its state lands selections — and when still-pending transfers to several western states are finished — the government will have given the states more than 328 million acres.

In addition to the education lands, the government in the 19th century made substantial land grants to help states finance roads, canals, and other internal improvements. Congress made other large grants to corporations that were building railroads, beginning in 1850 with the Illinois Central Railroad from Chicago to Mobile. In 1862 Congress granted the Union Pacific and Central Pacific railroads alternate sections of public lands up to 10 miles (later enlarged to 20 miles) on both sides of the transcontinental railroad route across the continent. In all railroad grants amounted to 94 million acres when the last grant was made in 1871.

Public Land Disposals
1781-1981

	Acres
Homesteaders	287,500,000
Railroads	94,400,000
Military veterans	61,000,000
Land grants by foreign governments before U.S. acquisition	34,000,000
Sold under 1878 Timber and Stone Act	13,900,000
Sold or granted under 1873 Timber Culture Act	10,900,000
Sold under 1877 Desert Land Sales Act	10,700,000
State land grants:	
to support common schools	77,600,000
to reclaim swamplands	64,900,080
to build railroads	37,100,160
to support universities, hospitals, asylums, etc.	21,700,000
to build public improvements, reservoirs, irrigation facilities	117,600,000
canals and rivers	6,100,000
wagon road construction	3,400,000
Total granted to states	328,400,000
Land sales, mineral entries, other methods	303,500,000
Grand total	**1,144,300,240**

Source: U.S. Department of the Interior, Bureau of Land Management, *Public Land Statistics 1981*, 5.

Most railroad lands eventually were sold to other owners. Similarly, state governments sold much of their lands, although some western states retained their holdings. One consequence has been a checkerboard pattern of land holdings in the West, with 640-acre sections of private lands and state-managed parcels mixed in with federal forests and rangelands.

Congress in the 19th century made several attempts to encourage public land development. An 1873 law offered 160 acres to any person who would plant 40 acres with trees, and an 1877 measure authorized sale of 640 acres to a settler who would irrigate it within three years. In 1872 the General Mining Act granted title to valuable minerals on public lands to any prospector who discovered a deposit and staked a claim. The law, still in effect in the 1980s, also offered full title to surrounding lands at $5 an acre. *(Minerals, chapter 8, p. 171)*

Failed Disposal Policies

Through those disposal laws, the government ultimately transferred two-thirds of the public domain to other owners. Constant access to a supply of free or cheap land and resources in the West promoted economic growth, broke down social barriers, and helped make Americans a restless people who rebelled at restraints on freedom and opportunity. Yet, from the start, public land policy in the 19th century was a sometimes tragic failure.

Federal land sales never realized officials' hopes in generating government revenues. Nor did the homestead law or other measures fulfill Jefferson's vision of populating the land with yeomen farmers tilling productive soil across the continent. Land policies written in Washington, D.C., by a government dominated by men from the eastern seaboard, never fully took account of the land's actual conditions in the nation's western territories.

Jefferson's grid system, for instance, drew on the experience of farmers on the humid eastern seaboard, where rainfall averages more than 40 inches a year, and rivers and streams keep the land well watered. The survey system worked successfully in the Midwest, but it broke down farther west on the drought-prone High Plains and desert basins where rain seldom approaches 20 inches annually. In that country, a 160-acre homestead was simply too small for most "nesters" to make a go of it.

Some early western observers, notably John Wesley Powell, recognized that public land policies were inappropriate in much of the West.

Powell, explorer of the Grand Canyon and later head of the U.S. Geological Survey, suggested in the *Report on the Land of the Arid Region* published in 1878 that the rectangular survey system be revised in the West to conform to watersheds and other physical features of the terrain. Powell argued that stockmen needed to receive four sections, 2,560 acres, to have sufficient lands for ranching. And he contended that cooperative measures would be essential to build dams and canals for irrigation.

The government ignored Powell's proposals, although Congress in the Reclamation Act of 1903 authorized federal construction of western irrigation projects to promote settlement. Through various laws, culminating in the Stockraising Homestead Act of 1916, Congress enlarged homesteads to 320 acres and finally to a full section. But the only result was a last wave of homesteaders after World War I who plowed up the High Plains just before the droughts of the 1920s and 1930s. "The soil uprooted by the homesteaders' efforts to 'prove up' their claims blew all the way to Washington during the dust storms of the 1930s," Dana and Fairfax noted. [10]

In the West the government's reverence for the homesteading myth produced incredible human hardship and disastrous destruction of native grasslands. Federal land policies all but invited fraud, and early cattlemen and sheepmen established large ranches by ignoring or violating the law. Cattle barons staked homesteads around water holes or widely scattered riverbeds, thus establishing effective control over dry lands for miles around that remained in federal ownership. Some had their cowboys file phony homesteads on critical lands, then bought the lands up to consolidate enormous holdings. University of Texas historian Walter Prescott Webb, in his 1931 study *The Great Plains*, reported that the early western cattleman "violated every land law made, in order that he might survive." [11]

That necessity fed Westerners' contempt for federal land authority. It also produced destructive overgrazing on federally owned rangelands as ranchers eager to profit from grazing public lands increased herds beyond the capacity of the range. The struggle continues as ranchers resist efforts by BLM and the Forest Service to cut grazing levels to give federal rangelands time to recover their vigor.

The Conservation Era

The year 1890 was a benchmark in the American nation's development. The U.S. Census director reported that that year's population surveys showed that settlers had moved into the nation's farthest frontiers. Three years later, in his famous 1893 essay "The Significance of the Frontier in American History," historian Frederick Jackson Turner concluded that expansion onto the vast western expanses of free land had been completed.

Settlement in fact continued for two or more decades, as homesteaders struggled to fill in the broad gaps that remained on the western plains and deserts. But frontiersmen already had claimed nearly all the most desirable farmlands that the public domain had contained. In the years after 1890 the U.S. government began designating some remaining public lands for continued federal control.

Congress set the precedent in 1872 by putting aside two million acres in Wyoming, Montana, and Idaho as Yellowstone National Park. Montana residents, escorted by the U.S. Cavalry, had explored the region in 1870; the expedition's leaders sought congressional action to head off commercial expansion by private developers who might file claims to the spectacular waterfalls, geysers, and mountain wilderness they had found. On March 1, 1872, Congress reserved those public lands, withdrawing them from the public domain open for disposal and dedicating them as a "pleasuring ground for the benefit and enjoyment of the people."

Congress provided no funds to administer the park, and the Army by default was left with responsibility for protecting the area. The disposal philosophy still prevailed on the remaining public lands. But concern was building, at least in the East and California, that other federal lands were being rapidly squandered.

Throughout the 19th century, American writers and artists had celebrated North America's wild beauty and warned against its destruction. In the decades after the Civil War, scientists and naturalists, following the lead of geographer George Perkins Marsh, warned against deforestation and overgrazing that were depleting resources and compounding the natural dangers of fires and flooding. Toward the century's end, political reaction set in against big business monopolies that were gaining control over much of the nation's timber and mineral resources. In California, naturalist John Muir intensified a crusade for preservation of wild places unspoiled by human use.

Those sentiments merged into an American conservation movement. Professional foresters, many trained in Germany, warned that the nation would quickly run out of timber if the wasteful logging already depleting the Great Lakes' forests continued. Private timber companies showed little interest in conservation practices, so foresters argued that only the government could manage scientifically the nation's forests by keeping them in public hands.

Congress ignored Powell's proposal to classify public lands by climate, soil, topography, and water supply and allocate them to their best use for timber, mining, grazing, or irrigated agriculture. In the 1870s and 1880s Congress gave only fleeting support to efforts by some federal officials, notably Secretary of the Interior Carl Shurz, to crack down on illegal timber cutting on federal lands and to force livestock operators to tear down barbed wire fences they were building across public range-lands. But in 1879 a report by a Public Land Commission created by Congress at least pointed out the need to adapt policies to the different conditions and capacities of the public lands.

Almost inadvertently, Congress in 1891 laid the groundwork for a permanent land management system. In writing a bill revising public land laws during the closing days of its 1891 session, a House and Senate conference committee slipped in a section that authorized the president to establish forest reserves from federal lands. The House and Senate accepted the language with little discussion, even though neither body had included a forest reservation provision in the original legislation. Congressional intent was surrounded by confusion, although members had been discussing the concept of forest reserves for years.

Presidents Benjamin Harrison and Grover Cleveland set aside 17.5 million acres of public lands in forest reserves between 1891 and 1893. But Congress had made no provision for government management of the reserves, and Interior Department officials concluded that no use could be permitted. That angered western stockmen, miners, and loggers, although many Westerners supported the first reserves' creation to protect the watersheds originating on federal forests.

In February 1897, 10 days before leaving the presidency, Cleveland proclaimed 13 new forest reserves in the West, more than doubling the total area of protected forest. Cleveland's action followed recommendation by a National Academy of Sciences panel, most of them eastern academics, who hastily drew up the boundaries of 21 million acres of reserves after spending three months touring the West by train.

Cleveland acted without consulting Congress or state governors. The new reservations included towns, cities, and other developments, as well as potential farmlands. Despite bitter protests, Congress backed

27

away from measures to repeal the reserves. Instead, three months after William McKinley entered the White House and called a special session, Congress passed a landmark law that finally gave the government authority to protect and manage the federal forests.

That measure, the Organic Act of 1897, defined the reserves' purposes as preserving forests, maintaining watershed flows, and furnishing a continuous timber supply. The act contemplated both use and preservation, and it empowered the government to sell federally owned timber and to regulate private use of public resources. It set the stage for active government management of the federal lands in the public interest. *(Timber, chapter 6, p. 131)*

Roosevelt and Pinchot Conservation Policies

By the turn of the century, federal law thus had begun to provide for permanent government control over large parts of the public domain. Many Westerners, particularly ranchers and loggers who always had used public lands without restriction, continued to protest that all public lands rightfully should be turned over to private ownership. But Theodore Roosevelt, after taking over the presidency in 1901 following McKinley's assassination, committed the government to bold and vigorous efforts to protect public lands and conserve the nation's resources.

Roosevelt, himself a noted outdoorsman, made resource conservation a central theme of his administration. Allied with Pinchot, a Yale University graduate who had studied forestry in France and Germany, Roosevelt relied upon an expansive view of presidential power to implement the Progressive movement's commitment to scientific management of public resources by high-minded civil servants.

As president, Roosevelt again vastly expanded the national forest reserves, created the U.S. Forest Service, began federal wildlife protection, and reserved large areas for national parks, monuments, and game refuges. His administration also began withdrawing public lands bearing coal, potash, and other valuable minerals from availability under the homesteading and other disposal statutes. After winning election in his own right in 1904, "Theodore Roosevelt rewrote the rulebook on presidential power, effectively reversed the nation's thinking on resources, and saved a land birthright for the American people," Interior Secretary Stewart L. Udall wrote in his 1963 book *The Quiet Crisis*.[12]

During Roosevelt's term Pinchot set the foundations for the modern U.S. land management system. Even after the 1897 Organic Act, the forest reserves taken out of the public domain had remained under Interior Department control. But beginning in 1876 the Agriculture Department had been responsible for studying forestry and recommending conservation practices. While Interior's General Land Office retained authority to administer the forest reserves, the Agriculture Department's Bureau of Forestry employed most of the government's professional foresters. Pinchot, the bureau's chief beginning in 1898, persuaded Congress in 1905 to transfer the reserves' administration to the Agriculture Department.

Pinchot reorganized the forestry bureau into the U.S. Forest Service. In a letter addressed to himself, then signed by the agriculture secretary, Pinchot laid out the conservation principles that were to guide the Forest Service into the 1980s. Pinchot maintained that forest resources be put to their most productive uses, not simply preserved undeveloped. He instituted a decentralized management structure, largely relying on rangers and forest supervisors to manage the separate forests by taking local conditions into account. And while stressing that national forests be managed for the public good, not for the benefit of individuals or private companies, he nonetheless insisted that forest resources contribute to the economic stability of ranchers, miners, timber and agricultural interests, and the surrounding communities that depended on them.

Pinchot won a major victory by successfully imposing regulation of livestock grazing on the forests. Politically powerful stockmen resisted Pinchot's decision to charge fees for grazing use that previously had been free. But two 1911 Supreme Court decisions, *Grimaud v. United States* and *United States v. Light*, upheld grazing regulations and confirmed congressional authority to establish the forests and assign the Forest Service to manage them.

But western congressional delegations remained hostile to the Roosevelt conservation program, and in 1907 appropriations legislation Congress prohibited new forest reserves in six western states without congressional approval. Roosevelt was unwilling to veto the appropriations measure, but the Forest Service quickly drew up plans adding 16 million acres to the reserves. The president signed the proclamations just before signing legislation forbidding him to create new reserves.

Roosevelt's maneuver enlarged the national forest system in the West to roughly its current extent, about 140 million acres. President William Howard Taft dismissed Pinchot in 1910 after the Forest Service chief feuded publicly with the interior secretary. But Pinchot's zealous commitment to scientific resource management endured as the Forest Service earned a lasting reputation as one of the federal government's most professional and best-managed agencies.

In 1911, after Pinchot's departure, Congress authorized the service to acquire private timberlands and add them to the national forest system. Using that power, which was expanded in the 1920s and 1930s, the Forest Service bought up 24 million acres of forests in the South, East, and Midwest that private owners had allowed to deteriorate. Those acquisitions, along with national grasslands that the government reacquired for homesteaders during Dust Bowl days, extended the national forests into 41 of the 50 states. In the process, the Forest Service broadened public recognition of its role and political support for its policies.

National Parks and Wilderness

From the beginning wilderness preservation advocates led by Sierra Club founder John Muir were uneasy with Pinchot's insistence that conservation meant wise use of public resources. Muir's continuing crusade to save the nation's wild and spectacular lands from logging, mining, and livestock grazing eventually opened a bitter political split that haunted federal resource policy for decades afterward.

Differences over use and preservation sharpened in the early 1900s as Muir campaigned to block a dam across the Hetch Hetchy Valley in Yosemite National Park. The Forest Service was not directly involved, but Pinchot endorsed plans by California water interests to turn the valley into a reservoir providing water and hydroelectric power for San Francisco. Ignoring other potential sites, Congress in 1913 approved the Hetch Hetchy dam. Muir died a year later, but the Hetch Hetchy loss inspired his supporters to push for a formal management system to protect the parks against more intrusions.

In the four decades after Yellowstone National Park was created in 1872, Congress had established 13 additional national parks. Using authority provided by the Antiquities Act of 1906, Roosevelt had proclaimed 18 national monuments to protect historic and scientific landmarks, including the Grand Canyon and three other places that Congress later made national parks. Park superintendents reported independently to the interior secretary, but Congress had provided no overall policy or management framework for the parks.

The Forest Service had sought to bring the national parks under its control. But at the urging of preservation advocates such as noted landscape architect Frederick Law Olmstead, Congress in 1916 established the National Park Service within the Interior Department to regulate use of the parks and similar reservations. In a passage drawn up by Olmstead, the law directed the Park Service to administer the system "to conserve the scenery and the natural and historic objects and the wildlife therein and to provide for the enjoyment of same in such manner and by such means as will leave them unimpaired for the enjoyment of future generations." That mandate gave the Park Service a preservationist philosophy clearly distinct from the Forest Service's.

The Interior Department and the Forest Service had been at odds frequently ever since Pinchot won transfer of the forest reserves to the Agriculture Department. The National Park Service emerged as a strong competitor with the Forest Service for appropriations, public and congressional support, and for control over land and resources. The rivalry sometimes forced both agencies to modify land management policies to protect their funding and territory.

Determined to expand the park system, Stephen T. Mather, the first Park Service director, emphasized construction of hotels, roads, concessions, and other facilities to lure tourists and build public support for its program. Railroads, the American Automobile Association, and park concessionaires contributed critical backing for park expansion despite opposition in western states. The early Park Service boosterism solidified the agency's standing with Congress, but it enormously complicated later efforts to redirect park management toward preserving sensitive environments.

As the park system was expanded, many new park units were carved from national forests. The Forest Service, eager to hold onto its lands, responded by stepping up construction of camp grounds, picnic areas, and other recreational facilities. At the urging of ecologist Aldo Leopold, then a forester on the Gila National Forest in New Mexico, and other foresters, the Forest Service in the 1920s and 1930s began formally designating extensive roadless regions within the forests as primitive areas to be preserved, at least temporarily. Bob Marshall, a Wilderness Society founder and Forest Service Recreation and Lands Division chief in the late 1930s, pushed through new regulations that afforded more permanent protection of wilderness areas designated by the agriculture secretary.

Interagency rivalries grew in the 1930s as President Franklin D. Roosevelt's New Deal expanded federal conservation programs. A 1933 executive branch reorganization enlarged the Park Service role by giving that agency jurisdiction over military parks and cemeteries, public buildings, as well as national parkways and monuments, including some surrounded by national forests. Harold Ickes, Roosevelt's interior secretary, angered Forest Service leaders by persistently campaigning to create a new federal Department of Conservation that would bring the national forests and Interior Department lands together.

During the 1930s growing concern about dwindling wildlife prodded Congress to pass the Pittman-Robertson Act of 1937 funneling funds from federal firearms taxes to state fish and game management programs. Franklin Roosevelt also expanded federal wildlife refuges, and his administration took some steps to mitigate wildlife habitat damage from federal dam and other New Deal construction projects. In 1940 Roosevelt merged the Agriculture Department's Bureau of Biological Survey and the Commerce Department's Bureau of Fisheries to form a new agency, the U.S. Fish and Wildlife Service, within the Interior Department.

Before the 1930s the U.S. government had taken little responsibility for managing wildlife, even on federal lands. Following the English common law tradition that game animals belonged to the sovereign, the federal government generally deferred to state government laws regulating hunting and fishing. But President Theodore Roosevelt had established a national system of game refuges, and federal legislation in the early 1900s prohibited interstate trade in wild animals and birds taken in violation of state game laws. Drawing on the federal power to make treaties with foreign governments, Congress did protect migratory game birds in 1913. And beginning in the 1890s the Agriculture Department's Bureau of Biological Survey began hiring hunters and trappers to conduct campaigns to eradicate coyotes, wolves, mountain lions, and other predators that preyed on livestock on western rangelands.

Closing the Western Range

By World War II broad national support had assured permanent federal control over the national parks, forests, and refuges. But three decades into the 20th century, the rest of the public domain in the West still was being dismissed as "lands that nobody wanted."

Long after the turn of the century, the western range was a kind of lawless frontier, beyond reach of federal authority. The government held legal title, and the Interior Department's General Land Office administered a hodgepodge of archaic land disposal laws that still applied to most leftover public holdings. The best lands had long since been claimed, but homesteading entries peaked in the first decades of the 1900s as settlers made last desperate attempts to carve farms out of the dusty plains. Prospectors roamed freely across the public domain, including the forests, searching for strikes where they could stake out claims that automatically would confer title to the lands as well as the minerals. And cattlemen, after half a century of grazing federal lands with no government supervision, had grown accustomed to free use of rangelands they felt were rightfully theirs simply because nobody else had claimed them.

Westerners knew that the range was federal land, but the government's authority was rarely evident. Early ranchers turned their cattle loose to roam freely across public grasslands surrounding their privately owned ranchhouses, corrals, and watering holes. In some parts of the West, cattlemen fought off homesteaders and nomadic sheepmen who dared to intrude on public lands they had used by custom. Barbed wire was invented in the 1870s, and some stockmen strung fences that stretched for miles across federal as well as private ranges.

Congress outlawed fences on public lands, but the Interior Department could never fully enforce those edicts. After the forest reserves were created, Pinchot successfully forced stockmen to pay fees to lease grazing rights. But, trying to build western political support for Forest Service programs, Pinchot resisted Muir's demands to ban sheepmen and their "hoofed locusts" from the forests. Ranchers also fended off proposals to regulate grazing on the unreserved public domain for 30 more years, until 1934, when heavy use had brought the federal grasslands almost to the brink of ruin.

Western opposition to any limits on access to public lands and resources continued. Still, after two decades of debate, Congress in 1920 broke with past resource disposal laws to set up a system for leasing instead of selling or granting increasingly valuable federal minerals. Under the Mineral Leasing Act enacted that year, the government leased private individuals and companies the right to develop coal, oil and gas, potash, and other sedimentary deposits.

Since the early 1900s conservation-minded administrations had been attempting to reserve valuable minerals under government control to head off speculative claims to the lands that held them. At Theodore Roosevelt's instructions, the Interior Department between 1905 and 1909 reserved 80 million acres of public lands thought to hold coal deposits. About half those lands were made available for homesteading again after the government classified them as without coal potential. But Roosevelt's administration also withdrew lands from disposal laws to protect oil and potash deposits and keep potential dam sites under federal control. Congress in 1910 passed the Pickett Act granting President Taft's request to approve previous withdrawals and confirm presidential authority to withdraw other lands to protect the public interest. *(Further discussion of presidential authority to withdraw lands, pp. 40-41)*

Before setting up the mineral leasing system, Congress turned down proposals to authorize federal agencies to develop public resources themselves. The measure also left the 1872 mining law system in effect for hardrock minerals such as gold, silver, and other deposits. Still, the new leasing system strengthened federal control over development by giving the Interior Department discretion to approve or disapprove requests to lease public resources. It also required private companies to pay the government a return for its resources in royalties.

Out on the open range, ranchers still were the only organized group with direct interests in public land conditions. As a consequence, federal regulation became possible only as Dust Bowl droughts in the 1930s made it plain that some restriction on total livestock grazing on public lands would be essential to the industry's survival. In the late 1920s Montana stock operators' experiment with a grazing lease system had demonstrated that range conditions could be dramatically improved.

In 1934 the Taylor Grazing Act authorized the Interior Department to set up grazing districts on 142 million acres of public range and established a federal Grazing Service to lease forage resources to established stockmen. But to persuade Congress to keep the lands under Interior control, Ickes promised the livestock industry that grazing fees would be kept low and grazing administered without an extensive bureaucracy such as the Forest Service. Those conditions assured that the Grazing Service would be a weak, under-funded agency dominated by district advisory boards composed of influential stockmen. Until the 1970s, well after President Harry S Truman had merged the Grazing Service with the venerable General Land Office to form the Interior's Bureau of Land Management, congressional support for a determined livestock industry weakened the government's regulatory hold on the public rangelands.

The Taylor law provided for minimal grazing regulation "pending final disposition" of the remaining public domain to other owners. But after the law was passed, Roosevelt issued executive orders withdrawing all public lands within the contiguous 48 states from homestead entry. Disposal laws remained on the books another 40 years, and homesteading still was permitted in Alaska. Nonetheless, the grazing act effectively closed the 175 million acres of public domain outside Alaska to major disposals. It ended the disposal era and began a shift toward federal retention of most remaining public lands.

Notes

1. Stewart L. Udall, *The Quiet Crisis* (New York: Holt, Rinehart & Winston, 1963), xi.
2. *Kleppe v. New Mexico*, 1976.
3. Pinchot used the phrase in a letter, addressed to himself, that gave instructions for administering the national forests after they were transferred to the Department of Agriculture. The secretary of agriculture signed the letter and returned it to Pinchot on the day the transfer legislation was signed into law.
4. Wallace Stegner, "Land: America's History Teacher," *The Living Wilderness* (Summer 1981): 5.
5. Roderick Nash, *Wilderness and the American Mind* (New Haven: Yale University Press, 1967), 43.
6. Samuel T. Dana and Sally K. Fairfax, *Forest and Range Policy* (New York: McGraw-Hill Book Co., 1980), 3.
7. Kentucky, formed from Virginia's western counties, never was part of the public domain.
8. Daniel K. Boorstin, *The Americans, The Democratic Experience* (New York: Vintage Books, 1965), 419.
9. Ibid., 73.
10. Dana and Fairfax, *Forest and Range Policy*, 23.
11. Walter Prescott Webb, *The Great Plains* (New York: Grosset & Dunlap, 1981), 428.
12. Udall, *The Quiet Crisis*, 131.

Alaska's enormous natural resources kicked off a bitter struggle between environmentalists and economic developers before passage Nov. 12, 1980, of the historic lands bill that restricted future development on 100 million acres. Mount Igikpak, crowning the Brooks Range at 8,500 feet, was designated a wilderness area as part of the Gates of the Arctic National Park.

Chapter 3

A COMPLEX TASK:
MANAGING THE PUBLIC LANDS

Fifty years after the homesteading era ended, the U.S. government remains by far the nation's largest landowner. The federal lands are still so immense, and in many places so wild, that the government has yet to survey more than half of its public domain to mark off the 640-acre sections that Thomas Jefferson envisioned almost two centuries ago.

But by the 1980s Congress had devised a system for managing most of those lands, to their farthest extent, under permanent federal ownership. Four government agencies, with 60,000 employees in all, wield authority to administer the public lands. In combination, those agencies control 599 million acres, which Congress has dedicated to preserving natural conditions and to producing resources for all Americans.

The government has set its most spectacular lands aside, off limits to development. It has opened the rest for multiple uses — by ranchers, loggers, and miners, and also by hunters, fishermen, campers, river runners, and adventurous back-country explorers. The Agriculture Department's U.S. Forest Service and the Interior Department's Bureau of Land Management (BLM), the government's principal land agencies, earned taxpayers more than $2 billion a year in the early 1980s, primarily by leasing energy minerals from public lands and selling timber from federal forests. In the same period Interior Department revenues from leasing federally owned offshore oil and gas rights climbed close to $12 billion one year. *(Chart, p. 67)*

The federal domain is "the people's land," Secretary of the Interior James G. Watt proclaimed in a 1983 *Newsweek* interview, "and the people of this country have many, many diverse interests." [1] In theory the government manages most of its lands, more than 60 percent of its holdings, under "multiple-use" policies that attempt to balance all those often-conflicting interests. More and more, however, federal land

37

managers must make tough choices — for instance, between mining coal and preserving wildlife habitat — where developing a resource or conserving natural values inevitably rules out almost all other uses.

Congress, using its virtually limitless power over public lands, has designated millions of acres for special protection in national parks, wildlife refuges, and national forest wilderness. The Forest Service, along with the Interior Department's land agencies, has withdrawn other vast tracts by administrative decisions that sharply curtail resource development. Responding to new federal environmental and land management laws, the Forest Service and BLM have begun tightly restricting access to remaining multiple-use lands to preserve wildlife and other natural values. *(Controversy over withdrawing public lands, box, pp. 40-41)*

As the government tried to balance conflicting demands on its lands and resources after World War II, public land controversies multiplied. Congress itself has attempted to settle some disputes through laws that have vastly expanded the national park, wildlife refuge, and wilderness systems. By applying federal environmental standards to public lands — then demanding careful land-use planning by Interior and Forest Service officials — Congress also has imposed broad central goals for managing federal lands that sprawl to the far reaches of North America.

But to administer those lands Congress still relies on decentralized agencies that confer decision-making authority out "on the ground" to forest rangers and BLM district managers. In granting the Forest Service and BLM new authority under federal land laws in the 1970s, Congress directed both agencies to consult conservationists, sportsmen, commodity producers, and state and local officials while drafting plans for long-term federal management. Despite its unchallenged authority to set federal land policy, Congress "specifically declined to impose its will, in preference to that of interested citizens, on the public lands" when it wrote BLM's 1976 organic act, University of California professor Sally K. Fairfax has suggested.[2]

That deference has opened federal land management to the full play of competing political pressures from conservation and commodity interests. Even Interior's National Park Service and U.S. Fish and Wildlife Service, "single-use" agencies with narrow mandates to preserve scenic splendors and save wildlife habitat, have faced growing conflicts between protecting natural ecosystems and giving Americans a chance to behold them. But BLM and Agriculture's Forest Service have been struggling ever since World War II to balance multiple — and in some places irreconcilable — demands to produce natural resources and to preserve public lands unimpaired for future generations. As Watt remarked in a 1982 television interview, ". . . the secretary of the interior is sitting on a department filled with conflict." [3]

Federal Land Systems

Those four agencies together manage almost a million square miles, more land than in Mexico. Those holdings make the Interior Department and the Forest Service the nation's principal conservation authorities — and the government its most diversified producer of resources. In addition to its land-managing programs, Interior holds responsibilities for encouraging mineral and water resource development even in federally controlled offshore waters. Congress rounded the federal land system into basically permanent form in 1980. That year, a month after conservative Republican Ronald Reagan defeated conservationist President Jimmy Carter, a Democrat, in the November election, the House accepted the Senate version of landmark legislation allocating federally owned lands making up most of the country's largest state to various public land management systems. The law also cleared the way for Alaska's state government and Alaskan natives to finish selecting nearly 150 million acres of public lands that Congress granted after admitting the state to the Union in 1959.[4]

The Alaska land measure more than doubled the U.S. national park and wildlife refuge systems. It tripled the acreage that Congress has protected formally against development in the federal wilderness system. It also mapped out the public lands that remain open for multiple-use management under Forest Service and BLM administration. *(Federal lands in Alaska, map, p. 43)*

In the early 1980s Watt ordered Interior officials to convey 13 million acres a year to Alaska state government ownership. Transfers to Alaskan natives were proceeding more slowly, at perhaps 4 million to 5 million acres a year, as officials negotiated which lands would fill the congressional grant of 44 million acres. The process was expected to take years, most likely to beyond the turn of the century. Utah and some other western states also were pressing outstanding land claims still unfulfilled from their statehood grants.[5]

By Interior Department estimates, the U.S. government still will own 636.9 million acres after Alaska land transfers are completed. That federal property includes post offices, courthouses, and other buildings in

Withdrawing Public Lands . . .

For 191 years, from 1785 through 1976, the objective of most national land laws was to dispose of the public domain. Yet Congresses and presidents, almost from the nation's earliest days, have used various procedures to designate large tracts for continued federal government control, unavailable for homesteading, mining, or other private claims to public lands and resources.

Those procedures took two forms:

● A *withdrawal*, by statute, executive order, or by administration decision, which made a parcel of public land unavailable for any private claims. Withdrawals could be temporary or permanent; they could remove lands from application of all disposal laws or only from specified statutes.

● A *reservation*, also by law or by executive action, which withdrew lands from disposal but also dedicated them to a specified purpose, generally considered permanent.

Both Congress and presidents can make withdrawals and establish reservations. Since the early 19th century, presidents have claimed and used an implied executive power to withdraw public lands in the public interest. As commanders-in-chief of the armed forces, presidents set up military reservations for forts and other facilities on the public domain. Between 1855 and 1919, they also set aside about 23 million acres from the public lands as Indian reservations for Native American tribes.

Congress itself has retained authority to withdraw and reserve lands for national parks, wilderness areas, and wild and scenic rivers. Congress also has reserved lands by law for other purposes, including some national wildlife refuges. Through other statutes, Congress has authorized the president to withdraw lands for specific purposes. In 1891, for instance, Congress gave the president power to establish forest reserves, which

towns and cities across the land. The Defense Department alone holds 30.4 million acres in sprawling military bases, weapons testing sites, and 8.2 million acres that the Army Corps of Engineers administers at federal navigation and flood control projects. The U.S. Bureau of Reclamation,

... A Continuing Controversy

eventually became the national forests. In 1906 the Antiquities Act empowered the president to reserve lands to protect ancient ruins, scenic qualities, or scientific curiosities. President Theodore Roosevelt, claiming expansive withdrawal powers, in the early 1900s withdrew large federal tracts to prevent claims to their coal and petroleum deposits. At the request of Roosevelt's successor, William Howard Taft, Congress in the Pickett Act of 1910 delegated the president a general authority to withdraw public lands to protect the public interest. That law turned out to be unnecessary when the U.S. Supreme Court, in a 1915 decision (*United States v. Midwest Oil Co.*), ruled that Congress, by failing to challenge a host of 19th century executive withdrawals, had in effect acquiesced to earlier presidents' claims that they held broad implied powers to withdraw public lands from disposal.

Congress, still jealous of its authority over public lands, in the Federal Land Policy and Management Act (FLPMA) of 1976 inserted language aimed at reversing the 1915 decision by abolishing the president's implied withdrawal authority. The law also required congressional review of Interior Department withdrawals of more than 5,000 acres, subject to congressional veto after 90 days. FLPMA further directed the interior secretary to review all withdrawals in the 11 western states by 1991 and report to Congress on which lands should be reopened for mining or other development. The law permitted the secretary to withdraw lands for three years in emergency situations.

Withdrawals continue to be controversial. The Carter administration in 1978 withdrew 161 million acres in Alaska, including 56 million acres that the president designated as national monuments, to prevent development after Congress failed to meet its self-imposed deadline for classifying federal lands in the state for federal retention in national parks, wildlife refuges, and other reservations.

part of the Interior Department, manages 6.6 million acres in 17 western states where it has built dams, reservoirs, and irrigation systems. Other U.S. agencies, from the Central Intelligence Agency to the American Battle Monument Commission, own research centers, prisons, office buildings, and other facilities that occupy large tracts of land.[6]

But the Interior and Agriculture departments manage by far the bulk of federal holdings through the four agencies that Congress created primarily to administer the government's undeveloped public lands. In combination, those agencies control 598.6 million acres, reaching into all 50 states, of lands that probably will remain permanently under federal control. *(Federal lands, U.S. map, chapter 1, p. 3)*

They include:

National Parks. With the addition of those Alaska lands that Congress assigned to the National Park Service in 1980, the park system expanded to 73.6 million acres built around 48 national parks. Those national parks, most in Alaska and the West, commonly have been called the nation's "crown jewels," preserving its most spectacular vistas and unique natural wonders. But in recent decades Congress has rapidly enlarged the system to include 78 national monuments, 64 historic sites, national recreational areas and preserves, lakeshores and seashores, parkways and trails, some of them in the midst of crowded metropolitan areas. The Park Service, with 10,000 full-time employees, manages the system with a $1 billion budget, roughly half for park operations.

Wildlife Refuges. The wildlife refuge system takes in nearly 89 million acres, with just more than 76 million acres in Alaska. It includes 772 units in all 50 states and some U.S. territories, with 103 in North Dakota and 53 in Montana. Its 413 refuges provide habitat for migratory waterfowl and mammals, including the National Bison Range in Montana. In addition, the system includes waterfowl production areas, fish hatcheries, wildlife research stations, and other facilities. The U.S. Fish and Wildlife Service manages the system with 5,400 full-time employees and a $490 million budget.

BLM Lands. Interior's principal land management agency, BLM in 1983 administered roughly 310 million acres. Those lands are almost entirely the remaining western public domain, in vast sections of Alaska and 11 states from the Rocky Mountains west to the Pacific coastline. BLM's holdings have been shrinking with Alaska land transfers to the state, Alaskan natives, and other Interior land agencies, which eventually will reduce bureau lands to around 70 million acres — perhaps fewer — in Alaska, with another 174 million acres spread across the West. (As of July 20, 1983, BLM had conveyed 73 million acres to Alaska and 28 mil-

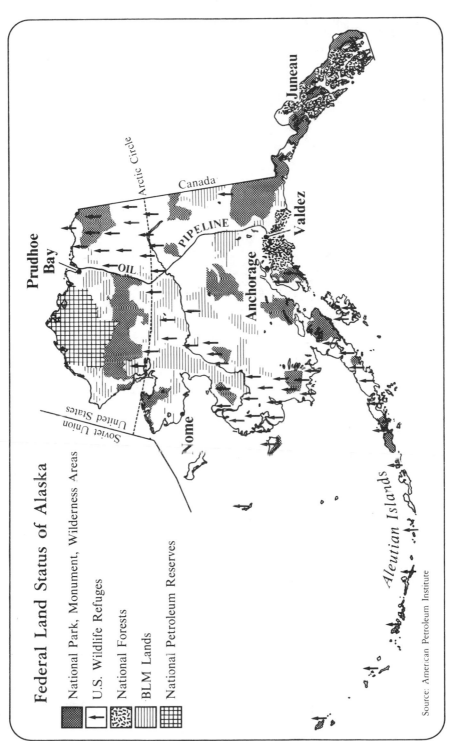

Federal Land Status of Alaska

National Park, Monument, Wilderness Areas

U.S. Wildlife Refuges

National Forests

BLM Lands

National Petroleum Reserves

Source: American Petroleum Institute

lion acres to Alaskan natives. The federal government at that date still owed the state another 31 million acres and natives another 16 million acres.[7]) BLM employed about 9,000 full-time workers, operating with a budget of around $570 million.

National Forests. The government's 155 national forests, along with 19 national grasslands, made up the bulk of a 190.8 million-acre system in 44 states, Puerto Rico, and the Virgin Islands. While also concentrated in the West, the system includes 50 national forests in 23 eastern states that make important contributions to timber production, recreation, and open space in New England, the South, and parts of the Midwest. The U.S. Forest Service managed the system, and it also conducted forestry research and cooperative state and private forest programs, with a $1.9 billion budget, 37,000 permanent employees, and another 6,000 seasonal workers.[8]

Each public land agency operates under its own legal mandate, with a distinctive tradition and management style. But collectively they share responsibility for lands that are, by and large, still wild or at least little developed by humans. Still, mining has deeply scarred some lands, and energy exploration crews have blazed roads that criss-cross some otherwise empty regions. Ranchers have strung fences across national forests and rangelands, built windmills, and bulldozed stock watering holes. Loggers have clear-cut ugly swaths through some national forests, and the Forest Service has replaced ancient trees with carefully planted and fertilized stands. For a century, concessionaires have been building hotels, restaurants, and gas stations within national parks — and gaudy tourist attractions just outside park boundaries.

Yet roughly a fifth of the public lands remain relatively untouched, never penetrated by roads. Congress, since enacting the federal Wilderness Act of 1964, has designated 80 million acres for preservation, more than 50 million acres in Alaska. In the 1980s Congress was working its way through Forest Service and BLM proposals that could add another 30 million acres or more to the wilderness system. Roderick Nash, historian of the American wilderness movement, predicted in 1982 that one-third of Alaska eventually will be set aside as wilderness. "Another third of Alaska," he added, "will, in the foreseeable future, be wild by default of development" in remote, inhospitable country.[9]

But public land policy, administered by the four agencies, ultimately will determine the fate of vast areas. In balancing the conflicting demands for use of the federal lands, government officials will make decisions that determine where natural forces will continue to rule and where human intrusions will alter the landscape. Even in formally protected wilderness areas, federal land managers more and more are imposing controls over access by back-country enthusiasts who pound heavily traveled trails with heavy hiking boots, race to claim choice campsites, and line up for permits to run wild rivers. Except perhaps in regions such as Alaska, with its intemperate climate and sparse population, "wild land will remain wild only as the result of deliberate human choice," Nash noted. "The time when wilderness was leftover land, preserved because nobody wanted it for anything else, is fading fast." [10]

Regional Distribution

Public lands are truly national lands, and all Americans possess interests in their management. But the impact of public land policies is felt more keenly in some regions than in others. The four agencies manage lands literally across the map, from New England to California, Alaska to Florida. Their holdings range from 1,240 acres in three Rhode Island wildlife refuges to nearly 224 million acres in Alaska's national parks, refuges, forests, and BLM lands — almost 60 percent of the nation's largest state.

BLM holds lands almost exclusively in Alaska and 10 western states from the Rocky Mountains to the Pacific. But the other three agencies have important holdings in other regions. The national park system in 1982 extended to every state except Rhode Island, Delaware, and Illinois, taking in parks and recreation areas in highly populated metropolitan areas. The Fish and Wildlife Service manages units in all 50 states, including a single 183-acre wildlife refuge in Connecticut but much larger holdings in Florida, Georgia, North and South Dakota, Texas, Louisiana, Hawaii, and other southern and midwestern states with significant waterfowl and other wildlife populations. [11]

The Forest Service also manages 24 million acres in 50 eastern national forests, made up of lands that the government bought up during Depression years in New England, Appalachia, the South, and the Great Lakes region. In some areas the eastern forests make important economic contributions through timber supplies to local sawmills. But their greater value may lie as green and wooded counterpoints to the sprawling cities and privately held farms that occupy most of the country's longer-settled regions. Some eastern and midwestern states, notably New York,

Pennsylvania, and Wisconsin, themselves have set aside large forested tracts in state forests or parks. But in Virginia, Indiana, Illinois, Ohio, and a few other states, "there are no other public lands but the national forests," William E. Shands, author of a Conservation Foundation study on eastern forests, commented in 1983. "So their biggest values are as recreation sites and open space" in otherwise developed countrysides.[12]

More than 90 percent of federally owned lands lie in the West and Alaska. Alaskan lands alone account for more than 35 percent of federal landholdings, and the government also owns 86 percent of Nevada, nearly two-thirds of Idaho and Utah, and roughly half of Oregon and Wyoming. Even in California, the nation's most populous state with major industrial and population centers along its coastline, the U.S. government holdings in the high mountains and barren interior deserts make up 46 percent of the state's land base. *(Federal land acreage in the West and Alaska, table, next page)*

Arizona, New Mexico, Colorado, Montana, and Washington have lower percentages of land under federal control. But even in those states national forests and rangelands occupy heavily used areas — including ski resorts, picnic grounds, and hiking trails — that in places abut the city limits of fast-spreading urban centers such as Denver, Colo.; Albuquerque, N.M.; Phoenix and Tucson, Ariz.; Las Vegas and Reno, Nev.; Salt Lake City, Utah; and Boise, Idaho. Outside these metropolitan areas, national forests and BLM lands spread across mountain ranges and lower elevation plains that hold most of the West's undeveloped resource potential. Many BLM lands, left over after 19th century grants to railroads, homesteaders, and states, lie in "checkerboard" patterns with state and private sections. Most western ranches are made up of scattered 640-acre sections of public lands that in effect control use of intermixed state holdings and private lands owned by the ranchers themselves.

As a consequence, federal land agencies have enormous influence over the West's economic and social development. In past decades, Westerners themselves dominated decision making by forest rangers and BLM range managers who lived in western towns and consulted with the ranchers, miners, and others who most often used federal lands. But since the 1960s environmental policies and resource development pressures have imposed central national goals for public land management that more and more outweigh Westerners' local interests. Decisions by Congress and public lands agencies — to lease federal coal, to designate a federal wilderness, to approve a national forest ski area, to improve

Federal Land Acreage, Alaska and 11 Western States
(thousands of acres)

State	BLM	Forest Service	National Park Service	Fish and Wildlife Service	Total Federal	Percent Federal
Alaska	73,600.0[a]	23,119.5	51,015.2[b]	76,058.9[b]	226,200.0[a]	60.3
Arizona	12,588.9	11,271.9	2,696.0	1,588.4	32,014.3	44.0
California	16,609.4	20,413.0	4,500.0	234.5	46,702.1	46.6
Colorado	7,993.1	14,431.2	600.0	56.9	23,607.9	35.5
Idaho	11,945.9	20,427.5	86.9	85.2	33,759.6	63.8
Montana	8,141.6	16,764.4	1,220.5	1,137.7	27,740.6	29.7
Nevada	48,844.8	5,149.8	697.6	2,362.7	60,506.1	86.1
New Mexico	12,840.5	9,347.7	248.5	383.0	25,873.7	33.3
Oregon	15,745.1	15,617.2	171.3	507.4	32,313.7	52.7
Utah	22,052.6	8,046.0	2,009.2	101.7	33,530.2	63.6
Washington	311.2	9,053.7	1,909.9	181.1	12,472.2	29.2
Wyoming	17,793.1	9,254.7	2,391.1	74.2	30,329.6	48.7
West subtotal	248,467.0	162,896.6	67,546.2	82,771.8	585,050.5	52.3
U.S. total	248,887.7	190,839.5	73,626.2	88,774.7	636,929.6	28.1

[a] Lands expected to remain federal after state of Alaska and Alaska native selections are completed, BLM estimate as of March 1982.
[b] Lands after enactment of Alaska National Interest Lands Conservation Act of 1980, agency estimates as of March 1982.

Sources: U.S. Forest Service, *Report of the Forest Service, Fiscal Year 1982*; *Current Issues in Natural Resource Policy* (Washington, D.C.: Resources for the Future, 1982), 16.

wildlife habitat on BLM lands — can produce jobs and economic prosperity across a wide region. Yet those same decisions also can pollute the West's air and water, overtax roads and public services, and irreparably disrupt the slow-moving quality of life that many western natives and newcomers alike have found attractive. "Decisions now made in Washington have more effect on us than decisions by our legislatures in important areas," Colorado Gov. Richard D. Lamm, a Democrat, declared in a 1979 *National Journal* interview.[13]

But the West also benefits from federal resource production. The U.S. government turns half its mineral leasing revenues over to states and counties, plus another 40 percent to the federal reclamation fund that finances western water projects. The Forest Service pays the states 25 percent of national forest revenues, and the Interior Department returns 12.5 percent of grazing fees to state and local governments, with another 50 percent spent for rangeland improvements. In 1981 those payments to the 13 western states totaled $474.1 million. Western state governments also collected large revenues — $283.4 million in 1980 — by imposing mineral severance taxes on coal, oil and gas, and other resources produced from federally owned lands.[14]

Institutional Conflicts

Public policy decisions are influenced by institutional conflicts and rivalries within the federal land system. The Interior Department, long dominated by western officials and congressional delegations, traditionally has brought a pro-development slant to federal land operations. While the Forest Service has built a broader nationwide constituency, it also customarily has made providing timber and other resources for local communities one of the main goals of national forest management. The Forest Service and Interior agencies continue their historical struggle for control of lands and congressional support for funding.

BLM, little known to most Americans outside the West, usually has fared poorly in bureaucratic infighting with other Interior agencies for budget resources. The Forest Service, on the other hand, continues to be regarded as one of the government's most efficient, disciplined agencies. As the Agriculture Department's largest agency, the service enjoys considerable autonomy from department officials and has resisted steadfastly proposals that it be transferred to Interior.

Federal environmental laws since the late 1960s have brought more balance into Interior and Forest Service decision making. But Congress still assigns them contradictory programs. In addition to agencies that manage land surface, for instance, the Interior Department takes in the U.S. Geological Survey, Bureau of Mines, and Minerals Management Service, agencies whose primary duties are to map the nation's mineral wealth, explore ways to produce it, and lease the government's offshore oil and gas resources. Interior's Bureau of Reclamation, founded in 1903, built and operates most of the giant federally financed dams and reclamation projects that provide water and power to most of the West's growing cities. BLM itself, in addition to managing the remaining public domain, leases rights to minerals beneath those lands, most of the national forests, and nearly 66 million acres of private lands where the government retains mineral rights. The Forest Service, in addition to administering national forests, conducts forestry research and provides assistance to state and private forest owners.

Even the Park Service and Fish and Wildlife Service, with their specialized missions, must cope with conflicting objectives. The Park Service since the early 1960s has stressed preserving native plants and wildlife in undisturbed natural condition, but that objective often is difficult to balance with making the parks accessible for millions of visitors each year. Since the 1960s, moreover, Congress has steadily expanded the park system by adding seashores, lakeshores, and urban parks where conditions and goals necessarily must be different from those in remote western national parks.

The wildlife refuges, while dedicated to preserving habitat, also are open for grazing, hunting, and potentially mining. The Fish and Wildlife Service, in addition to managing refuges, also administers the federal endangered species program. But the agency's Animal Damage Control Division conducts programs to trap and hunt down coyotes, mountain lions, and other animals that may damage crops or kill livestock. "All these activities make Interior one of the most controversial and sensitive departments in the government," political analyst Elizabeth Drew concluded in a 1981 *New Yorker* article.[15]

Public Land Politics

The United States has fought its most emotional conservation battles over protecting national parks or saving threatened wildlife. But in the decades since World War II national resource controversies have spread steadily to the vast federally owned lands, once all but ignored, in the national forests and rangelands.

Federal control over those lands always has been politically sensitive in the West, because they hold so much of the region's resources. But in the postwar prosperity Americans from other regions as well began to recognize the public lands' value for recreation and commodity production. As a result, local conflicts broadened during the last 40 years into full-scale national debates over the government's public land policies.

Congress, responding to surging recreation use and spreading environmental concern, has vastly expanded the national park, wildlife refuge, and wilderness preservation systems. Interior and Forest Service officials, using executive authority that presidents have claimed since at least the 1830s, have "withdrawn" other large tracts from mining and other uses to prevent destructive development. Those steps, along with continuing Forest Service and BLM studies of potential wilderness lands where no roads have penetrated, have sparked endless controversy over how much land the government should "lock up" for protection and how much it should keep open for grazing, logging, mining, off-road vehicle travel, and other activities that inevitably will mar, at least temporarily, the landscape.

As a result, BLM and the Forest Service have been caught in the middle of bitter fights over their efforts to balance multiple uses. A well-organized, politically astute environmental movement developed during the 1960s and succeeding years to challenge agency policies that critics contended were too receptive to resource development. But new restrictions also outraged Westerners who had grown accustomed to using public lands in earlier years with little government regulation.

Those conflicting pressures converged in the 1970s. The decade began with environmentalists celebrating Earth Day and wound up with Westerners mounting a Sagebrush Rebellion against BLM and Forest Service management. The western rebels initially demanded that the federal government turn most public lands over to state governments. But the resulting uproar also drew national attention to what Frank Gregg, President Carter's BLM director, in 1979 termed "the real issue, which is how to manage the land, and what kind of management system can best respond to the needs of the West itself." [16]

Commodity Producers' Influence

Since the late 1950s Congress consistently has endorsed Forest Service and later BLM multiple-use objectives. But multiple use remains a vaguely defined concept, open to conflicting interpretations. It leaves well-organized public land interests ample room to bring political pressure to bear on Forest Service and BLM decisions.

The philosophy of managing public lands to produce a variety of resources on a sustained basis goes back to the turn of the century when the founder of the Forest Service, Gifford Pinchot, instructed that the national forests provide "the greatest good for the greatest number in the long run." But the Forest Service actively promoted the concepts of multiple use and sustained yield in the 1950s to help counter timber industry demands for increased national forest harvests. Beginning in 1960 Congress wrote the multiple-use/sustained-yield standard into new federal laws updating Forest Service and BLM authority.

In several public land statutes, Congress has defined multiple use to include recreation, range, timber, minerals, watershed, fish and wildlife, as well as scenic, scientific, and historic site values. Those laws invariably grant Forest Service and BLM land managers wide discretion to decide how much of each of those uses public lands can provide without permanently destroying their productive capacity. Interior Department economist Robert H. Nelson, a critic of the current federal land system, concluded in a 1982 assessment for Resources for the Future that "multiple-use management is really management by agency administrative discretion in response to individual proposals." [17]

But in the Forest Service, and more lately within BLM, multiple-use doctrine provides foresters, range scientists, and other resource professionals with unifying principles and a professional ideology that justifies relying on their judgment and skills in managing public lands. To agency employees, the multiple-use philosophy generally has meant managing large tracts of land for an optimum mixture of uses, combining scientific measurements with their own knowledge to hold each activity to a level that accommodates other uses without damaging the land's biological capacity.

That balancing act always has been difficult, even when demands on the public lands were limited. But managing multiple-use lands has become immensely more complicated — and agency decisions subjected to relentless second-guessing — in postwar decades as Americans in ever growing numbers began using the federally owned lands. With the U.S. economy booming, commodity industries turned to the West for timber, coal, oil and gas, other minerals, and livestock forage provided by public lands. But as population shifted to far western and southwestern cities, newcomers to fast-growing towns and cities hunted, hiked, camped, and sought wilderness adventure in national parks, forests, and rangelands, including many of the lands that commodity producers coveted. Postwar prosperity gave millions the freedom to travel west to view the region's grandeur. Transportation improvements, along with technological innovations that produced lightweight tents, backpack, and other camping equipment, spurred renewed interest in exploring the back-country solitude of the country's remaining wild lands.

Over three decades, from the mid-1950s, those trends transformed the politics of public lands. Always before, western stockmen, timber and mining companies, and local sportsmen had held powerful, sometimes dominant, influence over Interior Department policy. The Forest Service, while enjoying more political independence, generally bent to prevailing local wishes in regulating use of the national forests. Of 11 postwar secretaries of the interior, including Watt, seven came from western "public land" states. Forest Service and Interior officials, both in Washington and in regional and district offices, often were themselves Westerners who shared the region's traditional optimistic faith that developing its natural wealth would bring progress and prosperity.

Western states' congressional delegations, while outnumbered in both the House and Senate, promoted federal resource development from powerful committee posts. Westerners generally dominated the House and Senate Interior committees, protecting their reelection chances by responding to the demands and complaints of stockmen, miners, and other public land users. During the 1960s, for example, House Interior Chairman Wayne N. Aspinall, a Democrat from Colorado's western slope, successfully drafted measures that authorized a massive federal dam and reservoir building program in the Colorado River and its tributaries. He also urged that commodity users be granted priority on public lands.[18]

Environmentalist Fervor Spreads

But in the 1970s the environmental movement matched, if not surpassed, commodity producers' influence on federal land policy. Old-line conservation groups expanded, and new activist organizations emerged to press legal and political cases against plans that would accelerate timber harvests, coal leasing, and other resource development on national forests and rangelands. Those environmental critics often questioned Forest Service and BLM decisions, and they built public suspicion that foresters' and range specialists' multiple-use training gave both agencies a bias in favor of developing resources for use and against leaving the land undisturbed to save ecological purity.

Some environmental groups traced their roots to the conservation movement that in the late 19th century backed creation of national parks and forests. That movement, led largely by professional foresters themselves, usually endorsed Forest Service policies for managing the forests and urged Interior to follow Pinchot's example. But conservationism grew more diverse in the 20th century, as pressures on public lands multiplied. Led by the Sierra Club and the Wilderness Society, conservation leaders increasingly sought preservation of undisturbed lands, not just government regulation of public resources; and they more and more challenged multiple-use agency decisions to develop public lands or build dams across western rivers.

In 1956 those groups demonstrated unprecedented political muscle. A conservationist alliance, led by Sierra Club Director David Brower and Wilderness Society Director Howard Zahniser, joined the Park Service to block U.S. Bureau of Reclamation plans to dam Utah's Green River at Echo Park, backing water up into Dinosaur National Monument. A well-organized lobbying campaign persuaded Congress to delete funds for the dam from legislation authorizing the massive Colorado River Storage Project, a system of dams and reservoirs that Aspinall was pushing to allow Colorado, Utah, Wyoming, and New Mexico to use their full share of water from the Colorado and its upper tributaries.

Although the Echo Park dam was abandoned, Congress approved construction of Glen Canyon Dam, at the Arizona-Utah border, which flooded intriguing canyons and amphitheaters the Colorado had carved in southeastern Utah before entering the Grand Canyon in Arizona. Still, the Echo Park victory symbolically reversed the decision to build Hetch Hetchy Dam in Yosemite National Park nearly half a century before. It also gave conservation groups new political momentum that carried over in following decades.[19]

Environmentalists' growing strength encouraged the government to enlarge the national park system and strengthen forest and rangeland regulation. In 1961 President John F. Kennedy appointed Stewart L. Udall, a Democratic member of Congress from Arizona with strong conservationist views, to serve as interior secretary. A month after taking office, Kennedy issued a message that declared the government should keep most public lands as "a vital reserve ... devoted to productive use now and maintained for future generations."[20] Udall stayed on at

Interior through President Lyndon B. Johnson's administration, and he backed legislation and administrative changes that pushed BLM into more active and balanced management.

Congress also devoted more attention to public lands. Conservation groups, following up on their Echo Park success, in 1964 achieved a longstanding goal by persuading Congress to create a federal wilderness system by statute, no longer relying on the Forest Service itself to designate wild and primitive lands for protection by administrative actions that officials could reverse. As part of the political bargaining over the 1964 Wilderness Act, Congress also approved Aspinall's proposal to set up a Public Land Law Review Commission to assess the confusing proliferation of laws regulating the public domain. Another 1964 law gave BLM temporary authority to pursue multiple-use policies while the commission reviewed federal land administration. Other 1960s legislation set the stage for federal agencies to acquire additional private lands, largely for recreation, to expand national parks, forests, and refuges. Congress in 1964 set up a Land and Water Conservation Fund to finance the purchases and support state recreation planning programs. In 1968 Congress expanded the program for authorizing use of offshore oil and gas leasing revenues to provide additional funding.

In 1972 a challenger running on an environmentalist platform unseated Aspinall in Colorado's Democratic congressional primary. The Interior Committee chairman's defeat demonstrated growing sympathy for environmental protection, even in the West, and signaled the end of an era when western interests held exclusive control over public land legislation. As interest grew in expanding parks and protecting federal lands from damage, members of Congress from the East, Midwest, and other regions took seats on House and Senate committees that considered Interior and Forest Service measures.

By the 1970s new federal environmental protection laws were being applied to the entire nation, including the government's own lands. The federal Endangered Species Act forced forest rangers and BLM managers to survey public lands for threatened wildlife and plants and to rule out uses that could disrupt their habitats. New laws ordered states to prevent degradation of clear air around national parks and other remote lands, and water pollution control measures authorized regulation of "non-point" pollution — resulting from widely scattered sources such as timber operations, livestock grazing, or other activities — that entered streams from water running off federal forests and rangelands. President

Richard Nixon in 1969 considered a proposal to create a new Department of Environment and Natural Resources, merging the Forest Service and government pollution control agencies into Interior. After well-publicized disputes with Interior Secretary Walter Hickel, the former Alaska governor, Nixon instead set up a separate agency, the Environmental Protection Agency (EPA), to monitor pollution and enforce federal mitigation laws.

But since 1970 a single law — the National Environmental Policy Act (NEPA) of 1969 — "has been at the cutting edge of change in public land management," George Cameron Coggins and Charles F. Wilkinson wrote in a 1981 casebook on federal land law. NEPA applied to all U.S. government agencies, ordering officials to draft an environmental impact statement (EIS) to assess potential damage to the environment from any major government action.

The president's Council on Environmental Quality (CEQ), an advisory group established by NEPA, drafted detailed guidelines for preparing the statements that placed heavy emphasis on public participation in agency analysis of environmental consequence and on public review of environmental impact statement documents. Those rules enormously expanded opportunities for litigation contending that agencies failed to follow proper procedures in drafting EISs or inadequately considered alternative actions.

Most early court cases filed under NEPA concentrated on massive federal projects, such as dams and highways. But within a few years, environmental groups were mounting NEPA challenges to routine government land management practices, notably Forest Service timber harvests and livestock grazing on BLM rangelands. NEPA's requirements, fleshed out by federal court decisions, transformed BLM and Forest Service decision making. In the process, Coggins and Wilkinson suggested, the drafting of environmental impact statements evolved into "the most important procedure in public land law...." [21]

The EIS process forced public land managers to broaden the interests and values they weighed in balancing multiple uses. It required rangers and district managers to justify resource development in written documents, open to public scrutiny. The Forest Service and BLM increasingly consulted other agencies, such as the Park Service and the Fish and Wildlife Service, before making decisions affecting large tracts of public lands. Both agencies also hired wildlife biologists, archeologists, recreation experts, and other specialists to assess public land values and defend specialized interests in agency deliberations. As a result, Paul J. Culhane noted in his book on public land politics, BLM and the Forest Service diversified their staffs, "counteracting some of the problems caused by the domination of some agencies by a single profession, such as foresters in the [forest] service." [22]

Most importantly, however, NEPA gave environmentalists a legally enforceable entree for participating in BLM and Forest Service decisions. They seized the opportunity, at both local and national levels. Well-organized groups used public comment requirements to prod local rangers and district officials to take account of environmental risks. Agency officials, anticipating environmentalist opposition, increasingly modified proposals to provide increased protection for wildlife and other values.

At the national level, conservation groups mustered well-financed staffs to lobby and challenge government policy through court action. The Sierra Club and Wilderness Society attracted new members and hired sophisticated Washington, D.C., staffs to lobby Congress as well as land agency officials. The National Wildlife Federation and Izaak Walton League, generally more conservative organizations that represent hunters and fishermen, took more aggressive stances on how public lands were managed. New environmental groups, notably Friends of the Earth and the Natural Resources Defense Council (NRDC), were formed to press environmentalists' conviction that protecting natural values outweighed economic development goals in federal government policies.

Major groups, some with private foundation funding, hired expert legal staffs to challenge government land management decisions through litigation. In the past, western courts traditionally deferred to BLM and Forest Service judgment in turning down legal challenges to their decisions. But federal judges grew more active in reviewing government agency decisions, and environmentalist lawyers successfully pressed numerous cases through federal courts in other regions, notably in the District of Columbia. The U.S. Supreme Court ruled on a 1972 Sierra Club lawsuit to block Walt Disney Corp. plans for a ski resort in California's Mineral King Valley (*Sierra Club v. Morton*). The decision expanded previous judicial doctrine to grant legal standing to sue the government to organizations that could demonstrate that their members used the public lands affected by agency actions.

Court rulings on Sierra Club, NRDC and other groups' litigation sometimes produced major changes in federal land administration. The

U.S. District Court for the District of Columbia, in a 1974 decision on an NRDC case (*NRDC v. Morton*), ordered BLM to prepare 144 separate EISs to assess livestock grazing on western public rangelands. In 1975 the U.S. Fourth Circuit Court of Appeals affirmed a district court decision that upheld the Izaak Walton League's complaint that the Forest Service violated its own 1897 Organic Act by allowing clear-cutting on West Virginia's Monongahela National Forest (*West Virginia Division of the Izaak Walton League of America v. Butz*).[23]

Those rulings, along with other court decisions on the government's coal leasing and wilderness programs, forced the Forest Service and BLM to tighten regulation of commodity production on public lands. But, while congressional committees, especially in the House, no longer responded solely to western demands, congressional delegations from public land states still were sympathetic to industry complaints. Western state governors in the late 1970s organized the Western Governors Policy Office (WESTPO) to present a united response to Interior and Forest Service decisions that influenced the region's economic growth. And wealthy conservative business executives poured money into private legal foundations that mounted court challenges to restrictive policies. Watt, after a stint as an Interior Department official, directed the Denver-based Mountain States Legal Foundation from 1977 to 1980, frequently challenging federal land policies before President Reagan named him interior secretary in 1981.

BLM, Forest Service Powers

As public land politics shifted in the 1960s and 1970s, Congress responded with new federal laws that strengthened BLM and Forest Service authority. Those measures generally confirmed the multiple-use objectives that both agencies adopted in postwar years. They also directed both agencies to proceed with long-term planning for balancing conflicting demands.

In rewriting public land laws, Congress, however, made no attempt to dictate the balance between resource production and land preservation. A series of measures, culminating with the National Forest Management Act (NFMA) and the Federal Land Policy and Management Act (FLPMA), both passed in 1976, spelled out goals and procedures but left federal land managers operating on the ground with authority to make most resource decisions. Those laws mandated

57

The Law's Language

".... 'Multiple use' means the management of the public lands and their various resource values so that they are utilized in the combination that will best meet the present and future needs of the American people; ... a combination of balanced and diverse resource uses that takes into account the long-term needs of future generations for renewable and nonrenewable resources, including, but not limited to, recreation, range, timber, minerals, watershed, wildlife and fish, and natural scenic, scientific and historical values; and harmonious and coordinated management of the various resources without permanent impairment of the productivity of the land and the quality of the environment. . . ."

—Federal Land Policy and Management Act (Oct. 21, 1976)

scientific land-use planning, but they also ordered full consultation — if not full compliance — with environmentalists, industry, state and local governments, and all parties with interests in federally owned lands. Although congressional authority on public lands "may be boundless in theory," Fairfax noted, "in practice Congress has essentially demurred and relied explicitly on a locally oriented negotiations process called land-use planning." [24]

Yet, merely by declaring that the U.S. government should keep most remaining public lands, Congress strengthened BLM authority to set permanent management policies on the public lands. By endorsing BLM and Forest Service multiple-use goals, moreover, the new laws encouraged the agencies' professional staffs to feel confident that the government would back up their decisions. Multiple-use mandates freed both agencies, in particular BLM, from relying on a single dominant constituency for political support. Forest rangers and BLM land managers became able to use the threat of environmentalists' opposition to pressure industry clients to accept agency decisions, "even though those policies originated at least as much in the agencies' progressive conservationist missions as in explicit environmental group demands," Culhane noted in his 1981 study of both agencies' operations. "The

Forest Service and BLM thus find themselves in a very powerful position." [25]

Forest Service Reputation

The Forest Service entered the postwar years much better prepared than BLM to cope with growing pressures. Since 1905 when Pinchot founded the agency, the Service had built a solid public reputation and strong congressional backing for its appropriations. The national forest system had been extended into the South, Midwest, and Northeast, expanding the agency's geographic base into the nation's most populous regions. The Forest Service campaign to prevent forest fires, featuring the now legendary Smokey the Bear, was broadcast on television sets throughout the nation.

Uniformed rangers, wearing green shirts and flat-brimmed hats, nurtured the Service's image as an efficient, "spit-and-polish" operation guarding the public interest. The agency still enjoys broad public support, in the West as well as in other regions. But since the 1950s even the Forest Service has been plagued by continuing controversy as it expanded timber harvests from national forests. Even as timber companies pushed for access to uncut lands, environmental groups attacked the Forest Service as reluctant to preserve wilderness or restrict logging operations to protect sensitive watersheds against ugly erosion.

The Organic Act of 1897 provided the government with authority to protect its forest reserves, to furnish continuous timber supplies, and to ensure the flow of water from mountain watersheds. But the Forest Service, pressed hard by timber, recreation, grazing, and wilderness demands in postwar years, asked Congress in the 1950s for new legislation to clarify its mission. Congress complied in 1960, passing the Multiple Use-Sustained Yield Act. The measure, written mostly by Service officials, defined multiple use to include outdoor recreation, fish and wildlife, and range as well as timber and watershed. The 1960 multiple-use law set no priorities, and it basically expanded Forest Service discretion to allocate national forest resources among competing uses. [26]

The Sierra Club was the only major conservation organization to oppose the 1960 multiple-use act, objecting that its failure to specify standards left decisions on preserving untouched lands up to professional foresters who had been trained to manipulate natural environments. In the following decade, similar concerns led Congress to establish a wilderness system within the national forests by statute, over Forest

Service objections. And by the 1970s an explosive controversy over ugly clear-cutting operations in national forests forced the agency to accept further restrictions on its policies.

In the 1964 Wilderness Act, Congress granted wilderness groups' demand that national forest wilderness be protected by law, not by revokable Forest Service administrative designation. Passed after nine years of deliberation, the measure granted immediate wilderness status to 9 million acres that the Forest Service had protected previously under 1939 regulations. Largely at Aspinall's insistence, the law kept national forest wilderness open for established livestock grazing, and even for aircraft and motorboat use. It authorized the Forest Service to fight fires and control insects as well as tree disease in wilderness areas, and to build roads and facilities for administration. It also allowed prospecting and mineral exploration through the end of 1983, permitting claims staked before that deadline to be worked in subsequent years.

The 1964 wilderness law required congressional action to designate other roadless, primitive areas within the national forests, or any additional wilderness in national parks, wildlife refuges, and BLM rangelands. But court and Forest Service decisions in the 1970s barred development of potential wilderness while the agency assessed possible additions to the system. The agency undertook two massive roadless area studies, ultimately recommending that Congress expand the national forest wilderness system to 33 million acres. By 1983 Congress had expanded the national forest wilderness system to 25 million acres, in addition to 35 million acres in national parks and 19 million acres in wildlife refuges, and it had protected other lands along national trails and national wild and scenic rivers.

In the meantime the development of another 36 million acres of roadless forest lands was held up while the Forest Service drafted forest management plans that would allow them to be managed for multiple uses.

Even as the wilderness debate continued, environmentalists and industry challenged other forest policies. Timber company officials and resource economists criticized Forest Service "non-declining, even-flow" timber harvest schedules, adopted in the early 1970s, that limited logging in Pacific Northwest "old-growth" forests containing huge volumes of wood (*Details, chapter 6, p. 131*).

But in the late 1960s and early 1970s, the most emotional forest controversies erupted over clear-cutting, the practice of stripping large areas of all trees, then allowing forests to grow back in even-aged stands.

The clear-cutting method generally was accepted by foresters as productive silvicultural practice. But in the 1960s, as the Forest Service expanded harvests from reclaimed Appalachian Mountain forests, public outcry mounted in West Virginia over unsightly clear-cutting scars in Monongahela National Forest. In 1970 a University of Montana School of Forestry investigation criticized Forest Service management practices, including clear-cutting, on Bitterroot National Forest. That report fed public alarm about Forest Service timber management and led to a Senate subcommittee investigation of clear-cutting methods.

The Forest Service and professional foresters acknowledged mistakes in Bitterroot timber management and clear-cutting practices. The agency accepted clear-cutting guidelines, designed to limit the practice on steep slopes, fragile soils, and watersheds, proposed in 1972 by the Senate Interior and Insular Affairs Subcommittee on Public Lands, chaired by Sen. Frank Church, an Idaho Democrat. Those "Church guidelines" allowed clear-cutting on limited areas shaped and blended into natural terrain, and they preserved most of the agency's freedom to select silvicultural techniques for national forest harvests.[27]

Yet clear-cutting controversies continued. In its 1975 decision on the Izaak Walton League's challenge to Monongahela clear-cutting, the US Fourth Circuit Court of Appeals in Richmond, Va., upheld a 1973 lower court ruling that clear-cutting on national forests violated provisions of the Organic Act of 1897 requiring that only mature, individually marked trees could be harvested. A week after that appeals court decision was handed down, the Forest Service suspended most timber sales in four southern states served by the fourth circuit. Fourteen months later Congress passed the National Forest Management Act (NFMA) reversing the Monongahela decision but also thoroughly revising Forest Service authority.

Forest Planning

Congress responded to forestry controversies of the early 1970s with new national forest laws that addressed touchy on-the-ground land management issues. Those measures nonetheless generally upheld the Forest Service's own policies and gave the agency continued discretion to apply them to national forest timber, wildlife, wilderness, and livestock grazing programs as it drafted forest management regulations and comprehensive plans for each national forest unit.

Those measures directed the Forest Service to launch an unprecedented effort to plan for long-term management of the national forests at local, regional, and national levels. Since then, national forest supervisors and rangers, in addition to managing current use of specific tracts of land, have held public hearings, gathered data, run computer studies, and compared alternative land-use decisions to plan for future balancing of resource development. In Washington, D.C., Forest Service headquarters now continuously assess nationwide demand for timber, livestock forage, and other renewable resources, from state and private lands as well as national forests. The ambitious goal, fully endorsed by Congress, was to weave management of the country's 154 national forests together to fulfill nationally defined resource goals. "In terms of geographic area, ecological complexity and interaction between social and physical system," that Forest Service planning effort "has no precedent, at least in the western hemisphere," one 1981 study concluded.[28]

The Forest Service traditionally has managed national forests from the ground up, basing decisions on foresters' assessments of what resources the land provides. Until the 1960s, management policy gradually evolved as forest supervisors and rangers applied standard forestry practices to meet rising resource demands. The agency began drafting district plans after Congress passed the 1960 Multiple Use Act, and by the 1970s it had begun drawing up plans for ecological units, such as separate watersheds or basins, within the national forests. But Congress, through new laws passed in 1974 and 1976, ordered the service to press ahead into full-scale planning at all administrative levels.

In 1974 the Forest and Rangeland Renewable Resources Planning Act (RPA) directed the government to prepare what would amount to a master plan for the nation's forests and rangelands. The Forest Service was to prepare an assessment, updated every 10 years, of nationwide demand for timber, recreation, livestock forage, wildlife habitat, and other values from all the country's forests and rangelands, not just those in the national forest system. It also required the Service to draft an RPA program, to be revised every five years, laying out national forest system goals for meeting expected demand for those resources. The program's objectives, broken down among timber management, wildlife habitat improvement, wilderness designation, and other functions, would set benchmarks for Congress to use in reviewing whether annual Forest Service budgets provided sufficient funds and manpower to meet the agency's mission.

Congress, in passing the NFMA two years later, formally linked the national RPA goals to grass-roots national forest administration at regional and local levels. NFMA amended the 1974 law to make it mandatory for the Forest Service to draft plans for managing each national forest, following procedural guidelines and public participation requirements specified by the law. Those plans, along with regional plans drafted by the nine Forest Service regional offices, provided data for national RPA planning and also set forth agency policies for allocating each national forest's lands among competing resource uses.

NFMA, in prescribing that the Forest Service draft regulations laying out planning procedures, also addressed some hotly debated forestry issues. In the wake of the 1975 Monongahela decision, the agency and timber companies sought quick congressional action to revise the 1897 Organic Law to restore clear-cutting authority. Environmentalists, trying to protect the advantage they gained from the clear-cutting decision, backed legislation offered by Sen. Jennings Randolph, a West Virginia Democrat, that sharply restricted Forest Service discretion in managing federal timber harvests. But Congress compromised, approving a bill, backed by Sen. Hubert H. Humphrey, D-Minn., that wrote into law policies that restricted clear-cutting, required that only mature trees be cut, directed that forest species' diversity be maintained, limited harvesting on marginally productive lands, and held annual national forest harvests to "non-declining, even-flow" levels that could be continued without ever falling *(Details, chapter 6, p. 131).*

NFMA, as enacted, carefully qualified all those standards with phrases that allowed the Forest Service to adjust them as officials determined necessary in writing regulations to implement the forest planning process. Yet by mandating planning through law, rather than agency administrative decisions, NFMA left open the door for litigation contending that Forest Service regulations and decisions exceeded the agency's authority or were made through improper procedures. "The NFMA will be the basis of lawsuits well into the 21st century," Fairfax and Samuel T. Dana noted in their 1980 text *Forest and Range Policy.*[29]

The 1976 law required the Forest Service to complete plans for 121 administrative units, including some combining small national forests, by the end of 1985. By 1983 the agency was putting final touches on nine regional guides, planning documents for each Forest Service region that set resource production goals to fulfill regional contributions to overall RPA objectives.[30] But the agency made its separate national forest plans, each one drafted as an environmental impact statement subject to EPA review, its principal decision documents. As of mid-1983 forest planners had filed only 22 forest plans with EPA, and officials were predicting that the Reagan administration's decision to once again review potential wilderness areas could delay completion of all 121 plans at least a year beyond the 1985 deadline. Proposals by John B. Crowell Jr., Reagan's assistant secretary of agriculture for natural resources and environment, to accelerate timber harvests from western "old-growth" national forests gave the Forest Service another potentially explosive issue to weigh in drafting forest management plans.

By mid-1982 R. W. Behan, dean of the Northern Arizona School of Forestry, dismissed the ambitious RPA and NFMA planning system as "a quagmire that transcends description." [31] Both the Carter and Reagan administrations held Forest Service budgets below levels envisioned by the RPA program. Fiscal 1982 funding, for example, amounted to 83 percent of RPA targets, with the largest curtailments below RPA goals absorbed by wildlife habitat management, trail construction, and other non-commodity programs.[32] Many observers remained skeptical that national forest planning efforts would yield improvement in forest management.

Behan noted that Forest Service officials had reported that the agency's planning costs had grown to $500 million annually. To draft national forest plans, supervisors assembled interdisciplinary teams composed of experts in wildlife, archeology, watersheds, recreation, and other fields as well as the agency's professional foresters. But environmentalists remained concerned that forest plans nonetheless would reflect the service's customary stress on making use of resources.

Timber industry critics, on the other hand, contended that early planning results arbitrarily curtailed the amount of forest land available for timber production, ignoring overall RPA harvest objectives.[33] Even within the Forest Service, former forestry students have grown frustrated with the time-consuming planning process, Elwood Miller, associate dean of the University of Nevada, Reno, School of Renewable Natural Resources, noted in 1983. "They have been so involved with the planning process that they are hardly getting anything else done," Miller said

"... At the grass-roots level, they're not convinced that the plans are going to amount to anything." [34]

BLM Struggles

Despite such misgivings, the Forest Service entered the 1980s with broad political support and a firm sense of mission. In contrast BLM — still little known outside the West — was struggling to overcome a checkered past as a timid, usually ineffective, land manager historically dismissed by conservationists as "the bureau of livestock and mining."

BLM manages a huge area, mostly leftover public domain that homesteaders passed up as too dry for farming. It administers roughly 300 million acres, pending further transfers of Alaskan lands, compared with the 191 million acres managed by the Forest Service. BLM also leases minerals beneath another 200 million acres in national forests and private lands. Yet the bureau operates with less than one-third of the Forest Service's manpower and budget, and it suffers from what Culhane described as "an unfortunate — and currently inaccurate — image as the Forest Service's embarrassing stepsister." [35] *(BLM and Forest Service Land Revenues, table, p. 67)*

Congress in fact has bolstered substantially BLM's potential authority since the early 1960s. In 1976 FLPMA gave the bureau a permanent mandate to manage its public lands for multiple uses, matching the Forest Service's mission. FLPMA declared, presumably once and for all, that Congress intended to keep most of the remaining public domain and to back up the bureau's authority to determine how those lands should be used.

FLPMA enhanced BLM powers, but the bureau still has trouble using them. Environmentalists distrust the agency's commitment to land protection, while ranchers, miners, and other Westerners have resisted stiffer public land regulation. BLM suffers from inadequate budget and staffing levels, and Watt's rapid shift away from conservationist policies clouded its long-term objectives. As a result, Sally K. Fairfax concluded in a 1982 paper, BLM remains an "unconvincing goliath" poorly equipped to impose the federal will on reluctant western interests. [36]

Bureau of 'Livestock and Mining'

Compared with the Forest Service, and the Park Service as well, BLM is a relatively new and inexperienced federal agency. President

65

Harry S Truman formed the bureau in 1946 by executive order, merging a discredited U.S. Grazing Service with the Interior Department's antiquated General Land Office (GLO). Three decades later, BLM still was burdened by their legacy of inept public land administration.

The old GLO, founded in 1812, processed the paperwork for surveying and disposing of most of the public domain through 19th century land laws. In that role, the land office earned a reputation as an inefficient agency, prone to corruption by speculators who acquired public lands through bribery and fraud. After the merger, BLM assumed GLO's control over remaining public lands in Alaska and in western Oregon forests that the government had reclaimed from the Oregon & California Railroad. The new bureau also took responsibility for leasing minerals from public lands, a function that GLO had handled since the 1920 Mineral Leasing Act.

But initially BLM's major responsibility was to administer livestock grazing on 142 million acres of public rangelands organized after Congress passed the Taylor Grazing Act in 1934. The law set up the Grazing Service, within the Interior Department, to regulate overgrazing on the public domain by leasing permits to ranchers. But western congressional delegations, dominating the House and Senate Interior committees, kept the Grazing Service poorly staffed and funded to assure minimal government intervention. Western stockmen themselves effectively controlled Grazing Service decisions at the local level, through advisory boards whose members held more power than the government officials who administered grazing districts on public lands. Truman disbanded the Grazing Service after Congress cut its budget by 85 percent in retaliation for the agency's proposal to raise livestock grazing fees from nominal levels *(Chapter 7, grazing discussion, p. 155)*.

For three decades thereafter, BLM's dubious heritage handicapped its efforts to pattern public domain management on the Forest Service's multiple-use example. The bureau operated without clear authority from Congress, administering more than 3,500 public land statutes, many left over from the homesteading era, enacted over a century and a half with no consistent objectives. The 1934 Taylor Act, BLM's primary mandate, was a single-use law, authorizing the government to regulate livestock grazing on public lands "pending disposition" by Congress. The Mining Law of 1872 gave prospectors the right to explore the public lands, without the government's consent, and, when hard-rock minerals were discovered, to file claims for adjoining lands, removing them from BLM

BLM and Forest Service Land Revenues, Thousands of Dollars

Bureau of Land Management	1980	1981	1982
Mineral leases and permits (onshore)[1]	$ 682,130	$ 821,950	$1,420,569
Timber sales	216,110	215,744	87,401
Livestock grazing fees	24,602	24,834	20,879
Sales of lands, materials	7,756	4,829	3,599
Miscellaneous fees, rents	47,818	73,996	97,837
Subtotal onshore receipts	978,416	1,141,443	1,630,285
Outer continental shelf oil and gas leasing[2]	4,100,871	11,988,516	7,038,794
BLM total	$5,079,287	$13,129,959	$8,669,079

Forest Service	1980	1981	1982
Timber sales	$ 625,407	$ 581,441	$ 251,022
Roads built by loggers in lieu of cash	164,226	189,559	164,128
Livestock grazing fees	15,850	14,889	12,426
Mineral leases and permits[3]	40,472	62,080	57,885
Recreation fees	18,317	19,416	25,352
Miscellaneous receipts, rents, sales	1,190	8,710	9,517
Deposits for timber salvage sales, reforestation work, etc.	203,663	208,210	140,266
Forest Service total	$1,069,125	$ 1,084,305	$ 660,695

[1] Includes revenues from leasing minerals beneath national forest lands reserved from the public domain.
[2] Collection of offshore oil and gas lease revenues transferred to Interior Department's Minerals Management Service, effective in fiscal 1983.
[3] Mineral leasing revenues from national forest lands acquired from private owners that were not part of the public domain.

Sources: U.S. Bureau of Land Management, *Public Land Statistics, 1980* and *Public Land Statistics, 1981*; U.S. Bureau of Land Management, *Managing the Nation's Public Lands, Jan. 31, 1983*; U.S. Forest Service, *Report of the Forest Service, Fiscal Year 1982, February 1983*.

control. The bureau leased rights to mine coal and drill for oil and gas, but officials generally offered those minerals only when requested by petroleum or mining companies.

Through the 1950s BLM's performance earned it a reputation as a "captive" agency, subservient to the public land users it was supposed to supervise.[37] The bureau, funded by Congress, had to rely on political support from predominantly local constituencies who demanded minimal government regulation of public resources. BLM grazing district managers, often from ranching families themselves, still relied heavily on the judgment of stockmen's advisory boards. Most bureau officials, even those who moved up to BLM state offices or Washington, D.C., posts, shared the rural, independent values of the western communities where BLM district offices were located.

But during this time BLM also began to attract more professionally trained range specialists who were eager to improve federally owned rangelands degraded by decades of overgrazing. Western universities offered more sophisticated range science programs; and the Society for Range Management, formed in 1948, began publishing a journal and promoting a common professional philosophy among bureau employees and academic rangeland experts. Congress still paid little attention to BLM programs, refusing to schedule hearings when Interior officials submitted legislation providing BLM with authorities similar to those the Forest Service received under the 1960 Multiple Use Act.

Growing conservation concerns turned attention to public lands in the 1960s, and BLM began moving into more aggressive multiple-use management. As Interior secretary, Udall encouraged the bureau to adopt even-handed policies, protecting wildlife and other values in addition to livestock grazing. Congress in 1964 finally granted the bureau's request, at least temporarily, for authority to evaluate its lands and classify some for permanent multiple-use management.

Aspinall steered that law, the Classification and Multiple Use Act of 1964, through Congress as part of maneuvering over the federal Wilderness Act enacted that year. In return for accepting the wilderness measure, Aspinall won approval of his long-sought proposal to establish a Public Land Law Review Commission, dominated by members of Congress, to study ways of overhauling federal land management laws and policies. Aspinall agreed to enlarge BLM's authority in the meantime, pending release of the commission's recommendations.

The Classification and Multiple Use Act directed the secretary to gather information about the public federal lands and resources and to draw up criteria for deciding which lands should remain under federal ownership. A separate measure at the same time gave the bureau power, for the first time, to sell lands at fair market value for community expansion or economic development. Both measures were temporary, and they expired when Aspinall's Public Land Law Review Commission (PLLRC) reported its findings in 1970. But BLM, interpreting its new authority broadly, continued to pursue multiple-use objectives in following years while Congress debated more permanent legislation.

Aspinall chaired the PLLRC, and its recommendations reflected his commitment to productive use of the public lands. The commission's report, entitled *One Third of the Nation's Land,* suggested that Congress review most federal lands, including national forests and monuments, to determine whether the government should retain them. It generally favored commodity use of the lands, including controversial proposals to designate the most productive public lands, for example the best timberlands, for "dominant use" for timber harvests.[38] Congress ignored the PLLRC proposals, and its report produced little public interest. By the time the commission released its findings, moreover, its views were out of step with the prevailing congressional mood in favor of environmental protection.

Beginning in the mid-1960s environmentalists' growing complaints that livestock overgrazing had left public lands in deteriorated condition broadened public backing for more balanced BLM range management. Using its 1964 land classification authority, the bureau began drawing up "management framework plans" setting out long-term goals for resource units within BLM grazing districts. BLM range managers persuaded many ranchers to agree to "allotment management plans" that specified when livestock could be turned out to graze on federally owned range and when the land could be rested. The bureau hired better-trained rangeland specialists, most of them graduates of western state universities.

New federal laws in the early 1970s expanded the bureau's responsibilities. In addition to the endangered species and pollution control laws, a bill was passed by Congress in 1971 that protected wild horses and burros on BLM rangelands and national forests, outlawing roundups by ranchers and professional "mustangers" who sold the animals for dog food. The law corrected undeniable abuses, but it also complicated BLM efforts to restore its lands to productive condition as fast-breeding wild horse bands rapidly multiplied in numbers.

Ranchers out on the range still stubbornly resisted BLM's grazing management plans. The bureau stressed a cooperative "rest-rotation" system that officials maintained ultimately would provide more forage for livestock. In 1973 NRDC filed a lawsuit challenging BLM's plan to draw up a single environmental impact statement to assess grazing on all 170 million acres of public rangeland. The NRDC lawsuit, while filed against BLM, sought grazing reductions that many bureau officials themselves thought necessary. Top-ranking BLM officials, seeking ways to prod Congress and the White House Office of Management and Budget (OMB) to increase funding for rangeland management, sensed an opportunity to form a tacit alliance with environmentalists behind more balanced public land policies.

In September 1974 BLM Director Curt Berkland released an internal bureau report, prepared the previous spring, that detailed the agency's past failure to prevent excessive grazing in Nevada, the state with the largest expanse of federal rangelands, to the detriment of wildlife, recreation, and other uses. Release of the Nevada report, Interior Department economist Nelson recalled in a 1980 study, marked "a pivotal event in shifting the BLM from a livestock grazing agency to an agency with a broader constituency...." [39]

NRDC attorneys introduced BLM's own report as evidence, and U.S. District Judge Thomas A. Flannery in his Dec. 30, 1974, ruling ordered the bureau to prepare 144 separate livestock grazing EISs on western rangelands by 1988. In the following nine years, the bureau's district offices devoted major staff and funding resources to writing grazing statements, producing lengthy documents assessing a whole range of characteristics — including wildlife, landforms, vegetation, historic stage stations, Indian ruins, scenic vistas, and recreation qualities — on public lands where the government leased grazing rights. The bureau's data, often gathered in one-time range surveys by inexperienced workers, was challenged frequently by ranchers and by rangeland scientists employed by western state universities and their agricultural extension services. But the EIS process required BLM to expand its grazing district staffs by hiring biologists, archeologists, engineers, geologists, and other specialists to assess previously ignored rangeland values — and argue forcefully for their protection through more stringent grazing management. Those new employees, many from outside the

West, brought new blood to BLM and infused the agency with their commitment to multiple-use management as they moved upward into state offices and Washington, D.C., headquarters. As Utah State University professor Bernard Shanks pointed out in 1979, "Many of the best natural resources students of the Earth Day era ended up employed by the BLM." [40]

In FLPMA, passed late during the last night of its 1976 session, Congress finally granted BLM permanent authority to manage the public lands. That measure, adopted after six years of maneuvering among environmentalists and public land users, formally established the bureau by law and gave it full "organic" authority to carry out its programs. It provided the agency with general authority to acquire, sell, exchange, or lease lands, replacing the confusing and limited powers to engage in real estate transactions under earlier land laws.

Other provisions for the first time gave BLM officials authority to enforce federal laws on public lands, required persons holding unpatented mining claims on federal lands to record them with the bureau, established a 25-million-acre California Desert Conservation Area under BLM control, and ordered the bureau to review roadless lands for possible wilderness designation. The law provided for congressional review of public land withdrawals that restricted access for mining or other ventures. To underscore rising congressional interest in the public lands, it required that BLM's director be appointed by the president, not by the Interior secretary, subject to Senate confirmation.

The 1976 law, also known as the BLM organic act, in general granted the bureau a full range of multiple-use powers matching the Forest Service mission. It directed BLM to continue planning for managing public lands for the long term, basing resource management decisions on scientific data, public participation, and consultation with state and local governments. The resulting statute often was ambiguous, with numerous references to making BLM policy consistent with state and local preferences.

Yet FLPMA ended an era that had been dying slowly since the 1934 Taylor Grazing Act. It repealed more than 2,000 public land laws, including the 1862 Homestead Act itself, that were relics of 19th century disposal policies. "It's the closing of the West, for real, for final, for absolute," Bill Bishop, a New Mexico packtrip guide and Sierra Club member, noted in 1977.[41]

Resource Policy Shifts

But neither FLPMA nor NFMA ended battles over national forests and rangelands. Nor did expanded legal authority ensure either the Forest Service or BLM the budgets and manpower — or the political savvy — to fully impose scientific multiple-use management. In the years following passage of these two acts in 1976, both agencies were whipsawed as the government abruptly shifted its resource policy goals. By 1979 the West was being swept by the Sagebrush Rebellion against federal land policy.

It fell to Jimmy Carter, a former Georgia governor elected with environmentalists' strong support in 1976, to implement both measures. Carter, a Democrat, defeated Republican President Gerald R. Ford in a close race without carrying a single western state except Hawaii. Early on in his four-year term, Carter's administration displayed an environmentalist bent that dismayed western public land interests.

Carter appointed Cecil D. Andrus, previously Idaho's moderate Democratic governor, to serve as interior secretary. Andrus made it clear from the beginning that, despite his western roots, he intended to move Interior away from what environmentalists viewed as an unqualified sympathy with public resource development. Andrus appointed environmental group activists to top-level Interior positions. A month after he took over, the department deeply offended Westerners by releasing a "hit list" of federally funded water projects that the administration wanted to cancel.

Carter also named M. Rupert Cutler, a forester and former Wilderness Society official, as assistant secretary of agriculture for natural resources and environment, in charge of the Forest Service. Cutler alarmed western interests again by announcing plans to broaden the Forest Service review of roadless lands eligible for wilderness protection.

Those steps fed Westerners' suspicion that Carter had written off the West, with little concern for the region's special stakes in federal land and resource policy. As the Forest Service and BLM moved ahead with long-term forest and rangeland plans, ranchers and other public land users blamed the new administration as they realized their long-time dominance over federal lands was slipping away. Andrus took every opportunity to warn that BLM must improve its past performance. "The initials BLM no longer stand for Bureau of Livestock and Mining," the secretary declared before the National Wildlife Federation in 1977. "The days when economic interests exercised control over decisions on the public domain are past." [42]

On Capitol Hill congressional sympathies continued to shift toward environmentalist goals in public land management. In the House, Rep. Morris K. Udall, an Arizona Democrat and brother to the former Interior secretary, took over as Interior and Insular Affairs Committee chairman in 1979. Udall held strong conservation views and enjoyed close relationships with national environmental organizations. Rep. John F. Seiberling, an Ohio Democrat who also supported environmental controls, became chairman of the Interior Subcommittee on Public Lands and National Parks.

Andrus took a year before selecting Gregg, former New England River Basins Commission director, as BLM director. A Colorado native, Gregg took over the bureau in 1978 and sought accommodation with all public land interests — including commodity producers as well as conservationists — on range management, coal leasing, and other BLM-managed programs. The bureau reached cooperative agreements to consult with western state governments on coal and other energy development. Gregg also fashioned a broad-based coalition, including stockmen as well as environmentalists, behind a 1978 law authorizing additional BLM funds for range improvement projects.

BLM's staff expanded, especially in district offices, as the bureau implemented FLPMA's planning mandate. But while Congress, alarmed by the threat of new energy crises, pumped new funding into the bureau's energy leasing programs, the Carter administration's campaign to balance the federal budget cut spending on BLM resource conservation and planning efforts far below what officials thought was needed. "It was an enormous strain," Joellen Murphy, Gregg's deputy BLM director for policy analysis, recalled in 1983. "Out in the districts, BLM was never adequately staffed." [43]

Even so, Westerners resented BLM's expanding role in determining how public resources should be used. Ranchers' smoldering anger about possible grazing cutbacks burst out in stormy exchanges with BLM employees, in Roswell, N.M.; Escalante, Utah; Kingman, Ariz.; Battle Mountain, Nev.; Challis, Idaho; and other small ranching towns and cities. As grievances accumulated, ranchers in 1979 launched the Sagebrush Rebellion as the Nevada Legislature passed a bill demanding that the U.S. government turn all BLM lands in the state over to state government control.

73

Other state legislatures passed similar claims, arguing that continued federal control denied western states equal standing under the Constitution with eastern states that had few federal lands within their borders. Legal scholars found little merit in that position, and Congress was not about to give up vast western energy reserves by turning public lands over to state or private ownership. Except for Nevada Gov. Robert List, a Republican, western governors kept their political distance from the rebellion; public opinion polls suggested that most Westerners, especially residents of fast-growing cities, supported federal control of lands they used for recreation.

Yet the West voted heavily for Republican Ronald Reagan in his 1980 landslide victory that ousted Carter from the White House. By naming Watt to lead Interior, Reagan signaled that he viewed his victory as a mandate to reverse the Carter administration's policies on resource development. A former U.S. Senate aide, director of Interior's Bureau of Outdoor Recreation, and eventually a Federal Power Commission member, Watt beginning in 1977 directed the Denver-based Mountain States Legal Foundation's court challenges to public land policies, which business executives had found unduly restrictive. The foundation's supporters, including Colorado brewery magnate Joseph Coors, recommended Watt for the Interior post after former U.S. Sen. Clifford Hansen, a Wyoming Republican, turned it down.

Watt, who was born in Wyoming, moved rapidly to implement controversial policies on public lands and resources. He proposed eliminating funds to expand the national park system and supported opening federal wilderness and wildlife refuges for oil and gas exploration. Other Watt policies accelerated federal coal and offshore petroleum leasing schedules. Reagan named Robert L. Burford, a conservative Colorado rancher and state legislator, as BLM director. The administration also appointed John B. Crowell Jr., a former timber company attorney, as the assistant agriculture secretary over the Forest Service.

Watt came to office vowing to "swing the pendulum back to center" between resource production and conservation.[44] His policies, and his frequently combative statements, enraged environmentalists and at times alarmed western governors and resource professionals. Watt finally resigned in October 1983. Congress had challenged Watt's coal-leasing and offshore oil and gas plans, and NRDC in 1983 had taken BLM back to court to challenge the Reagan administration's livestock grazing program. Watt's "overemphasis on destructive, extractive kinds of activities is going to degrade and destroy the public land base," Jay D. Hair, the National Wildlife Federation's executive vice president, contended. "Literally, he's taking away our national heritage." [45]

Notes

1. "Battle Over the Wilderness," *Newsweek,* July 25, 1983, 25.
2. Sally K. Fairfax, "Beyond the Sagebrush Rebellion: the BLM as Neighbor and Manager in the Western States" (Paper presented at the Western Political Science Association meeting, March 1982).
3. "Meet the Press," NBC News, Feb. 21, 1982.
4. For a fuller discussion of the Alaska lands bill, see *Congress and the Nation*, 5 vols., *Congress and the Nation, 1977 1980,* vol 5 (Washington, D.C.: Congressional Quarterly, 1981), 577.
5. Harmon Kallman, U.S. Interior Department public affairs officer, Aug. 9, 1983, telephone interview with author.
6. U.S. Interior Department, Bureau of Land Management, *Public Land Statistics 1981* (Washington, D.C.: Government Printing Office, 1982), 11.
7. Lee Barkow, U.S. Bureau of Land Management, Alaska program staff, Washington, D.C., Aug. 10, 1983, telephone interview with author.
8. U.S. Forest Service, *Report of the Forest Service, Fiscal Year 1982* (Washington, D.C.: Government Printing Office, 1983), 64, 164.
9. Roderick Nash, *Wilderness and the American Mind,* 3d ed. (New Haven, Conn.: Yale University Press, 1982), 315.
10. Ibid., 380.
11. U.S. Fish and Wildlife Service, *Annual Report of Lands Under Control of the U.S. Fish and Wildlife Service, as of Sept. 30, 1982* (Washington, D.C.: Government Printing Office, 1983).
12. William E. Shands, Conservation Foundation senior associate, Washington, D.C., May 19, 1983, telephone interview with author. See also Shands and Robert G. Healy, *The Lands Nobody Wanted* (Washington, D.C.: The Conservation Foundation, 1977).
13. Neal R. Peirce and Jerry Hagstrom, "Western Governors Seek Stronger Voice Over Energy Policy for Their Region," *National Journal,* Oct. 13, 1979, 1692.
14. U.S. Interior Department, Office of Policy Analysis, *Past and Projected State Revenues from Energy and Other Natural Resources in 13 Western States* (Washington, D.C.: Government Printing Office, 1981).
15. Elizabeth Drew, "Secretary Watt," *New Yorker,* May 4, 1981, 104.
16. Frank Gregg, U.S. Bureau of Land Management director, Washington, D.C., Nov. 30, 1979, telephone interview with author.
17. Robert H. Nelson, "The Public Lands," in *Current Issues in Natural Resource Policy,* ed. Paul R. Portney (Washington, D.C.: Resources for the Future, 1982), 35.
18. *Congress and the Nation, 1945-64,* vol. 1, 1063.
19. Nash, *Wilderness and the American Mind,* 200-237.
20. *Congress and the Nation, 1945-64,* vol. 1, 1041.

21. George Cameron Coggins and Charles F. Wilkinson, *Federal Public Land and Resources Law* (Mineola, N.Y.: The Foundation Press, 1981), 197, 226.
22. Paul J. Culhane, *Public Land Politics, Interest Group Influence on the Forest Service and the Bureau of Land Management* (Washington, D.C.: Resources for the Future, 1981), 56.
23. Coggins and Wilkinson, *Federal Public Land and Resources Law*, 226, 497, 569.
24. Fairfax, "Beyond the Sagebrush Rebellion."
25. Culhane, *Public Land Politics*, 336.
26. Samuel T. Dana and Sally K. Fairfax, *Forest and Range Management* (New York: McGraw-Hill, 1980), 64, 204.
27. John Hamer, "Forest Policy," in *Editorial Research Reports, Vol. II, 1975* (Washington, D.C.: Congressional Quarterly, 1976), 867.
28. Hanna J. Cortner and Dennis L. Schweitzer, "Institutional Limits to National Public Planning for Forest Resources: The Resources Planning Act," *Natural Resources Journal*, vol. 21, no. 2 (April 1981): 204.
29. Dana and Fairfax, *Forest and Range Management*, 335.
30. U.S. Forest Service, *Report of the Forest Service, Fiscal Year 1982*, 3.
31. R. W. Behan, dean, Northern Arizona University School of Forestry (Paper presented to symposium entitled "Natural Resource Economics and Policy: Exploration with Journalists," Montana State University Center for Political Economy and Natural Resources, Big Sky, Mont., July 15, 1982).
32. U.S. Forest Service, *Report of the Forest Service FY 1982*, 64-65.
33. U.S. Forest Service, *Principles of Land and Resource Management Planning* (Washington, D.C.: Government Printing Office, 1982), 314.
34. Elwood Miller, associate dean, University of Nevada, Reno, School of Renewable Natural Resources, June 1, 1983, telephone interview with author.
35. Culhane, *Public Land Politics*, 75.
36. Fairfax, "Beyond the Sagebrush Revolution," 15.
37. See Phillip Foss, *Politics and Grass* (Seattle: University of Washington Press, 1960).
38. Public Land Law Review Commission, *One Third of the Nation's Land, A Report to the President and the Congress by the Public Land Law Review Commission* (Washington, D.C.: Government Printing Office, 1970), 92.
39. U.S. Interior Department, Office of Policy Analysis, "The New Range Wars: Environmentalists Versus Cattlemen for the Public Rangelands" (Draft report prepared by Robert H. Nelson, 1980), 47.
40. Bernard Shanks, "BLM Back in the Spotlight After Years of Neglect," *High Country News*, Lander, Wyo., Jan. 26, 1979.
41. Bill Bishop, Albuquerque, N.M., 1977 interview with author.
42. Secretary of the Interior Cecil D. Andrus (Address to National Wildlife Federation annual meeting, March 26, 1977).
43. Joellen Murphy, Albuquerque, N.M., Aug. 30, 1983, telephone interview with author.
44. Tom Arrandale, "Access to Federal Lands," in *Editorial Research Reports, Vol. II, 1981* (Washington, D.C.: Congressional Quarterly, 1982), 693.
45. Jay D. Hair, National Wildlife Federation executive vice president, Albuquerque, N.M., March 20, 1983, interview with author.

Traveling at passenger-train speeds, such trains carry coal from remote mines, making the West's vast public coal resources competitive with supplies closer to populated consumer markets.

Chapter 4

FEDERAL ENERGY SUPPLIES:
MINING FOR THE NATION'S FUTURE

After the 1973 Arab oil embargo, the federal lands and offshore waters emerged as America's last energy frontiers. In the decade that followed, the nation turned — at times almost desperately — to public lands that held most of its remaining coal, oil and gas, uranium, oil shale, and other domestic energy resources.

Those reserves rose dramatically in value in the 1970s as the Organization of Petroleum Exporting Countries (OPEC) pushed world crude prices up from $3 beyond $30 a barrel. As energy values climbed — and motorists twice were forced to line up for gasoline outside U.S. service stations — the government and industry drafted ambitious plans for drilling for federal oil and gas, mining federal coal, developing uranium, and tapping geothermal reservoirs beneath public plains and deserts. Four presidents pledged to speed federal resource production to assure the country dependable energy supplies to replace costly crude oil imports.

Yet, 10 years after the 1973 embargo, Congress and the U.S. Interior Department still were trying to put together an orderly energy leasing program. Energy companies and environmental groups fought incessantly over plans to strip mine western coal, to drill in offshore coastal waters, and to open pristine federal wilderness in the West for oil and gas exploration. Governors pressed for state or regional control over national policies for developing energy reserves on public lands within their borders and federal Outer Continental Shelf (OCS) lands along their seacoasts. In New England and California, and all along the Rocky Mountain chain from Alaska to New Mexico, powerful economic and political forces collided over federal energy resource management.

The federally controlled offshore waters, Arctic mountains and plains, and western deserts and flatlands contained most of the nation's last undeveloped or unexplored energy riches. Estimates vary widely, but the U.S. government may own one-third of the nation's remaining oil and gas, 40 percent of its coal, 80 percent of untapped oil shale reserves, and large portions of uranium and geothermal resources. "In terms of western coal resource ownership, the federal government is close to a monopolist," Garrey E. Carruthers, assistant secretary of interior for land and water resources, noted in 1983 congressional testimony.[1]

Those holdings will give the government a major role in supplying fuel to the nation's economy well into the 21st century. Since the Mineral Leasing Act of 1920, the government has been leasing its energy minerals — except for uranium, a "hard-rock" mineral still open for prospectors to claim under the 1872 Mining Law — for exploration and production by drilling and mining companies. For each of the nation's major conventional fuels, again with the possible exception of uranium, the government will be "a major, if not dominant, future supply source," a 1980 U.S. Department of Energy study concluded.[2]

As a result, the study suggested, ". . . future supply depends critically on the direction of federal land-use policy." During President Jimmy Carter's administration, Interior Secretary Cecil D. Andrus drafted comprehensive government plans to match federal resource production to expected energy demand, while barring strip mining and drilling in fragile country. But after conservative Republican Ronald Reagan unseated Carter and appointed James G. Watt as interior secretary, federal energy policy rapidly shifted toward wide-open leasing programs to inventory the government's resources and to allow free-market demand to determine production levels. "The lands that have energy and mineral potential can have those resources explored — and developed and produced — without destroying . . . other qualities," Watt insisted. "To deny access to those lands for development is to deny the realization of some of their prime value."[3]

But Watt's aggressive stance intensified, for the time being at least, longstanding differences over federal mineral leasing policy. Environmentalists objected that all-out leasing would expose the nation's prime wilderness lands, invaluable coastal waters, and wide-open western spaces to risky oil-drilling operations and land-scarring coal strip mines. Governors complained that rapid leasing gave states and communities too little time to plan for boom-town energy development. And former Carter administration officials, joined by environmentalist leaders and resource economists, contended that Watt's leasing policies turned

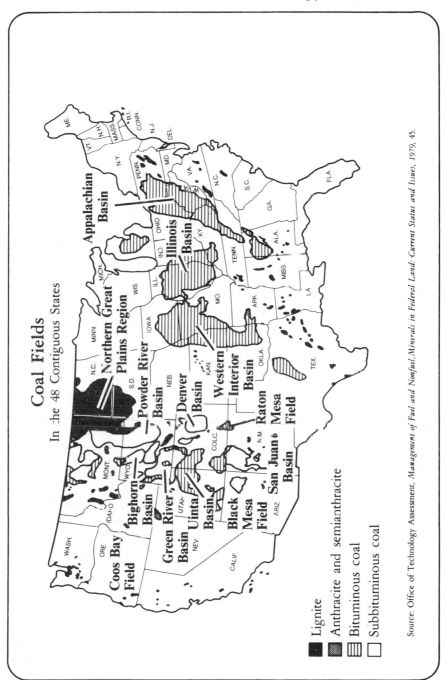

Coal Fields
In the 48 Contiguous States

Source: Office of Technology Assessment, *Management of Fuel and Nonfuel Minerals in Federal Land: Current Status and Issues, 1979,* 45.

Lignite
Anthracite and semianthracite
Bituminous coal
Subbituminous coal

precious resources over to private company control without sufficient financial return to the U.S. Treasury. "The secretary of the interior is acting as a trustee here," Frank Gregg, former director of Interior's Bureau of Land Management (BLM), pointed out in 1983. "He has an obligation to behave as a prudent manager." [4]

Federal Energy Development

The government's energy management responsibilities grew larger in the 1970s and early 1980s. U.S. oil production fell off after 1970, and the OPEC cartel demonstrated during the following decade the nation's vulnerable position as it relied heavily on imported crude. American energy companies, rapidly using up privately held fossil fuel deposits, turned eagerly to the public lands in their search for new reserves.

Those federally owned energy supplies included vast coal and oil shale deposits that had been mapped out early in the century. But producers had passed them by, at least while the nation enjoyed plentiful fuels from easily tapped deposits closer to energy markets. Since the mid-19th century, U.S. heavy industry had built up a base in the Northeast and Midwest, close by the Appalachian coal fields of Pennsylvania, West Virginia, Kentucky, and other states. And after the petroleum era dawned in the 20th century, Americans easily fueled automobiles, homes, and factories from giant oil fields that wildcatters found by drilling the flat, rolling terrain of Texas, Louisiana, the Permian Basin of western Texas and eastern New Mexico, and other petroleum-producing regions. *(Eastern v. western coal, box, pp. 84-85)*

Federally owned energy, in contrast, lay in hard to reach mountains and plateaus that made development too costly, or beneath plains and deserts too far from industrial and population centers. But as electricity demand rose — in the Far West as well as the Midwest and South — utilities looked to the government's low-sulfur coal for clean-burning fuel for their boilers. And as world oil prices climbed, major and independent oil companies alike flocked to the Rocky Mountains to drill thousands of feet beneath federal forests and rangelands in search of new oil and gas deposits. The government itself, alarmed by Middle East conflicts that threatened the nation's foreign crude supplies, began promoting projects to convert federal oil shale and coal into synthetic liquid fuels to power the nation's transportation system.

Those trends gathered strength in the 1970s. Mining from federal western coal reserves boomed after 1971, multiplying 10-fold in a decade.

Oil companies pressed the Interior Department to lease rights to explore promising public lands for potentially huge oil and gas reserves, both in the West and in federally controlled outer continental shelf waters. Major oil companies began investing in experimental coal and oil-shale conversion technology, while interest also grew in federally owned lands that lay over naturally occurring geothermal steam and hot-water reservoirs. As one result, law professors George Cameron Coggins and Charles F. Wilkinson noted in their 1981 textbook on federal land law, "some of the most powerful economic interests in the country have large stakes in the direction of public land policy." [5]

The government owns 60 percent of the West's low-sulfur coal, and those holdings control the development of another 20 percent in state and private reserves that cannot be mined separately from federal deposits. The U.S. reserves include most of the 142.5 billion tons lying in 120-foot-thick seams just beneath wind-swept Wyoming and Montana plains in the coal-rich Powder River Basin. [6]

Federal lands also hold most of the West's oil-bearing shales, including 80 percent of the 418 billion barrels of high-grade fuel locked into formations that stretch beneath 25,000 square miles of desert plateaus and basins in northwestern Colorado, Utah, and Wyoming. In addition to known coal and oil-shale reserves, public lands in the West may also provide plentiful uranium and geothermal resources. *(Oil-shale boom, box, pp. 94-95)*

Uranium mining, however, fell off in the early 1980s when utilities all over the nation scrapped plans for nuclear power plant construction as financial costs and concerns about nuclear safety grew. Similarly, geothermal power generation potential had yet to be widely developed except in California's long-operating Geysers region.

Energy Leasing System

Through the Mineral Leasing Act of 1920, Congress gave the secretary of interior discretionary power to lease federal energy reserves for production by private companies. The 1920 law, refined by subsequent measures, directed the Interior Department to sell rights to develop known coal, petroleum, and oil shale deposits through competitive bidding, making sure that the government received "fair market value."

In granting mineral leases, the government imposes diligent development requirements that allow a lease to be cancelled unless production gets under way within a specified period, usually 10 years. It also sets stan-

Environmental, Economic Factors...

The U.S. government owns major coal reserves beneath national forests and private lands in Kentucky, Alabama, Illinois, and other coal-producing eastern states. But the most extensive federally owned coal resources lie in the West, in easily mined deposits with low-sulfur content, beneath public plains and deserts in New Mexico, Utah, Colorado, Wyoming, Montana, and North Dakota.

Most eastern coals are hard anthracite or bituminous deposits, with high-carbon content and little moisture, that burn intensely to give off high energy levels from each ton. Those eastern coals, mostly in deep veins that are mined from underground tunnels, since the mid-19th century have supplied much of the fuel that the nation burned to heat homes and fire steel furnaces, industrial boilers, and electricity-generating plants in the eastern and midwestern industrial cities that grew up near Appalachian coalfields.

Western reserves, in contrast, generally are softer subbituminous and lignite coals, less desirable because high levels of water and other volatile materials reduce their heating value. The high costs of transporting heavy, bulky coal from isolated western fields also had discouraged shipments to industrial regions.

But eastern coals also hold relatively high levels of sulfur. When the coal is burned, the sulfur combines with oxygen to give off sulfur dioxide, a major air pollutant. Congress, in the 1970 Clean Air Act Amendments, directed the federal government to set emission standards for newly constructed plants at levels that barred burning of most eastern coals unless

dards for the pace of development, mining or drilling methods, and thorough recovery of resources from public deposits. In addition to bonus bids that companies pay to win leases at auction, the department charges rents for lands that operations occupy and royalties on the value of production set at 12.5 percent, or 16.5 percent for offshore petroleum in 1983.

Mineral revenues climbed in the 1970s as petroleum prices jumped and federal coal production accelerated. By fiscal 1982 BLM was collecting $1.4 billion from leasing minerals on national forests and rangelands, along with another $7 billion from offshore oil and gas

... Favor Western Over Eastern Coal

companies installed equipment to scrub sulfur dioxide from smokestack plumes.

Most western coal, including federally owned reserves, contains much lower percentages of sulfur. As federal clean-air standards went into effect, electric utilities in the Midwest and South began buying western coal that could meet federal air pollution standards without costly scrubbing equipment. In the same period railroad unit trains — hauling nothing but coal in long strings of hopper cars headed for the same destination — cut transportation costs to levels that also made western coal more competitive. Most western deposits, lying just beneath the surface, can be extracted by strip-mining methods that are less costly and require fewer miners than underground mining.

But Congress, in amending federal clean air standards in 1977, reduced western coal's competitive advantage by requiring that utilities install scrubbers on all new plants, regardless of the sulfur content of the coal used to fuel them. Federal strip-mining reclamation standards have raised western mining costs, while railroads have been increasing coal-hauling charges again since federal deregulation programs ended rate-setting restrictions. Those shifting trends, along with lagging energy consumption in Japan and other Far East nations once considered good prospects for western coal exports, may hold western coal production below forecasts made in the late 1970s. The resulting uncertainty complicated the federal government's plans for leasing its public coal reserves to meet future production requirements.

royalties.[7] As onshore revenues mounted, the government continued to share half its leasing receipts with state and local governments within whose boundaries public coal and petroleum were located.

But even as production and revenues grew, the government was confronted with tough decisions on leasing even more of its energy resources. As trustee of public lands, the interior secretary was under obligation to produce as much revenue as possible from development of the government's ever more valuable minerals. But the government also tried to make sure that fuel production from federal lands would be adequate in future years to fill the nation's demand for energy. As the wide policy shifts between the Carter and Reagan administrations confirmed, there was no political consensus in Congress or in the executive branch over how best to pursue those conflicting objectives.

Through its land-use planning process, the Interior Department also was trying to determine where wildlife habitat and other conflicting environmental concerns should rule out mining operations. In managing potential federal oil and gas reserves, the government was debating how rapidly to permit petroleum companies to explore sensitive offshore waters and forests and rangelands. Even for well-mapped reserves like oil shale and coal, the government remained divided over the timing and extent of development. And once reserves were cleared for sale, officials still faced difficult judgments on when to offer public resources on private markets, and what price to demand through competitive leasing.

Those decisions grew all the more complex in the early 1980s, as OPEC's disarray threw world energy markets into turmoil. At the same time, controversy over Watt's leasing policies revealed continued divisions within the United States over how efficiently the government was managing federal resources. "Clearly, a lot more creative thought could go into the way in which public resources are offered for private use," Phillip M. Burgess, director of the Colorado School of Mines Energy and Minerals Management Institute, suggested in 1983.[8]

Market demand for energy ultimately will determine how much fuel oil and coal companies extract from federally leased deposits. But the government's leasing policies will influence how much coal or other resources are available for mining, and how much consumers will pay to offset environmental and social costs of production. Like any landowner, the government will be tempted to conserve public resources for future development, when prices are likely to be higher. But, as the nation's sovereign authority, the government also must try to make sure that public energy reserves are available to fill the country's future need for dependable fuel supplies. "It really is a market-driven situation," Burgess went on in assessing 1983 controversies over federal coal-leasing policy. "If demand for coal exists in seven to ten years and it hasn't been leased, they're going to take a heavy rap" from hard-pressed energy consumers.[9]

Coal Leasing Controversies

The federal government owns 200 billion tons of coal, largely in thick low-sulfur seams just below the surface of federally owned deserts and plains in the Rocky Mountain region. Federal coal mining boomed in the 1970s as power plants and factories in the South, Midwest, and fast-growing West Coast turned to western low-sulfur reserves to supply dependable fuel for their boilers. Yet for 12 years federal coal policy was all but paralyzed by legal and political controversy. *(Federal coal production in six western states, table, p. 89)*

Federal coal production in 1982 jumped to 107 million tons, up from roughly 10 million tons a decade earlier. Yet for 10 years, from 1971 to early 1981, the Interior Department halted virtually all federal coal leasing while Congress, the courts, and BLM officials struggled to reshape coal management procedures. Two years after leasing resumed, Watt's efforts to rush federal reserves onto depressed coal markets created an uproar in Congress, environmental group headquarters, and western coal-state capitals.

By some calculations, the West will supply half of U.S. coal production by 1990, largely from previously leased federal deposits. But whether U.S. coal supplies can match national need for dependable fuels beyond 1990 may depend on critical judgments that the U.S. Interior Department must make.

It takes a mining company seven to 10 years to begin mining coal once leased, Burgess pointed out, and "it's anybody's guess what the market is going to be then." Any number of fast-changing forces — electric power demand, railroad coal-hauling rates, Japanese coal imports, federal clean-air and strip-mining regulations — could either curtail coal use or push it far above what the government's computers were forecasting. By marketing federal coal too soon, the government could lose revenue from higher bonus bids that coal firms might be willing to pay after resource values climbed higher. But if the government holds onto its resources too long, future shortages could force energy prices up and leave the country unable to rely on its own ample coal reserves to replace foreign oil imports.

Under Andrus, Carter's interior secretary, the department drew up a comprehensive coal management program to set leasing levels after careful land-use planning, computer coal-production forecasts, and consultation with western state governors. But Watt, taking over just as the government began leasing more coal, took a single-minded approach that accelerated sales to place federal coal reserves in industry control more rapidly. "We're leasing for reserves, to introduce competition between companies" by providing them with larger coal supplies to offer to electric utilities and other consumers, at prices set by market demand, Carruthers, Watt's assistant secretary, explained in a 1983 interview.[10]

But environmentalists challenged Watt's coal leasing plans in court, and Congress weighed holding up scheduled sales while it reviewed the government's coal management procedures. By offering so much coal, and at the same time cutting back on federal strip-mining controls, Watt "introduced a lot of uncertainty into a system that was nearing a point of stability," former BLM director Gregg suggested as the controversy mounted in 1983.

Coal Leasing Program

The U.S. government has been leasing coal since 1921. Western mines never produced a large share of the nation's coal output until the 1970s, when the region's production boomed to supply low-sulfur fuel to factories and electrical generating power plants in the South, Midwest, as well as in the West's own fast-growing markets. Federal energy planners at the same time eyed federally owned low-sulfur deposits as an immense energy reserve that the nation could easily exploit for new power plants and synthetic liquid fuel production.

Just as western coal mining took off, however, new legal and political pressures halted the government's coal-leasing program. Environmental groups challenged coal development plans that would permit giant earth-gouging draglines to rip across the West's wide-open spaces in destructive strip-mining operations. Congress ordered the Interior Department to manage federal lands for multiple uses, including wildlife, recreation, and wilderness preservation in addition to coal production. Western coal-state governors and community leaders raised an alarm about boom-town growth that could overload roads, hospitals, police forces, and other government services. Evidence mounted that speculators were keeping previously leased federal coal in the ground, hoping to profit from rising resource values.

The Interior Department responded by halting new leasing in 1971. The moratorium lasted a decade as government experts jockeyed to shape new coal management procedures that would strengthen the government's control over federal coal production and assure the nation larger financial returns from increasingly valuable public resources.

Before 1920 the government had offered its coal-bearing lands for sale. But the 1920 law directed the Interior secretary to retain the lands

Federal Coal Production and Reserves in Six Western States

Major federal coal states	1981 Federal production[1] (millions of tons)	Total federal reserves (millions of tons)	Federal percent of total state reserves	Projected total state 1990 production[2] (millions of tons)	1990 Total state percent of U.S. production
Colorado	11.5	9,900	61%	35.1	2.2%
Montana	15.4	77,200	64	109.7	6.8
New Mexico	8.9	3,700	82	64.1	4.0
North Dakota	0.2	3,200	32	50.8	3.1
Utah	8.6	5,600	85	48.8	3.0
Wyoming	49.9	40,400	73	256.5	15.8
Totals	94.5	140,000	66	565.0	34.9
Total 50 states	94.6	144,700	33	1,620.0	100.0

[1] Fiscal year 1981 production.

[2] Includes projected production of both federal and nonfederal coal in each state. The Energy Department projections are in the high range compared with other 1990 coal projections, particularly for the state of Wyoming. The state government of Wyoming itself forecasts that 1990 coal production will be 168 million tons.

Source: *Current Issues in Natural Resource Policy* (Washington, D.C.: Resources for the Future, 1982), 20.

and lease the coal for production by private mining ventures. The measure required competitive bidding on known federal deposits.

But outside of known energy reserves, the law allowed the government to grant companies rights to explore public lands for new discoveries, then reward successful finds with exclusive leases to produce the resources. That system remains in effect for oil and gas, but Congress in 1976 coal-leasing legislation repealed the preference-right prospecting system for coal resources because federal reserves already had been well delineated.

Once leases were granted, the government charged rents for the land and royalties of at least 5 cents per ton of production. The 1920 law granted 37.5 percent of coal-leasing revenues to state and local governments where mines were located.

By 1970 the government had issued more than 500 coal leases, and companies had filed with the Interior Department more than 170 preference-right lease applications for coal discoveries on federal lands. But BLM in 1970 reported that federal coal production in six western states actually had fallen to 7.4 million tons, from 10 million tons in 1945, even though the federal acreage under lease had grown 10 times during the postwar decades. BLM's report suggested that coal lease holders were keeping public resources in the ground, speculating that its value would rise, in the knowledge that the government never had enforced stipulations that coal be mined in timely fashion.

In response, Secretary of the Interior Rogers C. B. Morton in 1971 halted further leasing for two years; and the department in 1973 barred new prospecting permits and limited new leasing in reserves adjacent to existing mines that were needed to keep operations going. Interior officials set out to draft a new coal program and environmental impact statement to govern a long-term leasing plan encouraging production while also satisfying a growing environmental movement's fears that rapid coal development would ruin permanently large tracts of western land.

That turned out to be a time-consuming task. While Congress studied mineral leasing law revisions, the Interior Department put together a coal leasing proposal that was dubbed the Energy Minerals Activity Recommendation System (EMARS). Proposed in 1975, the EMARS system contemplated that the coal industry each year would nominate specific federal coal tracts that they wished to lease from the government. Western governors, environmentalists, and farmers opposed the Interior plan, however, and in 1977 the U.S. District Court for the District of Columbia declared in a lawsuit brought by the Natural Resources Defense Council (NRDC) that the department's final EMARS environmental impact statement was inadequate.

Congress in the meantime had introduced and passed new coal-leasing legislation. President Gerald R. Ford in 1976 vetoed the bill, contending that burdensome requirements would discourage production of federal coal and raise its cost to consumers. Congress overrode the veto, and the measure, the Federal Coal Leasing Amendments Act of 1976, became law. It abolished future preference-right leasing, directed that all coal be leased through competitive bidding, and required that accepted bids provide the government "fair market value." The law also raised federal royalties for strip-mined coal to a minimum of 12.5 percent of resource value and required lease holders to start production within 10 years or forfeit their leases. Other provisions raised state and local shares of federal coal lease revenues to 50 percent from the previous 37.5 percent and required the department to prepare comprehensive land-use plans before putting leases up for bidding. Congress in 1976 also passed the Federal Land Policy and Management Act (FLPMA) strengthening BLM's planning authority and followed up in 1977 with the Surface Mining Control and Reclamation Act (SMCRA) setting federal standards for strip-mining operations and reclamation.

The Carter administration officially scrapped the EMARS system in 1977. BLM during the following two years devised a coal management program, based on the new legislation, that relied on federal coal production goals, the bureau's land-use planning process, and regional coal teams made up of state and federal officials. BLM first studied existing and potential coal-lease tracts to screen out lands where low coal values, wildlife habitat, or conflicting uses made mining unsuitable. The federal Energy Department in the meantime proposed coal production goals based on computer demand estimates in each of the six western regions where federal reserves were concentrated. Calculating expected output from existing mines, the Interior officials set preliminary targets for leasing more federal coal to make up shortfalls below potential demand.

Regional coal teams, composed of BLM State Office directors and governors from the states concerned, reviewed the leasing goals and recommended adjustments. They also ranked potential leasing tracts that BLM had mapped out, considering its land-use plans and industry suggestions, in drawing up leasing schedules for the interior secretary to consider. As it leased new reserves, the department also would process pending preference-right lease applications by 1984 and cancel existing leases that had not been brought into production by 1986, 10 years after Congress approved the 1976 coal leasing amendments.

In its environmental impact statement on the coal management program, BLM contended that additional federal leasing was needed to meet national energy objectives and to "ensure that future western coal development is carried out as efficiently and with as little damage to the physical and human environment as possible." [11] The Carter administration designed its program to match coal-leasing levels to expected demand, as calculated by the Energy Department's computer model for future coal production, but erring on the high side of alternative forecasts. Western governors, environmentalists, and the coal industry by and large backed the Andrus system as a way to meet national coal-production needs while protecting western interests. "In the West, there is a lot of opportunity to reach compromise" on where coal development should take place, observed Douglas Larson, director of the Denver-based Western State Energy Board. "The only place you can do that is as close to the resource as possible, through the regional coal teams." [12]

Andrus in 1979 scheduled 1981-82 federal coal sales to lease nearly 1.5 billion tons, half of that in the Powder River Basin. But Andrus ordered that no leasing be conducted after 1984 except in areas where BLM had completed comprehensive resource management plans to replace earlier less detailed documents.

Gregg, who directed BLM during Carter's term, contended that such broad-based support ensured that coal could be put on the market in orderly fashion. "We could lease and produce far more coal than the market could possibly absorb," Gregg maintained in a 1983 interview, noting that preliminary leasing targets incorporated an ample 25 percent "fudge factor" to allow for unexpectedly high demand. By timing lease sales to expected mining, he went on, the government would have greater assurance that companies would bid up bonus payments and start paying royalties by putting coal into production as soon as possible. The program, he argued, "had a reasonable prospect — because of the greater possibility of timely development — of getting a reasonable return to the taxpayers."

Gregg conceded that the Carter program could have been improved by giving coal companies a chance earlier in the planning process to indicate which coal resources they preferred to mine. But critics went further, contending that government attempts to plan leasing on the basis of future energy demand estimates could not keep up with shifting market conditions. Interior Department economist Robert H. Nelson, in a 1982 assessment of public land policy published by Resources for the Future, noted that 1979 OPEC oil price increases, reduced electric power demand, natural gas price and production shifts, and changing synthetic fuel prospects in the late 1970s forced the Energy Department to sharply revise the coal production and demand forecasts on which leasing targets were based. "It is fair to say that central planning in this case turned out to be more like writing fiction than real planning," Nelson maintained.[13]

Before actual leasing resumed in 1981, the government's regional coal production goals swung wildly. In calculating regional leasing targets, Interior first used the Energy Department's 1987 medium production goal, increased by 25 percent for unexpectedly strong demand. Later, the department switched to the agency's 1990 medium production figure. In preparing for Powder River lease sales, officials finally settled on the high-range 1990 regional goal of 438 million tons per year.

Watt Leasing Efforts

The Interior Department in January 1981 leased its first coal under the Andrus program, in the Green River-Ham's Fork region in Wyoming and Colorado. By then, however, world coal markets were softening as electric power demand fell short of predicted levels. Over the following two years, oil prices slackened as OPEC, faced with internal bickering and an oil glut due in part to U.S. conservation efforts, fell into disarray. The Reagan administration took office and played down Carter's call for conservation and synthetic fuel development.

President Reagan named Watt to head Interior just as coal leasing resumed. Following the new administration's free-market philosophy, Watt moved quickly to accelerate leasing schedules and to streamline the Andrus coal management program. Watt's aides vastly increased the coal tonnage the department put up for bid, responding to coal industry requests for added reserves even though worldwide demand was depressed.

Watt and Carruthers made it clear that they put more faith in market competition to allocate public coal than in the government's planning capacities. In 1983 congressional testimony, Carruthers cited a

Long-awaited Oil-Shale Boom . . .

The Roan Plateau in many ways typifies the public lands still owned by the federal government. The plateau rises abruptly, in brown- and buff-streaked cliffs that climb 3,000 feet above the Colorado River's course through northwest Colorado. It stretches off to the north and west, across a bleak gray-green expanse of sagebrush and pinyon and juniper trees. Wild horses, elk, and mule deer roam across barren bluff sliced apart by dry arroyos draining toward Piceance Creek.

But the Piceance Creek Basin holds what well could prove the federal government's most valuable resources. Along with federal lands in adjacent northeastern Utah and southwestern Wyoming, those lands sprawl across the world's richest oil-shale deposits, containing more oil than in Saudi Arabia.

The Mahogany Ledge, a 100-foot-thick vein that crops out in the cliffs visible high above the Colorado River valley, contains 40 gallons of oil locked in each ton of satin-lustered rock stretching 30 miles to the north beneath the Piceance Basin. In that single region, the highest grade oil shale alone holds nearly 500 billion barrels of fuel. Those deposits, along with veins in a 25,000-square-mile region that includes parts of Utah and Wyoming, hold an estimated 1.8 trillion barrels of oil, six times the world's proven crude oil reserves.

The federal government owns 89 percent of the West's oil-shale riches. Experts suggest it could cost $60, perhaps even $100, to produce one barrel of oil from those rocks, actually marlstones that contain a solid hydrocarbon compound called kerogen. Despite those high costs, the government ever since the 1973 Arab oil embargo has been preparing to lease those well-mapped resources for commercial production. But in the early 1980s falling energy demand and oil prices dampened interest.

Before the 1920s prospectors staked 30,000 oil-shale claims in the West under the 1872 Mining Law, expecting that the deposits soon would be developed. The government also showed interest, but the giant oil field discovery in east Texas in 1930 flooded U.S. petroleum markets, depressing prices and making oil-shale production uneconomic. During World War II Congress authorized oil-shale conversion research, but cheap Middle East crude imports in the 1950s and 1960s discouraged further effort.

In 1974, after the Organization of Petroleum Exporting Countries (OPEC) began pushing world oil prices upward, the Interior Department leased four Colorado and Utah tracts for experimental oil-shale projects.

. . .Still Only a Distant Prospect

President Gerald R. Ford in 1975 proposed federal financial incentives to encourage development of a commercial oil-shale industry, and President Jimmy Carter, initially cool to synthetic fuel incentives, proposed a crash synfuel development program in 1979 after the Iranian revolution caused oil shortages. Congress approved Carter's plan for a Synthetic Fuel Corp. to grant subsidies for oil-shale and other synthetic fuel projects with revenues from federal windfall oil profit taxes.

Companies in the late 1970s accelerated work on at least 12 western oil-shale projects, both on federal leases and on private oil-shale claims. The Exxon-Tosco Colony project and Union Oil Co. began constructing underground mines to haul shale to the surface, where it would be heated in huge retorts to 900 degrees, inducing the kerogen to flow out of the rock. Occidental Petroleum Corp. sank two 2,000-foot shafts in the Roan Plateau to prepare huge underground chambers where blasted shale could be fired to produce oil, without bringing it to the surface.

But as of mid-1983 those techniques had yet to produce fuel on a commercial scale. In addition to rising costs, oil-shale ventures faced considerable uncertainty over their environmental and social impact on sparsely populated northwest Colorado. Full-scale commercial development posed the threats of overburdening water supplies in the arid region, polluting groundwater with toxic wastes, and dumping huge piles of spent shale into canyons and gullies near retort sites.

President Ronald Reagan's administration, committed to free-market energy policies, was less enthusiastic about federal support for synthetic fuels projects. A worldwide oil glut pushed crude prices down to $29 a barrel in 1983, far less than the cost of producing a barrel of fuel from shale. Occidental in 1981 mothballed its project, and Exxon the following year pulled out of the Colony venture. Exxon's sudden decision startled Colorado officials and threw thousands of workers out of jobs in Parachute, Battlement Mesa, and other nearby oil-shale boom towns.

Union Oil kept its project going, with $42.50-a-barrel price guarantees from the Synthetic Fuels Corp. The company expected to begin producing 10,000 barrels of fuel a day from shale by the end of 1983. Other experimental projects also were proceeding. But with companies reluctant to make massive investments in full-scale commercial projects, most experts expected that development of the government's oil-shale reserves probably would be delayed until the 21st century.

U.S. Geological Survey study that concluded that Andrus' "restrictive" leasing policies could cost the U. S. economy $2 billion a year by 1995. He also noted Justice Department advice that restrictive leasing could curtail competition by denying new firms entry into western coal production. "After a ten-year moratorium . . . the coal companies and consumers need the reassurance that a continuing supply will be forthcoming," Carruthers maintained.[14]

With the regional coal team's consent, Carruthers set leasing targets for the April 1982 Powder River lease sales at 1.6 billion tons, double Andrus' preliminary 1979 target. Interior also scheduled major sales for New Mexico's San Juan Basin, the Uinta-Southwestern Utah coal fields, and the Fort Union region of Montana and North Dakota. Carruthers rejected the Fort Union coal team's recommendation for lower leasing targets, but Interior scaled down its planned San Juan sale after New Mexico Gov. Toney Anaya, a Democrat, objected. The department also was planning a follow-up Powder River sale in 1984 for as much as 5.3 billion tons. In the meantime, officials were planning to finish processing by 1984 applications for 5.8 billion tons of coal that the department contended the government was obliged to lease under pending preference right applications.

Watt "is trying to put as much coal as possible in the hands of the coal companies," NRDC attorney Johanna Wald complained in mid-1983. "That's very clear." [15] NRDC filed suit to block further coal leasing under 1982 Interior regulations that Watt approved to replace the Andrus requirements. The Watt regulations based coal tract selections more closely on industry preferences while deferring BLM land-use planning intended to identify coal tracts unsuitable for leasing development.

By removing Andrus' 1984 deadline, the regulations permitted BLM to keep leasing coal under its outdated plans. The administration also cut the bureau's planning staff and budget to levels that forced the timetable for drafting comprehensive plans that Congress ordered in FLPMA to be stretched out. As a result, Larson charged, BLM was "making decisions on critical questions, such as coal leasing, based on inadequate plans."

The 1982 revised regulations initially relegated regional coal-leasing teams to an advisory role. But western governors, during a November 1982 meeting with Watt in Denver, persuaded the secretary to restore the teams' authority to recommend preferred leasing targets. Coal-state officials nonetheless were alarmed that federal coal development plans could overwhelm state and local governments' ability to process permits to control mining expansion and cope with boom-town growth. "The Interior Department under this administration views its trust obligation as being to get public resources into private hands so the market can determine what will be developed," Larson observed. "That's all well and good, but in state capitals that's only the beginning of the problem."

Coal Leasing Opposition

Watt's aggressive leasing plans rekindled concerns about federal coal development that the Andrus program had muted. Members of Congress and governors, who generally favored continued leasing, called for a temporary halt while the government made sure it was receiving adequate bonus bids, both for the federal Treasury and for state and local governments that shared half of federal coal-leasing revenues. Environmental group leaders, at the national and regional levels, questioned the need for any new leasing while U.S. coal markets were glutted. When Andrus prepared for more leasing, Wald remarked, "I didn't feel there was a need then and there's even less need now."

A 1983 furor over Powder River leasing in the previous year raised doubts about how well Interior was managing coal development. In April 1983, a year after the lease sales, a House Appropriations Committee investigations staff report charged that the government had offered 1.6 billion tons of public coal at "firesale prices" without requiring sufficient bidding competition. The staff questioned Interior's decision, made just days before the Powder River sale, to scrap its minimum acceptable bids in favor of much lower assessments of coal values.[16] The congressional General Accounting Office (GAO) followed up with its own study calculating that Interior accepted bonus bids for Powder River coal that fell $100 million short of fair market values.[17] In response, the full House approved an Appropriations Committee rider to the Interior Department's fiscal 1984 appropriations bill to halt new leasing for six months while a special commission studied the government's coal program. The Republican-controlled Senate went along, a major slap at Watt's policies.

Watt also defied a House Interior Committee resolution by going ahead with coal-lease sales in the Fort Union Basin, but a federal judge barred the department from actually issuing leases until 1984. Watt and Carruthers insisted that the government could best serve consumers in the long run by making reserves available to industry. Over time, Interior officials pointed out, land rentals and royalty payments as federal coal is mined provide much larger returns to the government. "The bonus bid is peanuts," Paul Applegate, BLM's Albuquerque, N.M., district manager contended in 1983. By holding up leasing, Applegate went on, "you're really losing out on the rental and royalty revenue." [18]

Continuing Coal Leasing Uncertainties

Congressional concerns about Watt's coal-leasing strategies cast new doubt on a program that already was clouded by the unpredictable swings in the U.S. energy outlook. The controversy unfolded as lagging coal demand undercut the government's coal production forecasts. And coal company plans to begin mining previously leased federal reserves suggested that production during the 1990s would be ample for the most likely levels of coal demand.

In a 1981 study the congressional Office of Technology Assessment (OTA) predicted that mining from 502 existing federal leases in the six western coal states would produce between 410 million and 500 million tons a year by 1991, depending on market demand, the success of synthetic fuel development projects, and construction of new railroad lines into coal fields. OTA found that coal demand for the Powder River Basin, where half of federal reserves were concentrated, most likely would range between 200 million tons and 225 million tons a year in 1990, well below Energy and Interior department projections. With the production capacity from existing mines and undeveloped leases approaching 350 million tons a year in the early 1990s, OTA found that "the potential for high overcapacity in the Powder River basin has caused questions to be raised about the timing, extent and location of renewed large-scale leasing." [19]

A 1981 study of western coal-export potential by the Western Governors Policy Office (WESTPO) found that only 57 percent of 1990 mining capacity in the region was committed to buyers under existing contracts. [20] Watt's critics contended that leasing more coal while future markets looked so uncertain sacrificed the government's discretion to hold reserves until coal demand would produce higher bonus bids for leases. "What we're seeing is the willingness of the administration to unload federal resources at a time when the primary benefit will flow not to the owner of the resource but to the coal companies," Norman Dean, a National Wildlife Federation counsel, contended. "With such a depressed coal market, it's inexcusable to be leasing more federal coal." [21]

But many observers, including western governors, supported at least modest federal leasing to gauge market demand and to keep existing mine operations going by giving companies access to adjacent tracts. "There are individual cases where it makes sense to lease additional coal," Larson noted — for instance, to replace existing leases where mining would be too destructive or to concentrate new mining growth in the vicinity of existing mines and power plants. "There are a lot of existing leases out in the middle of nowhere," he added.

Western state governors regarded the federal leasing system as fundamentally sound, but "repeatedly questioned the amounts of coal this administration is putting on . . . depressed coal markets," Montana Gov. Ted Schwinden, a Democrat, wrote in 1983.[22] Schwinden and Wyoming Gov. Ed Herschler, also a Democrat, supported the 1982 Powder River sales, assuming that fair market value requirements would produce adequate revenues and hold actual leasing to acceptable levels. But in view of continued market uncertainties, they favored a more cautious future strategy. "If you're going to err, it's better to err on the side of being conservative," Tim Gallagher, Schwinden's top energy adviser, suggested. "The coal's not going anywhere. . . . If anything, it's going to be more valuable." [23]

Notes

1. Garrey E. Carruthers, assistant secretary of interior for land and water resources, statement before the House Interior and Insular Affairs Committee, Subcommittee on Mining, Forest Management and Bonneville Power Administration, June 7, 1983, 98th Cong., 1st sess.
2. U.S. Energy Department, Energy Information Administration, *The Use of Federal Lands for Energy Development*, prepared by Edward Porter (Washington, D.C.: Government Printing Office, 1980), 1.
3. "How Interior Plans to 'Unlock' Public Lands," *Business Week*, March 23, 1981, 84L.
4. Frank Gregg, July 8, 1983, telephone interview with author.
5. George Cameron Coggins and Charles F. Wilkinson, *Federal Public Land and Resources Law* (Mineola, N.Y.: The Foundation Press, 1981), xxv.
6. U.S. Interior Department, Bureau of Land Management, *Final Environmental Statement, Federal Coal Management Program* (Washington, D.C.: Government Printing Office, 1979), 4-24.
7. U.S. Interior Department, Bureau of Land Management, *Managing the Nation's Public Lands* (Washington, D.C.: Government Printing Office, 1983), 17-18.
8. Phillip M. Burgess, director, Colorado School of Mines Energy and Minerals Management Institute, July 5, 1983, telephone interview with author.
9. Ibid.

10. Garrey E. Carruthers, assistant secretary of interior for land and water resources, July 6, 1983, interview with author.
11. Bureau of Land Management, *Final Environmental Statement, Federal Coal Management Program,* 2-63.
12. Douglas Larson, director of Western State Energy Board, July 8, 1983, telephone interview with author.
13. Robert H. Nelson, "The Public Lands," in *Current Issues in Natural Resource Policy,* ed. Paul R. Portney (Washington D.C.: Resources for the Future, 1982), 48.
14. Carruthers, statement before House Interior Subcommittee on Mining, June 7, 1983.
15. Johanna Wald, Natural Resources Defense Council counsel, July 11, 1982, telephone interview with author.
16. U.S. House Appropriations Committee Surveys and Investigations Staff, *A Report to the Committee on Appropriations, U.S. House of Representatives, on the Coal Leasing Program of the U.S. Department of Interior,* 98th Cong., 1st sess., 1983.
17. U.S. General Accounting Office, *Analysis of the Powder River Basin Federal Coal Lease Sale: Economic Valuation Improvements and Legislative Changes Needed* (Washington, D.C.: Government Printing Office, 1983).
18. Paul Applegate, district manager, U.S. Bureau of Land Management, Albuquerque, N.M., July 1, 1983, interview with author.
19. Office of Technology Assessment, *An Assessment of Development and Production Potential of Federal Coal Leases* (Washington, D.C.: Government Printing Office, 1981), 31.
20. Western Governors' Policy Office, Western Coal Export Task Force, *Western Coal Exports, Final Report,* December 1981, 77.
21. Norman Dean, National Wildlife Federation counsel, March 20, 1983, interview with author.
22. Montana Gov. Ted Schwinden, letter to Sen. Max Baucus, D-Mont., June 9, 1983.
23. Tim Gallagher, aide to Montana Gov. Ted Schwinden, July 8, 1983, telephone interview with author.

Most onshore oil controversies in the early 1980s centered on federally owned oil and gas discovered in the western Overthrust Belt, a geologic fault that twists north to south through the Rocky Mountains. Drilling rigs, such as this one in the Belt's northern Utah section, search beneath the rugged terrain for oil.

Chapter 5

FEDERAL OIL AND GAS:
EXPLORING THE LAST FRONTIERS

By the 1980s the United States' petroleum-producing potential had been explored more thoroughly than that of any other nation on Earth. Yet the country still possessed a few frontier regions with vast oil and gas potential, largely on public lands and offshore waters controlled by the U.S. government.

Between 1859, when the first oil well was drilled in Pennsylvania, and the 1970s, the United States had pumped more than 40 percent of the world's crude, largely from huge oil fields in Texas, Louisiana, California, and other western states.[1] U.S. crude discoveries peaked half a century ago, and natural gas finds have declined since the 1940s. The nation's crude output fell off in the 1970s because previously discovered fields were drained.

As world crude prices skyrocketed, U. S. oil and gas companies stepped up their search for new domestic petroleum reserves in unexplored or previously unpromising terrain, largely beneath public lands and waters. Estimates vary widely, but federally owned lands and Outer Continental Shelf (OCS) waters could hold 56 percent of the nation's undiscovered oil resources and 47 percent of its undiscovered natural gas.[2] But the only way to tell whether those lands actually hold vast oil and gas reserves is to drill costly wells thousands of feet deep under pristine coastal waters and some of the West's last wild mountains and deserts.

Managing the search for federal oil and gas as a result presents the U. S. government with "one of the toughest value judgments the nation has to make," Harvard Business School Professor Robert Stobaugh, co-editor of the book *Energy Future*, told *The Wall Street Journal* in 1981.[3]

But "wildcat" drilling for new oil and gas discoveries remains a risky, hit-or-miss business. Exploration firms often pour millions of dollars into drilling dry holes before they strike rich oil or gas deposits. The stakes can be huge, but oil people by nature are usually a gambling, opportunistic breed. Many find the government's system for leasing drilling rights in limited areas — while requiring careful measures to guard against environmental damage — too confining for a business that has built huge fortunes through trial-and-error exploration.

The federal government, which has leased public lands for oil exploration since 1920, opened OCS waters off the U. S. coastlines for drilling in 1954. Federally owned lands provided 4.7 percent of U. S. oil and 5 percent of the nation's gas production in 1980, mostly from well-known Wyoming and New Mexico oil and gas fields. Federal offshore holdings produced another 8.8 percent of national oil output and 23 percent of natural gas production. In all, the government by 1981 had leased nearly 122 million acres of its onshore lands, as well as roughly 12 million acres on the OCS, for oil and gas exploration and development.[4]

Yet actual OCS production still was limited to the Gulf of Mexico off Texas and Louisiana, along with long-known fields in Pacific Ocean waters off southern California. The industry just recently began exploring other promising offshore regions, notably along Alaska's long and con-voluted coastlines. Only since the late 1970s, moreover, has drilling in-tensified near giant Rocky Mountain Overthrust Belt discoveries beneath federal forests and rangelands in western Wyoming and eastern Utah.

A single oil drilling rig damages the land much less dramatically than a coal strip mine or experimental oil-shale production plant. But pe-troleum exploration can result in severe cumulative impacts as drilling crews build roads into empty back country and litter drilling sites with debris and equipment. Drilling in offshore water also poses the risks of catastrophic damage to marine life in the event of an oil-well blowout. One offshore accident, a 1969 oil spill off the Santa Barbara, Calif., coast, sparked a public reaction that helped launch the U.S. environmental movement of the 1970s.

But if oil drilling is risky, it also could produce huge payoffs in new reserves, thereby extending the American petroleum era. In the early 1980s companies reported giant oil and gas field discoveries from exploratory "wildcat" drilling under federal leases in the Santa Maria Basin off the California shores and in the western Overthrust Belt geologic province along the Rocky Mountains. Geologists and oil company officials likened the Overthrust finds to giant onshore oil field discoveries in east Texas in 1930 and Alaska's Prudhoe Bay in 1968.[5]

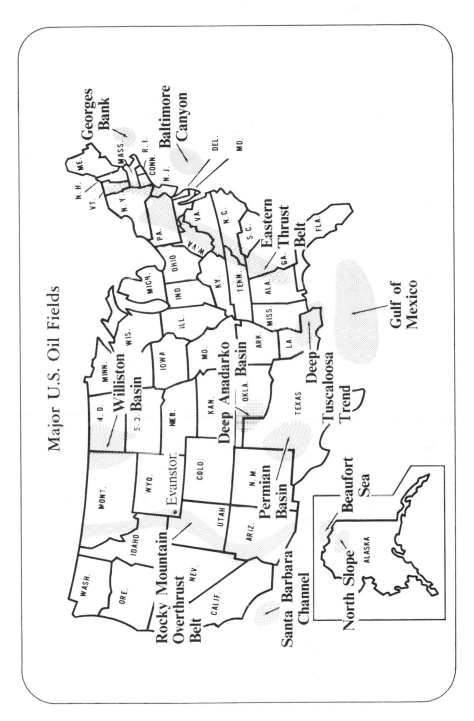

Major U.S. Oil Fields

James G. Watt, President Ronald Reagan's secretary of the interior, in the early 1980s accelerated federal oil and gas leasing. Watt contended that the nation, at the least, should permit oil companies to explore the government's lands and waters to find out how much petroleum they held. But environmental leaders and some state governors balked at Watt's efforts, especially at proposals to lease ocean basins off Alaska and California and to open forest and rangeland wilderness for drilling or seismic exploration. Petroleum reserves in those regions might some day be needed, Watt's critics acknowledged, but they contended that the government should encourage full development of private reserves and less sensitive federal lands before exploring its last untouched holdings. "If some future generation were to decide that the nation required the small amounts of energy contained in wilderness areas, these resources will still be there," Wilderness Society Chairman Gaylord Nelson, a former U.S. Democratic senator from Wisconsin, wrote in 1982. "If this generation determines to trade off the future for a fast return of dubious worth, then destroyed wilderness values will be gone forever." [6]

Offshore Exploration

The U. S. government controls mineral development on about 1.1 billion acres of submerged OCS lands along the country's 12,000 miles of coastline. The federal OCS begins three miles offshore — 10 miles off Texas' and Florida's Gulf of Mexico coasts — at the limit for state government jurisdiction that Congress decreed in 1953. The OCS extends out to sea for an undetermined distance; but geologists estimate that more than a billion acres lie in waters 2,500 meters or less deep, which was in the early 1980s the practical limit for oil and gas drilling technology.

Those federal offshore lands provide, in all probability, the best prospects for new giant oil and gas discoveries. More than half of the U. S. coastline runs along Alaska's deeply indented bays and peninsulas, in unexplored but geologically promising terrain.

By necessarily vague estimates, the federally controlled OCS eventually could yield one-third of the United States' still undiscovered crude oil and nearly one-fourth of new natural gas resources.[7] The sea bed floor, beneath waters up to 2,500 meters deep, includes unexplored basins and other structures off Alaska, California, and the Gulf and Atlantic coasts that geologists long have considered promising frontiers for petroleum exploration.

Federal Oil and Gas Production and Undiscovered Resources

Oil	1980 Production (millions/bbl)	Percent of 1980 U.S. production	1980 Royalties (millions)	Federal undiscovered resources[1] (billions/bbl)	Percent of U.S. undiscovered resources
Offshore, lower 48	277.4	8.8%	$ 837.2	14.8	18%
Onshore, lower 48	145.8	4.6	408.7	15.5	19
Alaska, offshore and onshore	3.9[2]	0.1	4.7	15.7	19
Total federal oil	427.1[3]	13.5	1,250.6	46.0	56
Gas	(trillion cubic ft.)		(millions)	(trillion cubic ft.)	
Offshore, lower 48	4.64	23.0%	$1,295.3	98.1	17%
Onshore, lower 48	0.95	4.7	209.1	95.3	16
Alaska, offshore and onshore	0.08[2]	0.3	6.2	83.4	14
Total federal gas	5.67[3]	28.0	1,510.6	276.8	47

[1] Geological Survey estimates of "undiscovered recoverable conventional resources" are based in part on subjective probability procedures. They are approximate estimates based on the best available geologic judgments at a given time. The figures shown in this table are mean estimates.

[2] Production during 1980 occurred onshore only.

[3] Does not include production from federal naval petroleum reserves. In 1980 such production was 52.6 million barrels of oil and 59.3 billion cubic feet of gas.

Note: Total U.S. oil production in 1980 was 3,147 billion barrels.

Source: *Current Issues in Natural Resource Policy* (Washington, D.C.: Resources for the Future, 1982), 19.

Congress confirmed the federal government's claim to OCS lands in 1953. The Interior Department began leasing offshore tracts a year later for drilling by U. S. oil and gas companies. By the end of 1981 OCS drilling had produced 5.7 billion barrels of oil and 53.5 trillion cubic feet of natural gas, just from Gulf of Mexico and southern California fields. OCS discoveries accounted for 10.3 percent of the country's known oil reserves and 19.8 percent of domestic gas reserves.[8] Alaskan, Atlantic Coast, and northern Pacific waters still were largely unexplored. But in the early 1980s Congress, environmental groups, and coastal state governments were challenging Watt's plans for opening virtually all the rest of the OCS for drilling operations.

The only way to inventory OCS reserves was through costly and risky drilling operations from platforms built in deep waters. As a result, no other federal resource development program stirred more controversy during the 1970s and early 1980s as the government debated how quickly to lease promising offshore regions for exploration and possible production.

The federally controlled offshore oil and gas resources offer "one of the most economically valuable and environmentally benign sources of domestic energy available to this country today," Secretary of the Interior Cecil D. Andrus maintained in 1980 as he announced the Carter administration's five-year OCS leasing schedule. But ever since the 1969 oil-well blowout in the Santa Barbara Channel blackened beaches just north of Los Angeles, killing thousands of fish and wildfowl, offshore drilling has drawn intense opposition from governors, local officials, and environmental groups in heavily populated Pacific coastal states where conservation sentiment is strong. Yet 1981-82 offshore oil discoveries, suggesting that a giant oil field lies beneath the Santa Maria Basin just 40 miles from the 1969 blowout, confirmed potentially huge payoffs in new energy supplies and federal leasing revenues from continued OCS exploration.

Federal Offshore Resources

By a compromise that Congress fashioned in the early 1950s, the U.S. government splits authority over offshore resources with coastal state governments. State governments control the sea bed floor from the low-tide level to three miles offshore, 10 miles off the Gulf coasts of Texas and Florida. The federal government, as the nation's sovereign power, asserts jurisdiction, but no claims to legal title, over the OCS and its resources as it slopes beyond the state jurisdiction limit to the vaguely defined continental margin 150 to 200 miles offshore. Federal control has given the government authority to manage most offshore oil and gas development — and reap $51.2 billion in royalties, rents, and leasing bids by the end of fiscal 1982.[9]

Oil drilling platforms were built in the shallow waters off Santa Barbara as early as 1897. But offshore exploration was limited until rapid drilling technology improvements after World War II made it possible to explore and produce petroleum from deeper waters despite rough seas and other hazards. From the nation's beginning, seacoast states had claimed title to the offshore sea bed floor; and during the 1920s California, Texas, and other states began leasing to private concerns oil, gas, and other mineral development rights.

The federal government began contesting state offshore sovereignty claims in the 1930s. The U.S. Supreme Court ruled in 1947 *(United States v. California)* that the federal government held "paramount rights in, and full dominion and power over, the lands, minerals and other things" under the ocean off California. Under pressure from coastal state delegations, especially from oil-producing regions, Congress in the Submerged Lands Act of 1953 ceded to the states offshore lands within three nautical miles of the coast. On the Texas and Florida Gulf coasts, the measure set the state limit at 10 miles. A few months later, President Dwight D. Eisenhower signed a separate measure, the Outer Continental Shelf Lands Act, that provided for federal administration of the sea bed beyond those limits and authorized the interior secretary to lease oil and gas deposits to private industry, charging 16.5 percent royalties.[10]

The Interior Department began leasing offshore oil and gas in 1954. In the following 25 years the department offered fewer than 12 million acres — roughly 1 percent of the OCS — leasing 5.3 million acres off both Texas and Louisiana and another 1.3 million acres along the Pacific Coast. The Bureau of Land Management managed the offshore leasing program, generally offering all tracts that oil companies nominated without government evaluation. Federal officials, eager for offshore oil revenues to help balance the government's growing budget, also encouraged the bureau to offer as much OCS land as possible. A 1973 University of Oklahoma study, funded by the National Science Foundation, concluded that the department held OCS lease offerings at a low rate to keep demand at levels that would increase bonus bids at OCS auctions.[11]

BLM in 1967 adopted an OCS tract selection process, which provided for the study of industry nominations before putting leases up for bid. Interior Secretary Walter J. Hickel temporarily suspended scheduled lease sales after the 1969 Santa Barbara oil spill. But the public uproar over the blowout's impact created a more lasting effect on offshore leasing as well as on other federal resource programs, by moving Congress to pass the National Environmental Policy Act (NEPA) later that year.

As world oil prices climbed in the 1970s the department came under pressure to improve OCS management and produce more federal revenues. The Nixon and Ford administrations, to cope with the serious national energy problems that emerged in the mid-1970s, drew up hastily conceived plans for stepping up OCS leasing. During the decade, the department continually changed OCS goals and schedules as it struggled to cope with shifting energy requirements and environmental problems. OCS leasing doubled during the decade, and the department opened up unexplored frontier areas off Alaska, the Atlantic, and eastern Gulf coasts. "Yet, the planned accelerated leasing goals of the 1970s were never achieved," the General Accounting Office (GAO) noted in a 1981 report, while Interior postponed or canceled planned lease sales in the Florida Straits and eight Alaskan basins that were considered promising frontier areas.[12]

The GAO report attributed leasing delays primarily to environmental concerns and limited industry interest in the regions that Interior actually offered. State government objections, hazards to fishing grounds, boundary disputes with Canada and Mexico, and Defense Department use of offshore waters kept large areas out of proposed sales or slowed the processing of leases once granted. Federal authority on the OCS itself was divided, with BLM managing the leasing program, the U.S. Geological Survey supervising drilling operations, the Environmental Protection Agency issuing ocean discharge permits, the Commerce Department's National Oceanic and Atmospheric Administration (NOAA) managing marine sanctuaries, the Army Corps of Engineers supervising platform construction, and the Coast Guard controlling navigation in coastal waters.

Revised OCS System

Leasing eventually proceeded in many regions, but initial drilling produced disappointing results in the Gulf of Alaska, the eastern Gulf of

Mexico, California's Outer Banks region, and the Baltimore Canyon off the Atlantic seaboard. During the Carter administration, Congress and Interior officials drafted a comprehensive OCS program that aimed at expediting leasing in new exploration frontiers while allaying oil-spill dangers. Congress rewrote the 1953 OCS law, approving 1978 amendments that tightened environmental controls, encouraged leasing competition, and gave states a larger role in recommending where leasing should proceed.[13]

In that measure, the Outer Continental Shelf Lands Act Amendments of 1978, Congress tried to provide mechanisms for balancing conflicting OCS concerns. The measure directed the government to draw up a five-year OCS leasing program to lay out the size, timing, and location of leasing, considering the relative sensitivity of ocean waters and marine life to drilling disruptions as well as assuring the government "fair market value" for its resources. Other provisions directed the interior secretary to ask the governors of affected states for recommendations on issuing new leases and to explain his reasons if he rejected their advice. Any party adversely affected by OCS leasing decisions was given standing to sue the government.

The 1978 amendments "legitimized the demands of all groups affected by OCS leasing and development," the GAO report concluded.[14] But the measure left open to interpretation the extent of its environmental protection and state consultation requirements inviting still more court challenges to Interior's leasing efforts. Environmentalists and industry continued to differ on how much oil-spill protection was sufficient, and several states demanded the right to review and approve federal leasing plans before sales were conducted. Alaska and California, in particular, maintained that the Coastal Zone Management Act of 1972 required that federal OCS leasing be consistent with state coastal management plans drafted under that statute. But Interior officials insisted that state approval would give states power to veto offshore leasing.

Operating under the new standards, Andrus in 1980 scheduled 36 OCS sales by 1985 to offer about 27.5 million acres for drilling. The Andrus schedule continued to target the Gulf of Mexico as the primary OCS leasing area but included 10 Alaskan sales making a total of 8.4 million acres available for exploration. The Andrus program envisioned an average of seven lease sales per year, double the 1970s pace. It excluded four areas — the Florida Straits, the Washington and Oregon coasts,

Alaska's Bristol Bay, and Alaska's southern Aleutian Shelf — that once had been considered for leasing. Andrus slated a 1981 lease sale off California's central and northern coasts, previously delayed more than two years, but a week before the 1980 presidential election the department excluded four untouched offshore basins along the state's rugged northern coast.

Environmental groups, along with California Gov. Edmund G. "Jerry" Brown Jr. and officials from other states, urged a go-slow approach to offshore drilling. Brown urged that 33 tracts in the northern reaches of the Santa Maria Basin be excluded from the 1981 sale on environmental grounds, including the threat from oil spills to migrating gray whales and the endangered California sea otter. Californians also objected to the potential impact on fishing and tourism along the scenic coastline between Los Angeles and San Francisco. Alaska officials meanwhile urged Interior to delay three out of 10 planned sales in that state's waters, while Massachusetts went to court to challenge proposed leasing in the Georges Bank fishing grounds in the north Atlantic.

Watt Leasing Plans

As he did with coal leasing, Watt escalated the OCS debate by expanding Andrus' program. After barely a month in office, the secretary startled California's congressional delegation by announcing that he would reconsider Andrus' decision to rule out leasing in the four Pacific basins along the state's northern coastline. Over the following year, Interior drafted a five-year leasing schedule that potentially opened the entire OCS for oil company drilling.

Watt's objective, he repeatedly insisted, was to inventory OCS oil and gas potential so the government would know how much energy potential its offshore lands actually provided. To that end, Watt scheduled 41 lease sales in the 1982-87 period, including 16 in Alaskan waters, while opening extensive OCS areas for industry nominations. Once the best prospects were identified, the government planned to focus its detailed environmental and economic studies on those areas, using streamlined procedures designed to speed leasing in frontier areas.

Under Watt's program, "nearly the entire Outer Continental Shelf — one billion acres — will be considered within five years compared to only 55 million acres under the Carter administration's proposal," David C. Russell, deputy director of Interior's Minerals Management Service, told a House subcommittee in 1982. "This does not mean that we will lease, necessarily, any more than we have been in recent years. Rather, and this is crucial, the market and not the government will decide which tracts are most promising and which merit a priority. . . ." [15] Under an Interior Department reorganization completed in 1983, the Minerals Management Service took over offshore leasing administration that had been shared by BLM and the U.S. Geological Survey.

Watt's OCS plans generated intense legal and political controversy. The Sierra Club, Natural Resources Defense Council, and other groups charged that accelerated leasing made careful planning and environmental studies impossible. Environmentalists and state governments kept pressing challenges, both to specific lease sales and the overall OCS program, through lawsuits and congressional measures that denied Interior funds for processing offshore leases.

Opposition from California's delegation forced Watt to put off leasing again in the four basins. A federal judge in Los Angeles in 1981 also blocked leasing in 29 tracts at the northern end of the Santa Maria Basin because of California's objections. California officials asserted that opening those tracts would be inconsistent with the state's coastal management plan, while Interior argued that just granting leases produced no environmental damage. Once leases were sold, the government's attorneys added, the department approved drilling plans only after consulting with state officials.

Congress followed in 1981 by accepting a House Appropriations Committee rider that barred Interior from using funds appropriated for fiscal 1982 to plan leasing in the four northern California basins. Congress renewed that ban in 1982, extending it to cover part of the state's central coastline as well. In drafting the fiscal 1984 Interior appropriations measure, the House panel agreed to a request by 23 of California's 45 House members to lengthen the area where leasing was banned to take in parts of the southern California coast. The divisions in the California delegation, along with oil strikes in the Santa Maria Basin, made the extension more controversial. Congress approved a modified version in its final bill, along with riders banning leasing off parts of Florida's Gulf of Mexico coast and in the Georges Bank area off New England.

Some members of Congress from California and Massachusetts proposed banning offshore leasing along their states' coastlines until the year 2000. Those measures had little chance of success, at least while Republicans controlled the Senate as they did in 1983. But state officials and environmental groups continued legal challenges to Interior's OCS procedures. One 1983 U.S. appeals court decision upheld Watt's 1982 leasing program, rejecting arguments by five states and several environmental groups that Watt had failed to assess adequately fair market value, protect environmental resources, and comply with the 1972 coastal zone law. The U.S. Supreme Court was expected to rule ultimately on various OCS lawsuits, including an appeal by Interior and oil companies to reopen the disputed Santa Maria Basin tracts.[16]

In setting the 1982-87 leasing schedule Watt dropped plans to open two Alaskan basins after negotiations with the state's Democratic governor, Bill Sheffield. Some critics urged Interior to defer leasing in northern coastlines and deep waters, contending that falling world oil prices would make oil companies less willing to bid for rights to explore in regions where drilling would be both risky and expensive.

As in the coal-leasing debate, the Reagan administration retorted that the need for stable energy supplies overrode the desire to produce maximum leasing revenues. Oil industry leaders generally had been content with the Andrus leasing schedule for the Lower 48 states, but they welcomed Watt's attempt to speed leasing in promising Alaskan waters. Companies needed at least seven years after leases were granted to find and begin pumping new discoveries from frontier regions, F. A. Seamans, Texaco Inc. vice president of exploration and production, told Congress in 1982 testimony. This made the industry reluctant to commit funds to OCS planning without assurance that the government will hold lease auctions on schedule. "To help insure stable domestic crude oil supplies for the next decade," Seamans said, "we must have a reliable leasing program in this decade." [17]

But political and legal maneuvering made OCS leasing prospects in the 1980s anything but certain. Despite Watt's initiatives, some sales were likely to be delayed as industry, environmentalists, and state officials fought over conflicting views of oil-spill risks and economic demand for new leasing. It was possible that procedural snags in Interior and other federal agencies could further slow the leasing process. And oil industry, once so eager to explore the OCS, could be less willing to bid on frontier areas and commit expensive offshore platforms to drilling unexplored regions, at least while falling crude prices reduced potential rewards.

Onshore Oil and Gas Resources

The U.S. government owns other important petroleum resources, deep beneath western mountains and plains and Alaska's far northern reaches. Federally owned onshore lands produce 5 percent of the nation's oil and gas, and they hold as much as one-third of its undiscovered reserves. Wildcat drilling in the late 1970s and early 1980s revealed potentially huge new finds beneath national forests and rangelands along the Rocky Mountains.

For most of the century the government gave the oil industry relatively free rein to drill on public lands in search of new discoveries. But after the mid-1960s federal wilderness laws and land management policies combined to keep seismic exploration crews and drilling rigs out of remote terrain that could hold giant oil and gas deposits. As a result the industry and environmental groups have battled over opening more federal lands for petroleum exploration.

Most controversies in the early 1980s centered on federally owned oil and gas prospects in the Western Overthrust Belt, a complex geologic fault that twists the length of the Rockies from Canada to Mexico. Wildcat drilling beginning in 1975 uncovered at least 16 major oil and gas fields along the Overthrust in southwestern Wyoming, eastern Utah, and southeastern Idaho. The oil industry began pressing the government to lease rights to nearby areas where the belt cuts beneath federally owned rangelands, forests, and wilderness regions near Glacier, Yellowstone, and Grand Teton national parks.

The government owns 60 percent of the land overlying the Overthrust Belt formations, and Congress as of 1983 already had designated 4 percent of those holdings as wilderness. The discoveries, therefore, brought new urgency to a continuing debate over drilling on federal lands.

Watt in the early 1980s prodded the U.S. Forest Service and Interior's BLM to speed leasing of the lands they managed in the region for oil and gas exploration. The secretary also backed industry requests for a chance to explore federal wilderness lands in the West before they were "locked up," unavailable for development. "If we are to put much of this area off limits to exploration and potential development, it should be done so consciously and with full recognition of the values to be foregone," Watt contended in a 1982 letter to Sen. Malcolm Wallop, a Wyoming Republican.[18]

Congress, in creating the federal wilderness system in the 1964 Wilderness Act, had given the minerals industry 20 years to explore those lands for petroleum and other resources. But the Forest Service and BLM, in managing both designated and potential wilderness areas, effectively excluded drilling and seismic exploration crews from most of those lands even as Congress enlarged the system. As the Jan. 1, 1984, deadline for wilderness exploration approached, Congress balked at Watt's plans to give the minerals industry more time to assess the lands.

As the debate unfolded, environmentalist groups raised an alarm about violating pristine country whose oil and gas potential remains unproven. Concerned by the precedent of allowing exploration in the wilderness system, they argued that even the most promising wild and roadless lands in the Overthrust region at best could contribute relatively small amounts to U. S. oil and gas production. "What we're talking about are supplies that can be measured in a few days of national petroleum consumption," Brant Calkin, then the Sierra Club's Southwest representative, commented in 1981. "That's not adequate promise to put in roads that are going to last a lot longer than the oil will." [19]

Onshore Leasing System

The public lands, including national forests as well as BLM-managed lands, produced nearly 150 million barrels of oil along with slightly more than one trillion cubic feet of natural gas in 1980. They held 4.5 percent of the nation's proven oil reserves, as well as 6.1 percent of recoverable natural gas reserves. But they sprawl across largely unexplored terrain, notably in Alaska and along the Overthrust Belt, that eventually could provide yet-to-be discovered petroleum fields to bolster U.S. resources.

In the century after former railroad conductor Edwin L. Drake drilled the first oil well near Titusville, Pa., huge reserves have been discovered in east Texas, Louisiana, California, Oklahoma, Wyoming, and the Permian Basin of west Texas and eastern New Mexico. The United States has pumped 100 billion barrels of oil from the 48 contiguous states, largely from privately owned lands on level and open terrain easily reached for drilling. But after U.S. oil discoveries peaked during the 1930s, production fell from its peak of 9.6 million barrels a day in 1970. As the Organization for Petroleum Exporting Countries (OPEC) forced world oil prices higher, the petroleum industry's interest grew in probing the little-explored mountains and deserts of federally owned western lands.

Since the turn of the century, as Americans began burning oil to heat homes, run factories, and power automobiles, the federal government has been regulating drilling on public lands. The U.S. petroleum

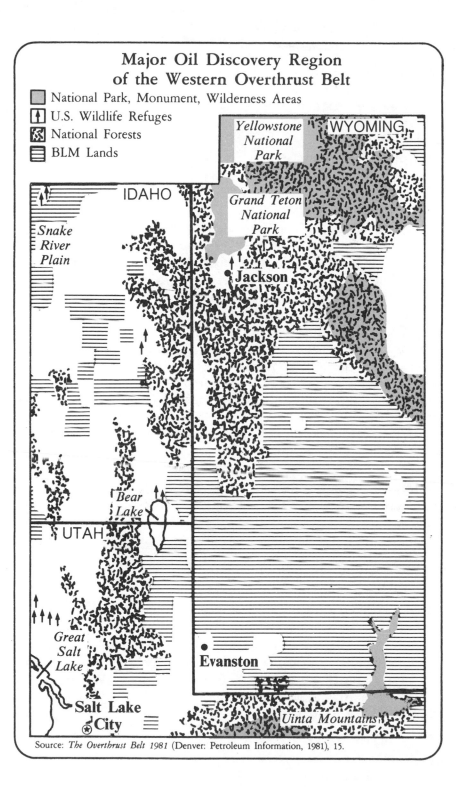

Major Oil Discovery Region
of the Western Overthrust Belt

- National Park, Monument, Wilderness Areas
- U.S. Wildlife Refuges
- National Forests
- BLM Lands

WYOMING

Yellowstone National Park

IDAHO

Grand Teton National Park

Snake River Plain

● Jackson

Bear Lake

UTAH

Great Salt Lake

● Evanston

Uinta Mountains

Salt Lake City

Source: *The Overthrust Belt 1981* (Denver: Petroleum Information, 1981), 15.

era dawned in the early 20th century, just as the conservation movement turned federal land policy away from its 19th century disposal goals toward retention in government ownership. The U. S. Navy at the time was switching from coal to fuel oil to power its ships, and crude reserves were becoming more valuable. Fearing that federally owned petroleum resources would be claimed quickly under homestead and mining laws, President Theodore Roosevelt began withdrawing oil lands from entry. President William Howard Taft, Roosevelt's successor, followed up by withdrawing three million acres in Wyoming and California. By 1924 the government had established four naval petroleum reserves and three oil shale reserves, and leases to E. L. Doheny's Pan American Oil Co. and Harry Sinclair's Mammoth Oil Co. to develop oil from the Elk Hills, Calif., and Teapot Dome, Wyo., reserves led to the Teapot Dome scandal that sent Secretary of the Interior Albert Fall to jail.

Congress in 1920 placed the remaining federal onshore oil and gas under the leasing system set up by the Mineral Leasing Act. That measure reopened federal petroleum deposits, except for the naval reserves, for leasing for exploration, development, and production by oil and gas companies. It gave the interior secretary discretionary authority to lease oil and gas rights, requiring competitive bidding for known deposits. But it provided noncompetitive leases to companies to drill for as-yet-undiscovered reserves and produce any petroleum found. In 1983 the law allowed the department to lease up to 10,240 acres for noncompetitive "wildcat" drilling, for a 10-year period, charging $1 an acre annual rent for the land and a 12.5 percent royalty on subsequent oil and gas production.[20]

Roughly 97 percent of federal oil and gas leases are issued for noncompetitive exploration. The Interior Department manages the leasing program, both on BLM public lands and national forests, which are under Agriculture Department control. Before 1983 BLM drew up and issued oil and gas leases, while the Conservation Division of the U.S. Geological Survey (USGS) made technical evaluations of federal petroleum resources, supervised drilling operations, and collected royalties. Under the Interior reorganization completed in 1983, BLM absorbed the old Conservation Division's regulatory functions to provide the industry with a "one-stop" leasing agency. A newly created part of Interior, the Minerals Management Service, assumed the USGS royalty collection responsibilities.

Restrictive Leasing Policies

BLM and the Agriculture Department's Forest Service divided responsibility for federal surface lands generally open for oil and gas development. Although the 1920 mineral leasing law did not require Forest Service consent to drilling operations, BLM issued national forest oil and gas leases only with the service's consent. Both agencies, responding to federal environmental laws and multiple-use mandates from Congress, during the 1960s and 1970s tightened regulation of drilling activity to protect recreation, prevent erosion, preserve archeological sites, or leave critical wildlife habitat undisturbed.

Oil exploration and drilling operations scar relatively few acres, certainly compared with coal strip mining and hard-rock mining ventures. Some early geophysical exploration can be done by seismic equipment that probes the earth for potential petroleum-bearing structures with no permanent surface disruption. But most searching, nonetheless, requires access to public lands, first to conduct geophysical studies and eventually to drill into the earth to find whether deposits actually exist. Both the Forest Service and BLM grew more reluctant in the 1960s and 1970s to permit industry crews access to remote lands where few if any roads had penetrated. Past oil and gas exploration in Wyoming's Red Desert, for instance, "scarred the landscape and left a network of roads and trails that are in conflict with open space, watershed and wildlife values," BLM's Rawlins, Wyo., district staff noted in a 1978 summary of planning in the region.[21]

To reduce those intrusions the Forest Service and BLM drew up increasingly detailed stipulations that officials attached to oil and gas leases before allowing exploration. Those requirements often specified routes where roads could be built, for instance, and how thoroughly crews must clean up drilling waste ponds. In some districts BLM directed oil companies to paint tanks and other buildings to blend with natural surroundings. "There's an awful lot of bureaucratic red tape involved, the kind of things that make it difficult to work on [public] lands," Peter Hanagan, the New Mexico Oil and Gas Association's executive director, commented in 1981.[22]

A 1981 GAO report on onshore oil and gas leasing pointed out that restrictive stipulations increased production costs and discouraged petroleum exploration. The report noted that agencies increasingly attached "no surface occupancy" stipulations barring companies from building rigs and other structures on the lands they lease, forcing expensive helicopter surveys or slant drilling from adjacent lands to explore oil and gas potential. Assessing petroleum leasing in five states, GAO estimated that at least a million acres under lease were subject to that restriction, including 345,000 acres of prime oil and gas prospects in the Wyoming Overthrust region.[23]

Both BLM and the Forest Service built up large backlogs of pending lease applications, and western oil and gas activity accelerated. Oil companies grew frustrated with time-consuming environmental, archeological, and other studies, accusing the agencies of needlessly delaying exploration. "Trying to get a permit for a well up there is something else," Owen Murphy, a Chevron USA spokesman in Denver, complained as the company stepped up its Wyoming drilling program.[24]

At Watt's orders, BLM reduced its backlog from more than 13,000 pending applications in January 1982 to fewer than one thousand a year later.[25] Both BLM and the Forest Service tried to upgrade their mineral staffs, but industry representatives worried that, in rushing leases through, the agencies were attaching vague or even inappropriate stipulations. Both agencies attached to some leases "contingent right" stipulations that gave the government the option of barring actual drilling once officials completed land-use plans for the area. With their planning budgets tight, the agencies also considered asking lease applicants to pay for environmental studies. Despite Watt's efforts, "there still are holdups," Alice Frell, public lands director for the Rocky Mountain Oil and Gas Association, reported in 1983. "Some leases have been pending for ages," she said, "and they just won't process them." [26]

Wilderness Exploration Debate

At the end of fiscal 1981 the government had nearly 110,000 oil and gas leases still in effect on more than 112 million acres of federal lands. BLM leasing was expected to triple by the end of fiscal 1983 as the agency speeded its procedures. In 1982 Interior began offering public lands in Alaska, including 4 million acres in the National Petroleum Reserve in that state, for oil and gas exploration and production.[27] Congress, in the 1980 Alaska lands law, authorized resumed petroleum leasing and seismic studies — but not drilling — on the caribou calving grounds in the William O. Douglas Arctic Wildlife Range.

Other promising federal lands remained off limits to oil and gas development. GAO, in its 1981 report, estimated that 64 million acres in the Lower 48 states were closed to drilling — 48 million acres by formal congressional or department withdrawals and another 16 million acres by various BLM or Forest Service administrative restrictions.[27] In a separate 1979 study the congressional Office of Technology Assessment (OTA) found that 11.9 percent of federal lands were closed formally to fossil fuel leasing in 1975, excluding Alaskan lands whose future management still was being debated by Congress. OTA noted that on another 9.9 percent, or 81.4 million acres, access was highly restricted by laws or administrative policies that effectively discouraged almost all mineral activity.[28]

Congress barred mineral leasing in national parks. The secretary of defense has closed nearly 23 million acres of military lands, while the U.S. Fish and Wildlife Service policies generally excluded petroleum drilling from national wildlife refuges. Those actions barred exploration of large areas, including some close to known oil and gas deposits, and also prevented drilling state and privately owned lands with considerable potential.

The 1964 wilderness law's cutoff on mineral development was due to take effect on Jan. 1, 1984, formally closing more than 25 million acres of national forest wilderness to leasing. In addition, Congress over the following decade was expected to consider extending wilderness status to perhaps another 40 million acres that the Forest Service and BLM had identified as roadless areas possibly qualifying for preservation. Congress still was working its way through the Forest Service's 1979 RARE II wilderness proposals, and BLM in 1980 identified 24.8 million acres of its lands for wilderness study areas. *(Discussion of RARE II, timber chapter, p. 149)*

Many designated or proposed wilderness areas have little oil or gas potential. They tend to be high mountain slopes or remote sites where seismic studies and drilling could prove prohibitively expensive. A 1982 analysis by the Wilderness Society's Economic Policy Department, updated in 1983, estimated that designated wilderness held 1 billion barrels of undiscovered oil reserves and 6.2 trillion cubic feet of undiscovered gas, while proposed wilderness contained 2.31 billion barrels of oil and 13.68 trillion cubic feet of gas in recoverable but undiscovered resources. In all, the study calculated that federal onshore lands held 23 percent of the nation's undiscovered onshore oil reserves, including only 3.9 percent in wilderness lands, and 19.3 percent of U.S. undiscovered onshore natural gas, with only 3.4 percent of the national total beneath wilderness areas. The Wilderness Society concluded "there simply is not enough oil and gas on wilderness lands to make a very significant contribution to total supply." [29] *(Federal lands and wilderness, table, next page)*

But, even with sophisticated seismic technology, the only sure way to test the oil and gas potential of unexplored regions is to drill wildcat wells. Many wilderness areas may indeed have little petroleum beneath them, but some roadless federal lands lie close to startling Overthrust Belt finds produced by deep drilling in country that previously yielded only dry holes. In the early 1980s the Overthrust region of western Wyoming and northeastern Utah became rapidly known as "elephant country," holding gigantic oil and gas deposits. *(Major oil discovery region of Western Overthrust Belt, map, p. 117)*

The Overthrust boom centered around Evanston, Wyo., a mid-19th century stop on the Overland Trail where westward migrants greased wagon wheels with oil that seeped to the surface. That region has produced crude oil from wells since the early 1900s, but drilling in the 1940s and 1950s was unsuccessful. Then, in 1969, the Union Pacific Railroad reached agreement with Amoco Production Co., domestic exploration subsidiary of Standard Oil of Indiana, to explore the railroad's land grants along the right of way of the transcontinental railroad built in the 1860s. American Quasar Petroleum, a Fort Worth, Texas, independent oil firm working on a "farm-out" arrangement with Amoco, struck oil, and in 1975 a 14,000-foot well opened Utah's Pineview field 40 miles east of Salt Lake City.

In the following years, drilling by major and independent oil companies brought in 16 large petroleum fields within a 100-mile-or-so stretch along the Idaho-Wyoming-Utah thrust belt. The Overthrust discoveries included six giant petroleum fields, a term applied by the American Association of Petroleum Geologists to a field that holds 100 million barrels of oil or 1 trillion cubic feet of gas. Early finds included one "supergiant" field, a classification that suggested it held the equivalent of 500 million barrels of crude or 3 trillion cubic feet of gas. As those discoveries were made, exploratory drilling quickly moved from the "checkerboard" of private and public lands along the railroad into the national forests and BLM rangelands that make up most of the region. Major finds in those public lands spurred industry interest in exploring northward from the railroad right of way into the mountains of western Wyoming, where the Overthrust Belt fault ran right through

Federal Lands and Wilderness
Oil and Gas Potential

	Oil (billion barrels)				Natural Gas (trillion cubic feet)			
	Identified Reserves	Undiscovered Recoverable Resources	Total	Percent	Identified Reserves	Undiscovered Recoverable Resources	Total	Percent
Designated wilderness	0.31	1.01	1.32	1.3	1.50	6.20	7.70	1.1
Potential wilderness	0.46	2.31	2.77	2.6	2.69	13.68	16.37	2.3
Other federal land	4.43	15.58	20.01	19.1	21.86	92.10	113.96	15.9
Subtotal	5.20	18.90	24.10	23.0	26.05	111.98	138.03	19.3
Nonfederal land	44.78	35.80	80.59	77.0	263.64	314.83	578.46	80.7
U.S. Total	50.10	54.60	104.70	100.0	289.80	426.80	716.60	100.0

Source: Wilderness Society, Economic Policy Department, *Potentially Producible Onshore Petroleum and Natural Gas in the United States (Revised Estimates) January 1983*.

123

Jackson, Wyo., near the foot of the Grand Teton Mountains. Exploration suggested that huge deposits lay beneath national forests and BLM lands around Grand Teton National Park, including wilderness lands already designated for protection by Congress and in roadless country that was being considered for preservation.

In 1981-83, for instance, four wildcat wells near LaBarge, Wyo., uncovered significant natural gas deposits on lands that bordered wilderness study areas (WSAs) BLM was considering for its wilderness system.[30] In Wyoming alone, the 1981 GAO study estimated that 483,000 acres of proposed BLM wilderness and 1.3 million acres of recommended national forest wilderness had oil and gas potential. In its study of public lands in six states — including Colorado, New Mexico, Utah, Nevada, and Mississippi as well as Wyoming, GAO estimated that wilderness lands could hold 387.4 million barrels of oil and 162.4 billion cubic feet of gas.

As Watt took over Interior in 1981 the Forest Service and BLM were under pressure to process accumulated lease applications for access to Overthrust wilderness regions. A 1980 U.S. district court decision in Wyoming — on a lawsuit that Watt had brought as president of Denver-based Mountain States Legal Foundation — had ordered the government to begin processing pending leases to either approve or disapprove industry requests.

In September 1981 BLM issued three oil and gas leases for exploration in New Mexico's Capitan Wilderness, by slanting drilling from outside wilderness boundaries on surrounding national forest lands. The Forest Service in 1981 released a draft environmental impact statement recommending oil and gas leasing in Wyoming's Washakie Wilderness and an adjacent roadless area just east of Yellowstone National Park. The document proposed opening 92,000 acres for leasing, with 72,000 restricted to slant drilling with no surface occupancy, and allowing seismic studies using underground explosives through most of the Washakie Wilderness, except for 85,000 acres of grizzly bear habitat.[31]

Oil and gas companies also asked for leases or expressed interest in Wyoming's Teton Wilderness, between Yellowstone and Grand Teton national parks; the West Elk Wilderness in Colorado; Glen Canyon National Recreation Area in Utah; Montana's Bob Marshall and nearby wilderness areas; the East Palisades wilderness study area of Idaho; and even Glacier National Park, Dinosaur National Monument in Colorado and Utah, and Theodore Roosevelt National Park in North Dakota. "It's just such a massive onslaught right now that we're losing everything," Bruce Hamilton, the Sierra Club's northern Great Plains representative, lamented in 1981. "Apparently now, they'll go a couple of steps farther and go after designated wilderness areas and even the national parks." [32]

But Congress stepped in over the following three years to halt wilderness leasing efforts. Environmentalists and their congressional allies pressed their case, arguing that the industry should concentrate its resources on exploring less sensitive lands first. "There are only so many drill rigs available for exploration," noted Andrew F. Wiessner, counsel to the House Interior Subcommittee on Public Lands and National Parks. "It will take years to explore the Overthrust Belt, so why not explore the less fragile areas first?" [33]

Invoking an emergency provision of Federal Land Policy and Management Act, the House Interior Committee in 1981 withdrew the Bob Marshall Wilderness from possible leasing, thus blocking industry requests to detonate dynamite along 200 miles of seismic lines through grizzly, bald eagle, elk, and mountain goat habitat. Congress in 1982 and 1983 agreed to House Appropriations Committee amendments to Interior appropriations bills that forbid the department to process leases in national forest wilderness and wilderness study areas. Congressional leaders and environmental groups also vehemently objected to Watt's 1982 proposal to bar drilling and mining in existing and proposed wilderness through the year 2000 — but to allow seismic studies and core sampling within the wilderness system and to expedite release of BLM study areas and RARE II areas in the national forests for leasing within several years.

The Reagan administration backed away from those efforts after the 1982 congressional elections demonstrated environmentalists' growing political muscle. Watt on Dec. 30, 1982, announced he would make no effort to "slip things through" in the last months of 1983, if the appropriations amendments barring wilderness leasing expired before the 1984 deadline in the Wilderness Act. "That's it," Garrey E. Carruthers, assistant secretary of the interior for land and water resources, remarked in July 1983. "We quit. What we wanted was exploration. But it's become so . . . politically explosive that we determined that you can't jeapordize all our leasing programs on exploration in a limited number of areas." [34]

Congress in the meantime still was debating whether newly proposed wilderness areas should be explored before designation.

Conservative Republicans were likely to attempt to redraw the boundaries of Forest Service recommendations for new wilderness preserves to exclude possible mineral deposits. The U.S. Geological Survey in mid-1983 was drafting an analysis of oil and gas potential in wilderness areas, and industry geologists could reveal proprietary company studies showing major petroleum potential beneath wilderness lands in efforts to persuade Congress to keep them open. Watt in late 1982 removed 805,000 acres from BLM's wilderness study program, including tracts with fewer than 5,000 acres, some that qualified only because they lay adjacent to other potential wilderness, and other areas with "split estates," where the government owned the surface and private parties owned mineral rights beneath them. Environmentalists challenged that decision in court, however, and Congress in 1983 considered barring leasing in BLM study areas even though Watt had agreed to refrain from issuing leases.

At the end of fiscal 1982 the Forest Service held more than 3,000 unprocessed applications for energy-related leases in its wilderness areas, including 1,400 in existing wilderness, 500 in wilderness study areas established by Congress, 1,000 in lands that the agency had recommended for preservation in RARE II and another 400 in areas that were proposed for further wilderness planning.[35] Some roadless lands could be opened up automatically as Congress completed action on Forest Service wilderness. "If we can get RARE II cleared out in the next two years, it will give ample ground for exploration outside of wilderness that industry is going to need," Rep. Larry Craig, an Idaho Republican who sits on the House Interior Committee, noted in 1983.[36]

A future Congress could, of course, revise the 1964 law to reopen all wilderness lands for exploration. But with the wilderness system enjoying broad political support, especially in the Democratic-controlled House and its Interior and Appropriations committees, that move would be unlikely except in a severe national energy crisis. "In a real national emergency, nothing will be withheld," the Sierra Club's Calkin said in 1981. "But I always thought the last things to go would be the national parks and wilderness."[37]

Notes

1. E. N. Tiratsoo, *Oilfields of the World* (Beaconsfield, England: Scientific Press, 1973), 216.
2. Rich Jaroslovsky, "Reagan's Drive to Open More Public Land to Energy Firms May Spark Major Battles," *Wall Street Journal*, April 1, 1981.

3. Robert H. Nelson, "The Public Lands," in *Current Issues in Natural Resource Policy,* ed. Paul R. Portney (Washington, D.C.: Resources for the Future, 1982), 18.

4. U. S. Department of the Interior, Bureau of Land Management, *Public Land Statistics 1981* (Washington, D.C.: Government Printing Office, 1982), 99-102.

5. Tom Arrandale, "Western Oil Boom," in *Editorial Research Reports, Vol. I, 1981* (Washington, D.C.: Congressional Quarterly, 1981), 392-394.

6. Gaylord Nelson, "Oil and Gas in Wilderness: Not Necessary," *National Journal,* Feb. 13, 1982, 309.

7. U. S. Department of Energy, Energy Information Administration, *The Use of Federal Lands for Energy Development,* prepared by Edward Porter as vol. 8 of *Energy Policy Study* (Washington, D.C.: Government Printing Office, 1980), 3-9.

8. U. S. Department of the Interior, Bureau of Land Management, *Managing the Nation's Public Lands* (Washington, D.C.: Government Printing Office, 1983), 35.

9. Ibid., 35.

10. *Congress and the Nation,* 5 vols., *Congress and the Nation: 1945-64,* vol. 1 (Washington, D.C.: Congressional Quarterly, 1965), 1401.

11. General Accounting Office (GAO), *Issues in Leasing Offshore Lands for Oil and Gas Development* (Washington, D.C.: Government Printing Office, 1981), 14.

12. Ibid., 24, 31.

13. *Congress and the Nation: 1977-80,* vol. 5 (Washington, D.C.: Congressional Quarterly), 485.

14. GAO, *Issues in Leasing Offshore Lands,* 73.

15. Statement before a joint hearing of the House Interior Committee's subcommittees on Mines and Mining and Oversight and Investigations, Sept. 28, 1982, 97th Cong., 2d. sess.

16. Patrick Crow, "Interior Sec. Watt Defends OCS Leasing Plan in Courts, Congress," *Oil & Gas Journal,* June 20, 1983, 57.

17. Ibid., 60.

18. James G. Watt, secretary of the interior, Jan. 22, 1982, letter to Sen. Malcolm Wallop, R-Wyo.

19. Brant Calkin, Sierra Club Southwest representative, 1981 telephone interview with author.

20. U. S. Congress, Office of Technology Assessment (OTA), *Management of Fuel and Nonfuel Minerals in Federal Land* (Washington, D.C.: Government Printing Office, 1979), 103-172.

21. U. S. Department of the Interior, Bureau of Land Management, *Wyoming Land Use Decisions, Seven Lakes Area* (Washington, D.C.: Government Printing Office, 1978), 10.

22. Arrandale, "Western Oil Boom," 404.

23. U. S. General Accounting Office, *Actions Needed to Increase Federal Onshore Oil and Gas Exploration and Development* (Washington, D.C.: Government Printing Office, 1981).

24. Owen Murphy, Chevron USA representative, 1981 telephone interview with author.

25. BLM, *Managing the Nation's Public Lands,* 33.

26. Alice Frell, Rocky Mountain Oil and Gas Association representative, July 29, 1983, telephone interview with author.

27. GAO, *Issues in Leasing Offshore Lands.*
28. OTA, *Management of Fuel and Nonfuel Minerals,* 215-220.
29. The Wilderness Society, Economic Policy Department, "Potentially Producible Petroleum and Natural Gas in the United States and the Western Overthrust Belt," February 1982; "Potentially Producible Onshore Petroleum and Natural Gas in the United States (Revised Estimates)," January 1983.
30. Richard B. Powers, U. S. Geological Survey, Oil and Gas Section, Denver, Colo., July 29, 1983, telephone interview with author.
31. Lawrence Mosher, "Wilderness System Is Under Siege by Oil, Gas, Mineral and Timber Interests," *National Journal,* Nov. 21, 1981, 2076.
32. Bruce Hamilton, Sierra Club Northern Great Plains representative, 1981 telephone interview with author.
33. Mosher, "Wilderness System Is Under Siege," 2080.
34. Garrey E. Carruthers, assistant secretary of the interior for land and water resources, July 6, 1983, interview with author.
35. U. S. Forest Service, *Report of the Forest Service, Fiscal Year 1982* (Washington, D.C.: Government Printing Office, 1983), 5.
36. Rep. Larry Craig, R-Idaho, July 28, 1983, telephone interview with author.
37. Brant Calkin, 1981 telephone interview.

A U.S. Forest Service employee inspects a stand of lodgepole pine, a common softwood used for timber, in Montana's Callatin National Forest.

Chapter 6

THE TIMBER RESOURCE:
CUTTING THE NATIONAL FORESTS

The Agriculture Department's U. S. Forest Service manages 191 million acres of land, mostly in national forests and grasslands. Only 89 million acres are commercial timberland, capable of economic wood production. But they hold half of the nation's crucial softwood sawtimber reserves, including huge volumes in the country's last virgin stands of centuries-old trees that tower from Pacific Coast mountain ranges.

The national forests make the U.S. government the nation's most important timber supplier. Along with prime timberlands that the Interior Department manages in western Oregon, they carry an immense inventory of sawtimber that Americans will draw on in upcoming decades to provide lumber for new homes and paper products.

"The national forest system is a tremendous asset which can contribute directly to economic well-being," John B. Crowell Jr., President Ronald Reagan's assistant secretary of agriculture for natural resources and environment, told Congress in 1982.[1] By the mid-1980s loggers were expected to cut more than 11.5 billion board feet of timber a year from the national forests. But pressure already was building on the Forest Service to double its harvests in following decades as the nation's forest products companies exhausted their own virgin stands in private Pacific Northwest forests.[2]

With lumber already accounting for 15 percent of the cost of building a new house, millions of Americans will have direct economic stakes in whether federal timber supplies will match rising demand for lumber, plywood, paper, and other wood products. Taxpayers also stood to benefit from wise management of a national forest system that in the mid-1970s was worth an estimated $42 billion, including $20 billion in standing timber.[3]

131

But the government manages its forests to protect their biologic potential, not just for economic efficiency. And as the Forest Service drafted forest management plans, critics were challenging federal timber management policies that experts contended left ancient trees to decay while destructive logging operations harvested less valuable stands. The debate grew heated in the late 1970s and early 1980s as lumber mills shut down in the Pacific Coast states while timber companies bid prices upward competing for limited federal harvests.

In its simplest terms, the debate boiled down to how much of the national forests should be kept wild and how much should be logged and managed to grow new timber stands. Both the Carter and Reagan administrations pushed the Forest Service to abandon cautious harvest schedules that limited cutting in the Northwest's stately "old-growth" Douglas fir stands. Those trees had been growing for 250 to 800 years on the western slopes of the Cascade Mountains in Washington and Oregon.

The Pacific Coast region alone holds more than half of the 1 trillion board feet of pine, spruce, fir, and other softwood trees that grow in the national forests. In addition, Interior's Bureau of Land Management (BLM) manages 2.4 million acres of timberland in western Oregon. Reclaimed by Congress from lands previously granted to the Oregon & California Railroad, those O & C lands hold 50 billion board feet of softwood sawtimber.

The Pacific Coast national forests take in some of America's most fertile timberlands. National forests in the Rocky Mountains and on Alaska's coast occupy much of those regions' commercial forests. Federal forests in the South, Northeast, and Great Lakes states make up much smaller percentages of timberland; but national forest harvests still make important economic contributions in some areas. Northern national forests supply some desirable hardwood timber, while southern timberlands support fast-growing pine stands that will become more important in the future. *(National forests, map, p. 135)*

In contrast to private timberlands, however, not even the best federally owned forests are dedicated solely to timber production. Congress in the 1976 National Forest Management Act (NFMA) affirmed the Forest Service's historic multiple-use mission. The agency had restricted or ruled out timber harvests in the 1960s and 1970s where logging and roadbuilding would harm watersheds, wildlife habitat, scenic vistas, recreation sites, and roadless wilderness. Those measures, along

Softwood Sawtimber Inventories
1976
(Million board feet)

	U.S. total	Pacific Coast region
National forests	1,009,287	544,581
Other federal, state forests	235,174	146,678
Forest industry lands	314,276	181,887
Farmer and other private lands	426,671	109,934
Total inventories	**1,985,408**	983,080

Source: U.S. Forest Service, *An Analysis of the Timber Situation in the United States 1952-2030.*

with stricter clear-cutting rules, curtailed the lands available for logging just as timber demands on national forests were rising.

The Forest Service was trying to balance timber needs with other non-commodity uses as it drafted 121 forest management plans that the NFMA had ordered. Congress meanwhile also was attempting to settle drawn-out controversies over expanding the national forest wilderness system, created by the Wilderness Act of 1964, where logging was prohibited. Assistant Secretary Crowell, former general counsel to Louisiana-Pacific Corp., the nation's second-largest timber company, was backing industry demands for accelerated national forest harvests. The future of the nation's timber supplies — and the prices they commanded — were at stake.

U.S. Timber Supplies

Even after centuries of logging, the United States remains a heavily forested land. Forests still cover a third of the country, and timber ranks with the nation's most valuable agricultural crops. A 1982 U.S. Forest Service analysis noted that logging, milling, processing, and marketing

133

timber-based products contributed about $48.5 billion to U.S. economic output in 1972, producing 4.1 percent of the gross national product. The nation harvested $6.4 billion worth of timber that year, with the South and Pacific Northwest each contributing roughly a third.[4]

Forests occupied about 737 million acres in 1977. They ranged in size from chaparral-mountain shrubs and pinyon-juniper growth in the arid Southwest to mighty redwoods and Douglas fir on rain-soaked Pacific Coast slopes. Virgin forests survived, mostly in western national parks and forests. But second-growth, even some third-generation, forests had been reestablished on lands that early colonists and settlers once had cleared for New England farms, southern cotton plantations, and Great Lakes logging operations.

Even with all that forested land, the United States faced an uncertain long-term timber supply. The mature Douglas fir forests in the Pacific Northwest provided 31 percent of the nation's 1976 sawtimber harvest. But private timber companies — including giants such as Weyerhaeuser Co., Louisiana-Pacific Corp., Georgia-Pacific Corp., Crown Zellerbach Corp., and Boise Cascade Corp. — rapidly were running out of trees on their own industrial forests in that region. Cautious Forest Service harvest schedules could keep Pacific Coast national forests from filling the gap while replanted industry forests slowly grew large enough to be cut again.

Without increased supplies, economists warned, rising demand could keep driving wood prices upward. A 1982 Forest Service analysis predicted that under existing price trends demands for wood products would double over the next 50 years, with the sharpest jump before the year 2000. As a result, the study suggested that a timber scarcity "will have significant and adverse effects on the economy, the environment and general social well-being."[5]

In the study the Forest Service classified 482 million acres of U.S. forests as commercial timberland in 1977, capable of growing 20 cubic feet or more of wood a year per acre. Nearly three-quarters of the commercial forests lay in eastern regions where American colonists found endless stretches of woodlands. Most were privately owned, including numerous farm woodlots and other small holdings growing well below potential.

Forest product companies owned 69 million acres of commercial timberland, including 36.2 million acres in the South. Timber companies assembled large tracts in the southern states after World War II and be-

U.S. Forest Service System

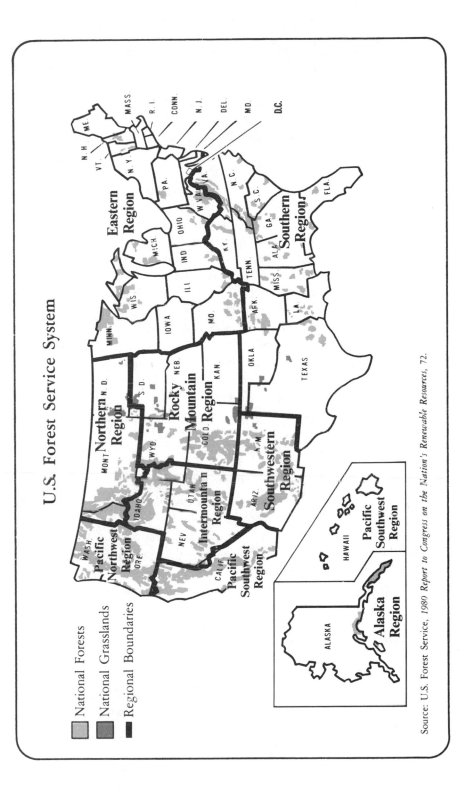

Source: U.S. Forest Service, 1980 Report to Congress on the Nation's Renewable Resources, 72.

gan managing them with intensive forestry techniques to supply regional sawmills and pulpmills. Southern timber harvests rose rapidly in the 1960s and 1970s, and the industry began shifting harvest operations to the South as it depleted its Northwest forests. The 1982 Forest Service study projected that southern sawtimber harvests would surpass Pacific Coast production during the 1990s. Southern national forests, only 11 million acres, supplied less than 7 percent of the region's harvests, although federal timber was important to timber production in some communities.

Most national forests lie in the West, in the Rocky Mountain and Pacific Coast regions. Rocky Mountain forests were marginally productive, lying at high elevations in rough terrain and dry climates. But on the Pacific Coast the national forests take in some of the country's most spectacular and productive timberlands. The Pacific region alone supplied half of U.S. timber harvests in 1977 and, in combination with Rocky Mountain states, produced 70 percent of the nation's softwood lumber and two-thirds of its softwood plywoods.

In 1977 more than 46 percent of the country's most productive forests, capable of growing 120 cubic feet or more of wood per acre each year, were in the West Coast region. Even after a century of harvesting, the region's forests held 983 billion board feet of timber, nearly 50 percent of the national inventory. The Douglas fir forests of western Oregon and Washington by themselves held 546 billion board feet, largely in the tall, thick "old-growth" stands in national forests where loggers never had harvested.

The forest industry owned 12.5 million acres of Pacific Coast timber, including 7.5 million acres in the Douglas fir region. Those lands generally held the region's most accessible forests, on the mountains' well-watered lower slopes. Timber firms have replanted most of their lands as they removed old-growth trees; but they cut too rapidly — while new forests have regenerated more slowly than anticipated — and industry inventories plunged nearly 40 percent between 1952 and 1976. As that trend continued, the Forest Service study forecast a 27 percent falloff in harvests from forest industry lands in the Pacific Northwest by the end of the century.

Forest Service Harvests

Forest Service timber sales jumped after World War II, nearly doubling between 1952 and 1976 both across the nation and in the Pacific region. Pacific Coast loggers once assumed that they could turn to national forest old-growth timber to keep mills running while industry forests grew a second crop of trees. Beginning in the early 1970s, however, the agency's commitment to sustained-yield forestry held harvests below potential levels.

Until World War II the Forest Service had treated national forest timber as reserves held for future development. In the early 1940s the agency sold only 1.5 billion board feet of timber a year; up until that time only 87,000 miles of road had been built into the forest system. The commercial timber industry, struggling to survive the Depression years, opposed federal timber sales that might drive lumber prices even lower. In the meantime the Forest Service built a shining public image by fighting forest fires and restoring once-abused eastern timberlands to more productive condition.

The Forest Service geared up for timber production in response to the post-World War II housing boom. Timber companies overcut private forests during the war, while the Forest Service planned for expanded harvests. "The Forest Service was, at the close of the war, thoroughly oriented toward production forestry in a way that it had never been previously," Samuel T. Dana and Sally K. Fairfax noted in *Forest and Range Policy*.[6]

Wood product consumption spurted in the postwar economic expansion. Improved fire control, heavy logging machinery adapted from military equipment, and federal tax-law changes treating timber sale profits as capital gains encouraged the forest products industry to make long-term investments in growing trees. Instead of discouraging competition from national forests, companies were eager to buy timber from the Forest Service to fill fast-growing demand. Some companies lacking their own forests invested in sawmills and other plants that were totally dependent on national forests for wood supplies.

The Forest Service responded by allowing timber harvests in previously uncut forests. The agency and timber purchasers built 160,000 miles of roads in the forests by 1960, primarily for logging trucks. In the next 20 years another 89,000 miles of road were built as harvests continued climbing. In the process total national forest timber harvests climbed to 3.5 billion board feet in fiscal 1950, 9.3 billion in fiscal 1960, and 11.5 billion in fiscal 1970. Timber cutting peaked at 12.3 billion board feet in fiscal 1973, then fell off over the following decade as housing markets lagged and the Forest Service balanced timber production with other forest uses.

In fiscal 1980 timber contractors cut 9.2 billion board feet from the national forests, including 3.6 billion in the Pacific Northwest. Nearly 2 billion board feet also were harvested that year from BLM's revested Oregon & California Railroad grant lands in western Oregon. In fiscal 1982 national forest harvests barely topped 6.7 billion board feet, the lowest level since 1958, while O & C harvests fell off to slightly more than 1 billion board feet.

But, expecting a sustained housing boom, timber companies in the late 1970s bid high prices to build up inventories of uncut national forest timber to ensure continued supplies for their mills. The volume of uncut timber under contract with the Forest Service reached 36.1 billion board feet in fiscal 1982, and some companies sought congressional relief from obligations to buy federal timber as sagging lumber prices made harvesting unprofitable.[7]

Even with that backlog, the Forest Service planned to increase timber sales in the mid-1980s for harvest later in the decade as wood demand resumed growing. In a report entitled "A Recommended Renewable Resources Program — 1980 Update," the agency suggested that, with intensive timber management, national forest offerings would rise to 12.5 billion board feet in 1985 and to 16.4 billion board feet 40 years later. The Reagan administration's proposed fiscal 1984 budget projected that timber sales would climb to 13.1 billion board feet in fiscal 1986, with actual harvests reaching 11.9 billion board feet in fiscal 1988.[8]

But top-level administration officials, with backing from timber industry leaders, were pushing forest supervisors and planners out in the field to study possibilities for accelerating harvests even more rapidly. Crowell, agriculture's assistant secretary who oversaw the Forest Service, told Congress in 1982 testimony that national forests could produce between 20 billion and 30 billion board feet a year if their timber inventories were harvested at the same rate as industry timberlands. "We are going to have to increase harvest rates on the national forests because of the increased dependency of the nation on those forests," Crowell contended. "This is the very purpose for which they were established back in the late 1890s and early 1900s."[9]

Old-Growth Harvest Debate

But proposals to step up logging on national forests threatened to set off a political struggle over the way the Forest Service calculated annual harvest levels. The nation could harvest that much timber only by rapidly drawing down over the next few decades the Pacific Northwest's huge inventory in old-growth stands. Once those giant trees were cut, "we're not going to see any old growth on those lands again," said Elwood Miller, associate dean at the University of Nevada, Reno."The economic models that we all live by will not allow [newly planted] trees to grow 300 to 400 years." [10]

For 80 years, since Gifford Pinchot founded the Forest Service in 1905, the agency's foresters had struggled with calculating how quickly western old-growth forests could be converted into new timber stands that could be managed to grow replacement supplies of wood. While old-growth forests provide irreplaceable vistas of towering trees that offer food and shelter vital for some wildlife, they grow slowly, if at all, and take up highly productive lands where younger stands could thrive. "In their own way," natural resources economist Marion Clawson contended in a 1975 study of forestry issues, "these forests are as unproductive as bare potential forest sites." [11]

After decades of accelerating harvests, the Forest Service in 1973 sharply curtailed future old-growth cutting. An emergency directive to forest supervisors that year restricted timber harvests to an average level over 10 years that could be achieved perpetually. That strict "non-declining, even-flow" method of calculating the yearly "allowable cut" from national forests in effect forced the Forest Service to spread the logging of old-growth timber volumes over many decades, regardless of timber demand and forest conditions. If mature stands were rapidly cut, harvest levels inevitably would drop. BLM also followed non-declining, even-flow policies on its western Oregon forests.

Congress wrote the non-declining, even-flow standard into law as part of the 1976 NFMA. But the measure provided a loophole by authorizing temporary departures from the harvest schedules "in order to meet multiple-use objectives." President Jimmy Carter in 1979 ordered the Forest Service to study temporary departures on 40 national forests where mature timber harvests could be increased to hold future wood prices down. The Reagan administration's Crowell in 1982 revised Forest Service planning regulations to make sure that management plans for all national forests at least assessed the potential economic benefits of departing from non-declining, even flow harvest limits. "In many cases, we feel that both environmental and economic objectives can be better achieved with departure from non-declining yield," Douglas MacCleery,

Crowell's deputy assistant secretary for natural resources and environment, noted in 1983.[12]

Allowable Cut Calculations

Since Pinchot's day, the Forest Service had based annual harvests primarily on biological, rather than financial, calculations. By computing factors such as available forest lands, their existing timber volume, potential productivity, and the age at which different species reach optimum growth, foresters attempted to set harvests at levels that would produce a maximum physical volume that could be cut without impairing future harvests. The objective always had been a sustained timber yield over the long run to meet national needs and to preserve the economic life of logging and lumber mill towns.

Few have quarreled with the sustained-yield goal. But finding the proper harvest level has been difficult, especially for national forests holding huge volumes of slow-growing, old-growth timber. Pinchot himself studied forestry in France and Germany, and in managing private timberlands in North Carolina he successfully followed the European forestry profession's rule that annual harvests cannot surpass the yearly wood growth on a forest. But that "cut-equals-growth" prescription, developed on fully managed forests that had replaced Europe's virgin timber centuries before, was inappropriate for New World forests dominated by old-growth stands that kept overall growth at low levels. As surveys revealed the silvicultural conditions on western forests, the Forest Service refined its sustained-yield approach to accommodate orderly liquidation of timber that already had surpassed the rotation age at which managed stands would be harvested. After the Depression, the agency also defined sustained yield to provide an even timber flow from national forests to industry mills.

By the 1970s, however, environmentalists were challenging steadily rising harvests. A 1969 Forest Service computer study of Douglas fir supplies found no combination of forest management, timber-age rotation, and road building that could sustain then-current harvest levels in the Pacific Northwest national forests after old-growth stands were converted to managed forests. With its even-flow goals in jeopardy, the agency strengthened in 1973 its policy to hold down harvest increases to strict non-declining levels. "The rationale for adopting non-declining even-flow has never been clear," three Center for Natural Resource Studies analysts concluded in a 1983 *Journal of Forestry* article. "... The policy seems to represent a middle-ground political position between a highly dependent timber industry and environmental critics." [13]

Timber industry foresters, along with some independent economists, quickly challenged the non-declining, even-flow restriction. The economists contended that the policy wastes national resources by postponing use of excessive old-growth volumes that Clawson calculated might be worth $12 billion.[14] Foresters complained that the restriction slowed conversion of decaying forests to thrifty young stands. Robert H. Nelson, an Interior Department economist, contended in a 1982 article that "by precluding any current harvests above the long-run level, the Forest Service literally wastes the foregone timber harvesting opportunities in the short run." [15]

On BLM lands in western Oregon, departure from non-declining, even-flow would allow timber cutting to rise 17 percent for three decades without reducing subsequent harvests below then-current levels, a 1977 Interior Department study concluded.[16] A 1974 analysis of timber management plans on Lassen National Forest in northern California for the Western Timber Association suggested that under Forest Service policy more than 1 billion board feet of timber essentially would be lost forever.[17] In addition, the study maintained, strict harvest limits on national forests simply ignored market demand and encouraged rapid price fluctuations. During the housing boom of the late 1970s, for instance, "industry was forced to bid unreasonably high stumpage prices — not because of a physical shortage of timber in the West, but because the owner of that timber imposed an artificial constraint called non-declining, even-flow," Ralph Peinecke, Boise Cascade Corp. vice president, complained in a 1982 symposium on sustained-yield policies.[18]

Environmentalists were alarmed by departure-from-harvest-schedule proposals. They argued that accelerated harvesting would devastate northwestern national forests while reducing housing costs by a minuscule amount. In 1979 Senate testimony opposing Carter's departure order, Sierra Club Director Brock Evans predicted that the result would be "an unwise acceleration of roading and logging into areas with high values for other resources. A great deal of the remaining uncut stands of old timber are on the steepest valleys, at the highest altitudes, where the soils are poorest. The environmental costs of extracting this timber, in the name of 'fighting inflation,' will be overwhelming, and permanent." [19]

The government previously had protected some Douglas fir old-growth forests in wilderness areas and in Washington's Olympic National Park. But environmental groups disputed contentions that the nation could cut most other virgin forests. Douglas fir old-growth represents an irreplaceable natural ecosystem, they argued, including vital habitat for northern spotted owls, wolverines, and martins. In hard winters, they added, the old-growth provides survival cover for elk herds in western Oregon. "A lot of people seem to be in an awful hurry to make decisions about something that is irreplaceable in our lifetime," Andy Stahl, a forestry expert for the National Wildlife Federation, commented in 1983. "It's not replaceable in the lifetime of our country." [20]

For its part the Forest Service was moving cautiously to assess potential departures. As of mid-1983 the agency had filed draft environmental impact statements on management plans for 21 national forests, including two in the Pacific Northwest and two in California. Only two of those draft plans — for Klamath National Forest in northern California and for Deschutes National Forest in Oregon — based the agency's preferred management alternative on departing from nondeclining, even-flow harvests.[21] The Deschutes plan projected a 38 percent increase in timber harvests in the first decade, mostly in old-growth ponderosa and lodgepole pine. The draft plan for the Klamath forest proposed stepping up harvests from Douglas fir and other species by 17 percent during the first two decades. In the third and fourth decades, timber cutting would fall off to 21 percent below current levels on the Klamath forest before recovering in the fifth decade, the draft plan predicted.[22]

The Forest Service in mid-1983 still was working on plans for western Oregon and Washington forests — including the Willamette, Umpqua, Rogue River, Olympia, Gifford Pinchot, Mount Baker, and Snoqualmie national forests — whose Douglas fir old-growth offered prime prospects for accelerated harvests. But early planning data suggested that other forests, such as the Mount Hood, Whitman, and Siuslaw national forests, would be unable to maintain even existing production goals because of lowered growth projections and stricter logging regulations. "Quite a few forests are coming in showing they can't meet today's allowable cuts," Stahl noted. "If that holds up, then the pressure to depart on forests like the Willamette will be much greater."

Logging Low-Quality Lands

Even as old-growth stands are converted to managed forests, the Pacific Coast national forests will continue to produce major supplies of timber. But most national forest lands, including some in the Pacific region, lie on rough and high terrain with steep slopes where trees grow much more slowly. As the Forest Service assessed its timber production goals, resource economists and environmentalists alike were challenging harvests on these low-quality lands as inefficient and environmentally destructive.

Under existing timber policy, Clawson charged in a 1976 *Science* magazine article, the Forest Service sold timber and replanted trees "in regions, on forests and on sites where timber values are so low that the areas should be abandoned for timber growing purposes." [23] A 1980 Resources for the Future study found that, even in the prime Douglas fir forests of the Pacific Northwest, 4.6 million acres of public timberlands could not be managed efficiently for timber production at foreseeable price levels. [24]

In fiscal 1980 the Forest Service lost roughly $440 million in its timber management activities after sharing harvest receipts with state and local governments. [25] Some critics contended that the deficit would mount to $1 billion a year under agency practices that exaggerated financial returns from managing less productive forests and sold federal timber at a loss to the government. In the process, they argued, national forest harvests kept timber prices artificially low and discouraged private owners from investing heavily to step up private forest production.

By applying stiffer economic standards to proposed timber sales, some economists argued, the Forest Service could step up federal timber harvests while setting aside more lands for wilderness, recreation use, and other purposes. "More timber could be cut, but it would be cut in different locations so that conflicts between timber harvesting and environmental amenities would be reduced," Barney Dowdle of the University of Washington Department of Forestry maintained in a 1981 critique of Forest Service timber management. [26]

'Allowable-Cut Effect'

In part, Dowdle and others contended, inefficient timber policies stemmed from the Forest Service's sustained-yield policy. The agency calculated a separate annual allowable timber cut for each of its 154 national forests. That limit applied to all commercial timberlands within the forest, including the low-quality sites as well as most productive lands. Under the non-declining, even-flow constraint, yearly harvests from each forest depended on the average growth rate of all the forest's timber stands. Forest supervisors could step up annual harvests under that policy only if overall timber growth increased.

The Forest Service could improve forest growth rates by planting new trees on idle lands, fertilizing reforested soils, thinning out young established stands, and other silvicultural practices. Those stands themselves would take decades to grow to sufficient size for harvesting. But investments in intensive forest management on those sites could pay immediate returns by raising the allowable cut in mature stands on other sites within the forest.

The Forest Service treated timber improvement projects exactly that way in its accounting procedures. The agency counted the revenues generated from harvesting additional mature timber as returns on new investments in forest management that produced increased growth. That practice showed lucrative immediate results from intensively managing forest lands that, on their own, might never yield profitable harvests.

Forest Service officials and timber industry spokesmen have used that twist, known as the "allowable-cut effect," to justify budget increases for timber stand enhancement. But critics argued that the practice obscured the true economic merits of heavy spending to improve timber growth on marginal lands where trees can be harvested only in the distant future. "It distorts public investment calculations," Nelson contended, "by showing large immediate returns to timber investments that in fact will not show any real timber yields for up to 100 years." [27]

As a consequence, economists suggested, the Forest Service committed federal funds to forestry projects on lands not really suited to long-term timber production. Environmentalists also supported intensive management on the best forests to free lower quality sites for other uses. In 1977 Senate testimony on Forest Service appropriations, Sierra Club Director Evans urged that reforestation efforts be focused "on those areas which have already been accessed by road systems and which in general contain the better quality timber growing areas." [28]

Timber Pricing System

Forest Service timber policies produced other inefficient results. The agency harvested timber stands when they reached the age when

U.S. Forest Service

Timber Sale Revenues and Costs 1974-78

Region*	Volume (thousand board feet)	Costs per thousand board feet		Average income per thousand board feet
		(100 percent of road costs)	(50 percent of road costs)	
1. Northern	5,189,991	$58.14	$42.22	$52.27
2. Rocky Mountain	1,577,753	56.60	44.36	19.84
3. Southwestern	2,045,942	86.70	70.22	96.46
4. Intermountain	2,181,000	45.86	35.95	41.55
5. Pacific Southwest	9,392,815	40.62	28.19	84.66
6. Pacific Northwest	22,829,192	32.03	22.45	86.25
8.** Southern	5,408,001	43.72	36.61	50.29
9. Eastern	2,460,883	41.84	36.95	15.76
10. Alaska	2,519,659	50.84	31.91	24.46
U.S. Total	53,640,659	40.31	29.59	67.68

* Forest Service regional map, p. 135.
** Forest Service Region 7 dissolved.

Source: Natural Resources Defense Council, *Giving Away the National Forests, An Analysis of U.S. Forest Service Timber Sales Below Cost*, 1980.

annual tree growth was at its maximum. That resulted in long forest rotation periods, often 100 years, from the time seedlings were planted to the
time mature trees were cut. But economists contended that trees should
be harvested at an earlier age, providing quicker returns on forestry
investments. And, even when timber was sold, the agency's methods for
setting prices often failed to ensure that the government recovered all its
costs.

As a result a 1980 National Resources Defense Council (NRDC)
study of 66 national forest units concluded that the Forest Service lost at
least $158 million on timber sales between 1974 and 1978. By NRDC's
calculations, timber sales during that period fell short of the cost of
reforesting lands, planning sales, building roads, and other timber
management projects in the East, Alaska, and the Rocky Mountains,
three of the nine Forest Service regional divisions.[29] *(Timber sale revenues
and costs, table, p. 145)*

Under its traditional practices, the Forest Service sold timber as it
stood, on the stump, through competitive bids by timber companies.
Most contracts gave loggers three to five years to cut trees down and
haul them out to sawmills, paying the government for timber as it was
harvested. In preparing timber sales, Forest Service appraisers first
examined tree stands to estimate what their value would be after trees
were cut and sawed into lumber or processed into pulp or plywood.
Then they subtracted an allowance for road building, logging, and
processing costs along with the contractors' profits. The agency also
computed an alternative minimum price that would cover an arbitrary
base rate, $3 per thousand board feet for high-priced species, along with
the government's expense in reforesting the lands after harvesting. The
Forest Service then set minimum bids at the higher of the two prices in
advertising timber sales.

At no point, economists contended, did that appraisal system take
into account the government's long-term timber production costs. The
unwieldy calculations, some foresters agreed, often produced unrealistic
estimates that varied widely from prices that loggers were willing to pay
for timber. The difficulty of setting accurate timber prices was com-
pounded when the agency auctioned forest stands that held several low-
valued species that grew amid more valuable softwood trees. In some
sales, in the Douglas fir region for instance, timber companies bid actual
prices far above Forest Service estimates. A 1982 House Appropriations
Committee staff investigation found that high bids for 24 timber sales

from the Willamette National Forest between 1976 and 1981 averaged 177 percent greater than the Forest Service appraisals. But in many federal timber sales, particularly in the Rocky Mountains and other regions where less desirable species are dominant and trees grow much more slowly, the government received prices far below levels that would justify managing the lands for continued timber production.

The 1980 NRDC study analyzed timber sales expenses by two methods, one allocating all road construction costs to timber activities and the other arbitrarily assigning 50 percent of road expenditures to other purposes. Even counting only half of road costs, the NRDC calculated that 56 percent of 118 national forest units studied failed to recover costs in 1974-78 timber sales. In the Pacific Northwest region, Forest Service timber receipts averaged $86.25 per thousand board feet (MBF), almost four times the estimated costs of $22.45 including half of road building expenses. But the Rocky Mountain region, including mostly Colorado and Wyoming national forests, took in an average of $19.84 per MBF, far below $44.36 per MBF that NRDC researchers assigned to timber management. The 16 national forests in the region took in an average of 35 cents in timber receipts for every dollar spent on timber management.

M. Rupert Cutler, Crowell's predecessor as assistant secretary for natural resources and environment in the Carter administration, acknowledged in 1980 that nearly 22 percent of Forest Service timber sales volume in 1978 was sold at below-cost prices.[30] Forest Service officials defended these sales as necessary in some areas to keep local lumber mills running, to thin out stands to allow improved growth, or to make use of damaged trees. They also contended that critics often failed to recognize that costly roads built for logging trucks may also provide access for campgrounds, wildlife habitat projects, fire protection, and for harvesting more valuable timber in adjacent stands. In some sales, the agency deducted the cost of roads that purchasers built themselves on national forest lands against the price of the timber. "What the Forest Service is doing is buying access," noted Miller, the University of Nevada, Reno, associate dean and forestry professor. "The only way they have to pay for a road is by selling timber." [31]

Congress ordered the Forest Service in the 1976 NFMA to give greater consideration to economic efficiency in timber management. The agency devised a more comprehensive cost accounting system and considered applying to all its forests an alternative appraisal method used in eastern forests based on comparisons with recent actual bids. In addition foresters tried to hold road costs down by reducing construction standards for roads expected to be abandoned after logging was completed. "When we put a sale package together, we have to do an economic analysis," said William Duemling, timber appraisal director in the Forest Service's Southwestern Regional Office. "In the past, projects would be undertaken to get the timber out. But in many cases, the cost of getting it out just wasn't worth it." [32]

Wilderness Controversies

The Forest Service in 1983 still was uncertain about how much national forest would be eligible for timber harvests. Twenty years after it created the national wilderness system, Congress had yet to decide finally which roadless national forest regions should be preserved in undisturbed natural condition. In the meantime Reagan administration officials and timber industry spokesmen complained that some valuable timber reserves were being kept out of production in forests under study for possible preservation. For more than a decade, Crowell told Congress in 1981, the wilderness debate had kept nearly a third of the national forest system "in a planning limbo of studies, lawsuits and repeated studies." [33]

In Oregon alone, more than 20.8 billion board feet of timber stood on Forest Service and BLM lands designated for wilderness status by legislation passed by the House of Representatives in 1983. That Oregon wilderness measure protected more than 1.1 billion acres, including 700,000 in the Douglas fir forests on the western slope of the Cascade Mountains. While the issue still was pending before the U.S. Senate in mid-1983, the House-passed version of the measure illustrated the potential stakes involved in Forest Service wilderness deliberations.

The debate was most intense in states such as Oregon, where timber provided much of the economic base but national forests also offered wilderness, wildlife habitat, watersheds, and other attractions that contributed to residents' quality of life. But the impact was likely to be felt across the nation as Congress worked its way, in state-by-state legislation, through the Carter administration's 1979 proposal to add 9.9 million acres in 36 states to the federal wilderness system. Congress in 1979-82 approved measures preserving 4.2 million acres, but it still was weighing controversial wilderness plans for other states, including timber-rich California, Washington, and Oregon.

The Reagan administration backed proposed legislation to release for multiple-use development all lands that the Forest Service had recommended be left out of wilderness preserves. But some environmental groups, dissatisfied with the agency proposals, lobbied Congress and took court action to keep logging out of forest areas not yet marred by roads while their merits as wilderness were again debated.

Cutler, a former Wilderness Society official, ordered the Carter administration's wilderness study in an attempt to finally determine how to manage the 62 million acres of Forest Service lands where roads had not yet penetrated. In the early 1970s the Forest Service had conducted a Roadless Area Review and Evaluation study (RARE I) that recommended 12 million acres out of 56 million acres inventoried be designated wilderness. But a Sierra Club lawsuit challenged the study, and the agency settled out-of-court by agreeing to draw up a land-use plan and environmental impact statement before approving any use that would alter any potential wilderness. With timber industry support, the Carter administration in 1977 launched a second roadless area review, dubbed RARE II, to again survey potential wilderness areas and draw up an environmental statement that would hold up in court as well as provide a final allocation of lands to wilderness and multiple-use management.

Carter's RARE II study proposed wilderness status for 15.6 million acres and further evaluation of another 10.6 million acres. Before sending the results to Congress, Cutler in 1979 directed the Forest Service to prepare for managing the 36 million acres found unsuitable as wilderness for multiple uses, including timber harvests. On Oregon national forests alone, forest supervisors drafted plans to sell 2.5 billion board feet in 1983-88 from roadless lands that the administration recommended be freed for logging.[34]

But RARE II, far from resolving the impasse, only further confused forest planning. Congress, not bound by the proposals, often extended wilderness measures to include regions that the Forest Service left out but wilderness advocates favored. Environmental groups criticized the 1979 RARE II environmental impact statement and filed lawsuits to block development in some roadless forests proposed for multiple-use management. In October 1982 the 9th U.S. Circuit Court of Appeals upheld a lower court decision in a lawsuit filed by the California state government and environmental groups to bar development in 46 roadless areas within that state. The court found that the Forest Service environmental impact statement had assessed inadequately the environmental consequences of non-wilderness designation.[35]

The Reagan administration responded in 1983 by throwing out the Carter RARE II recommendations and ordering the Forest Service to do yet another roadless area review as part of its forest planning process. With Crowell sympathetic to timber industry complaints about lack of access to national forests, the wilderness revisions presumably could drastically curtail timber reserves assigned to wilderness protection. But Congress, as the Oregon measure demonstrated, also could ignore any administration proposals and continue drawing its own maps of the wilderness preservation system.

In the meantime debate was mounting over how much land really was needed to meet national timber requirements. In a study published in 1981, Resources for the Future economist William F. Hyde examined potential timber yields from 169,000 roadless acres in southwestern Colorado's San Juan National Forest that the Forest Service had proposed opening for harvests. Hyde found that the government's costs in selling the timber would amount to $45.45 per MBF, including $30 per MBF just for road construction. But regional timber prices in 1976 averaged only $2.65 per MBF, and the highest annual average reached during the 1970s was $23.15.[36]

Based on such studies, economists and environmentalists more and more joined to urge that federal timber harvesting be confined to the most productive forests. By selling inferior timber at below-cost prices, they argued, the Forest Service only held lumber prices from rising to levels that would encourage private landowners to invest more heavily in managing their own lands to increase timber. The 1982 Forest Service timber assessment found that intensive management of 168 million acres of private and public timberland could increase annual wood growth by 12.9 billion cubic feet, a volume roughly equal to total 1976 harvests. In western Oregon's prime timber country, Stahl noted, 3 million acres of previously logged private lands stood idle, growing only brush.

"As long as the national forests continue to sell timber at low prices and engage in timber production on uneconomic, low-productivity lands, there will be no market incentive for private timber production," Wilderness Society economists Gloria E. Helfand and Peter M. Emerson said in a 1983 article.[37] Some experts argued that expanding wilderness reserves ultimately will enhance national timber production by removing marginal Forest Service lands from timber management. Many contended that large areas of commercial forests actually may have more value if set aside for recreation and other purposes. "An economically sensible policy would eliminate timber harvesting over wide areas of the Rockies, which happens to be one of the prime scenic and recreational attractions of the nation," Nelson asserted. Even in Washington, Oregon, and California, he said, "it would be economically beneficial to exclude timber harvesting from many higher elevation sites and to zone them for recreational or nontimber uses." [38]

Those arguments provided small comfort to timber companies trying to keep sawmills running and to loggers whose jobs were threatened. National forest policy likely will remain controversial for years to come, whatever the ultimate allocation of lands to wilderness and other uses. "It'll be back, maybe under a different name," Bruce Cooper, Forest Service RARE II coordinator for the Pacific Northwest region, commented in 1983. "Instead of wilderness, it may be old-growth harvests, wildlife habitat or something else," Cooper said. ". . . The issue is how the federal lands, the federal forested lands in particular, are going to be managed." [39]

Notes

1. Testimony before the House Appropriations Committee on fiscal 1983 Forest Service appropriations, April 27, 1982, 97th Cong., 2d. sess.
2. A board foot is the amount of timber equal to a piece of wood 12 inches square and one inch thick. A cubic foot is thus 12 board feet.
3. Marion Clawson, "The National Forests," *Science,* Feb. 20, 1976, 762-767.
4. U.S. Forest Service, *An Analysis of the Timber Situation in the United States 1952-2030* (Washington, D.C.: Government Printing Office, 1982), 2-5.
5. Ibid., xxiii.
6. Samuel T. Dana and Sally K. Fairfax, *Forest and Range Policy* (New York: McGraw-Hill, 1980), 175.
7. U.S. Forest Service, *Report of the Forest Service, Fiscal Year 1982* (Washington, D.C.: Government Printing Office, 1983), 12.
8. U.S. Forest Service, *A Recommended Renewable Resources Program — 1980 Update* (Washington, D.C.: Government Printing Office), 56-69.
9. April 27, 1982, testimony before the House Appropriations Committee.
10. Elwood Miller, associate dean at the University of Nevada, Reno, 1980 telephone interview with author.
11. Marion Clawson, *Forests For Whom and For What?* (Washington, D.C.: Resources for the Future, 1975), 165.
12. Douglas MacCleery, deputy assistant secretary for natural resources and environment, June 9, 1983, telephone interview with author.

13. B. Thomas Parry, Henry J. Vaux, and Nicholas Dennis, "Changing Conceptions of Sustained-Yield Policy on the National Forests," *Journal of Forestry,* (March 1983): 150.
14. Clawson, *Forests For Whom and For What?,* 101.
15. Robert H. Nelson, "The Public Lands," in *Current Issues in Natural Resources Policy,* ed. Paul R. Portney (Washington, D.C.: Resources for the Future, 1982), 49.
16. U. S. Department of the Interior, "Timber Harvest Policy Issues on the O & C Lands," prepared for the Office of Policy Analysis by Robert H. Nelson and Lou Pugliaresi (Washington, D.C.: Government Printing Office, 1977), 31.
17. John Keane, "Mimeo 6025," Western Timber Association, San Francisco, Nov. 11, 1974. Cited by William F. Hyde, *Timber Supply, Land Allocation, and Economic Efficiency* (Washington, D.C.: Resources for the Future, 1980), 28-29.
18. Ralph Peinecke, "Why Departures Should Be Permitted on the National Forests" (Paper delivered at the 1982 Conference on Sustained-yield Policies at Washington State University, Spokane, Wash.).
19. Statement submitted to Senate Agriculture, Nutrition and Forestry Committee, Subcommittee on Environment, Soil Conservation and Forestry hearing, June 22, 1979, 96th Cong., 1st sess.
20. Andy Stahl, forestry expert for the National Wildlife Federation, May 27, 1983, telephone interview with author.
21. George M. Leonard, director of Timber Management, U.S. Forest Service, June 9, 1983, letter to author.
22. U. S. Forest Service, *Draft Environmental Impact Statement, Deschutes National Forest* (Washington, D.C.: Government Printing Office), 24; U. S. Forest Service, *Draft Environmental Impact Statement, Klamath National Forest* (Washington, D.C.: Government Printing Office), 28.
23. Clawson, "The National Forests," 765.
24. William F. Hyde, *Timber Supply, Land Allocation, and Economic Efficiency* (Washington, D.C.: Resources for the Future, 1980), 181.
25. David H. Jackson, "Divestiture, Harvest Expansion and Economic Efficiency: The National Forests in the Early 1980s" (Paper delivered at the Wilderness Society Conference on Federal Lands and the U.S. Economy, Nov. 15-16, 1982).
26. Barney Dowdle, "An Institutional Dinosaur with an Ace: Or, How to Piddle Away Public Timber Wealth and Foul the Environment in the Process," in *Bureaucracy vs. Environment,* ed. John Baden and Richard L. Stroup (Ann Arbor: University of Michigan Press, 1981), 183.
27. Nelson, "The Public Lands," 50.
28. Statement submitted to the Senate Appropriations Committee, Subcommittee on Interior, April 19, 1977, 95th Cong., 1st sess.
29. Thomas J. Barlow et al., *Giving Away the National Forests, An Analysis of U.S. Forest Service Timber Sales Below Cost* (Washington, D.C.: Natural Resources Defense Council, 1980).
30. Nelson, "The Public Lands," 39.
31. Elwood Miller, June 1, 1983, telephone interview with author.
32. William Duemling, timber appraisal director in the Forest Service's Southwestern Regional Office, June 23, 1983, telephone interview with author.

33. Testimony before the House Interior and Insular Affairs Committee, Subcommittee on Public Lands and National Parks, June 12, 1981, 97th Cong., 1st sess.
34. Bruce Cooper, U. S. Forest Service RARE II coordinator for the Pacific Northwest region, June 24, 1983, telephone interview with author.
35. Joseph A. Davis, "Wilderness Issues Erupting Again in Congress," *Congressional Quarterly Weekly Report,* Feb. 12, 1983, 335.
36. William F. Hyde, "Compounding Clear-cuts: The Social Failures of Public Timber Management in the Rockies," in *Bureaucracy vs. Environment,* ed. John Baden and Richard L. Stroup (Ann Arbor, Mich.: University of Michigan Press, 1981), 186-202.
37. Gloria E. Helfand and Peter M. Emerson, "Timber Supply, Community Stability and the Wilderness Scapegoat," *Western Wildlands* (Winter 1983): 14.
38. Nelson, "The Public Lands," 40.
39. Bruce Cooper, June 24, 1983, telephone interview with author.

Cattle graze on an experimental range in Utah, where the U.S. Forest Service is testing the land for its optimum economic use. Restricted grazing allows forage to mature (foreground).

Chapter 7

TRAGEDY OF THE OPEN RANGE:
BLM AND THE LIVESTOCK INDUSTRY

Spread over stern and compelling country, across austere brown deserts, gray-green sagebrush plains, and golden short-grass prairies are the U.S. government's 251 million acres of rangeland — the last of the wide-open spaces. The lands roll right up to the edge of the sky, in places still unbroken by fences.

For a century the federally owned range has been ranching country, used chiefly for grazing livestock. Western families have built a regionally important industry — and preserved a colorful way of life — by turning sheep and cattle out to feed on the sparse grasses and brush of public range managed by the U.S. Interior Department's Bureau of Land Management (BLM) and the Agriculture Department's U. S. Forest Service. Yet for 50 years ranchers have been fighting government efforts to reverse the tragic deterioration of federally owned western lands caused by decades of overgrazing.

All over the West, much of the public range "remains in desperate condition, as wind, rain, and drought have swept over them and eroded their exposed soils," President Richard Nixon's Council on Environmental Quality (CEQ) concluded in 1970.[1] More than a decade later, stockmen and environmentalists continue to skirmish over BLM's campaign to cut livestock numbers to give the land time to recover. At stake is the future condition of sprawling public rangelands that make up a tenth of the entire country.

On both national forests and BLM lands, heavy livestock grazing has kept federally owned range in poor shape. The U. S. Forest Service, which has regulated grazing since 1906, has moved cautiously to cut livestock numbers on a case-by-case basis. Where ranchers have resisted, Forest Service officials usually have contained disputes at local levels.

But BLM's range improvement program has sparked controversy all over the West that has spread to Congress and federal courts. Since 1974 BLM has been under federal court order to draft 144 separate environmental impact statements (EISs) to assess the impact of livestock grazing on the rangelands. By late 1983 the bureau had filed only 80 of those statements, and its power to improve range conditions was under intense political challenge. Environmental groups have been pressing the bureau to follow up the statements by ordering stockmen to reduce the cattle and sheep herds to bring them in line with the government's estimates of long-term range capacity. But ranchers, in alliance with Interior Secretary James G. Watt, in the early 1980s still were vigorously resisting BLM range programs that they contended unfairly interfered with ranching operations.

"If a man lives on a ranch, derives a living from his ranch, he gets to have a feeling for the land," H. W. "Bud" Eppers, a southeastern New Mexico stockman, maintained in 1977.[2] Most ranchers in fact take good care of the range, on both public and private lands, out of pride and economic self-interest, BLM range specialists concur. But by opposing all grazing regulation, even where the range remains in poor shape, the livestock industry antagonized politically powerful environmental groups.

In 1983 the Natural Resources Defense Council (NRDC) and other environmental groups protested Reagan administration grazing policies that they contended "would in effect abandon the public's rangelands to the livestock industry."[3] NRDC also planned to take BLM back into court, contending that the bureau under Watt simply was going through the motions of drafting grazing EISs without ending range deterioration. Those steps renewed a long and bitter battle over rangeland erosion that some resource professionals considered one of the nation's most far-reaching and persistent environmental problems.

"We've never been able to get Congress to really understand what's at stake," former BLM Director Frank Gregg, director of the University of Arizona School of Natural Resources, lamented in 1983.[4] BLM lands, while less popular than national parks and forests, are used more and more for hunting, fishing, camping, hiking, off-road vehicle travel, and other recreation activities. Around fast-growing western cities that sprawl onto surrounding deserts and plains, federal rangelands provide critical watersheds that catch and hold sparse rainfall and absorb summer thunderstorm downpours that could send flash floods slashing down arroyos. Public rangelands provide key wildlife habitat for bear, mule

Wild Horses and Burros

Roughly 60,000 wild horses and burros run free across America's western rangelands. Since 1971 the U. S. government has been their legal guardian, a job that has saddled the Interior Department's Bureau of Land Management (BLM) with the difficult, highly controversial task of keeping fast-breeding bands from overrunning the public lands.

Congress, without a dissenting vote in either the House or Senate, passed legislation in 1971 protecting free-roaming horses and burros on federally owned lands as "living symbols of the historic and pioneer spirit of the West." The law ended undeniably cruel roundups by "mustangers" who made their living by corralling wild horses and burros and shipping them off to meat-packing plants. But with no natural predators, now that the wolves are largely gone from the plains, horses and burro populations quickly exploded to levels that posed a threat of overgrazing to environmentally sensitive ranges.

In response BLM and the U. S. Forest Service have conducted their own roundups, at federal expense, and put captured horses up for adoption by the American people. Between 1971 and 1981 the agencies removed 32,500 horses and 5,700 burros from the range, but they were only beginning to bring herd populations down toward numbers that range experts figured public lands could support. A number of animal protection groups — the American Horse Protection Association, Wild Horse Organized Assistance (WHOA), and others — mounted legal challenges to BLM roundups. Ranchers and state governments, on the other hand, have complained that the government was moving too slowly to keep horse and burro herds from damaging rangelands.

The controversy intensified when Interior Secretary James G. Watt proposed raising fees that the government charged persons who took part in the bureau's "adopt-a-horse" program. Horse protection groups feared that the higher fee would discourage adoptions, forcing the bureau to destroy healthy animals.

Wild horses and burros are not native to western rangelands. The fabled Spanish mustangs, animals that escaped from early colonists, vanished long ago. Present-day wild horses and burros are mostly strays or descendants of animals that ranchers turned loose when their operations went bankrupt during the Great Depression.

deer, sage grouse, fish, golden eagles, endangered black-footed ferrets, half the country's remaining pronghorn antelope, and even one of North America's last wild buffalo herds roaming in Utah's Henry Mountains.

Just as important, federal rangelands managed by BLM and the Forest Service serve as an irreplaceable economic base for the West's livestock industry. The cowboy era ended long ago, and ranching these days is a risky, sometimes unprofitable business; yet ranching families remain on the land, grazing livestock on the same range that their fathers, grandfathers, and even great-grandfathers used before them. They preserve, with fierce pride and stubborn independence, what novelists Wallace and Page Stegner have praised as "the most authentic and cherished way of life that has developed in the West."[5]

Range Livestock Industry

BLM alone manages 170 million acres of rangeland, virtually all of the remaining public domain in the lower 48 states outside national parks and forests. Those BLM lands generally lie at lower elevations, on the rolling western plains and intermountain basins that surround forested mountain ranges. The Forest Service also controls 50 million acres classified as range, generally at higher altitudes than BLM lands, along with 117 million acres of timberland within national forests where livestock graze in summer.[6] Other federal agencies also control rangelands, notably on military bases and testing ranges where the Defense Department permits some grazing. In all, those 251 million acres make up more than one-third of the government's land holdings, but they include terrain that has much lower economic value than other heavily forested, mineral-laden, or energy-resource-rich earth.

For a century, even longer, the federal range's main economic use has been for grazing sheep and cattle. The lands are dry, in many places receiving an average of 10 inches or less of rain a year. Even in good years, after heavy winter snowfalls and consistent summertime thunderstorms, the rangelands grow only sparse grasses, shrubs, and other low-growing plants. In combination, the vast expanses of BLM and Forest Service rangelands produce only 10 percent of the forage consumed by the U. S. livestock industry.

Western stockmen graze 1.9 million cattle and 2.3 million sheep on BLM lands, producing only 4 percent of U.S. beef and 28 percent of the nation's sheep.[7] Since the end of World War II, the country's livestock industry has been shifting to the South, where the well-watered pastures

Users of BLM Grazing Lands, 1981

State	Ranchers	Cattle	Sheep and Goats
Arizona	926	60,912	6,142
California	861	68,688	69,906
Colorado	1,817	122,508	214,149
Idaho	2,314	309,748	509,009
Montana	4,574	319,442	144,935
Nevada	720	284,374	232,261
New Mexico	2,585	155,337	118,197
Oregon	1,852	217,786	14,069
Utah	2,878	124,522	380,439
Wyoming	2,821	308,098	643,849
Totals	20,285	1,970,644	2,332,956

Source: U.S. Department of the Interior, Bureau of Land Management, *Public Land Statistics, 1981*, 78-79.

of Florida, Louisiana, east Texas, and other humid regions support more animals each acre. On typical public rangelands in the West, one cow needs more than 10 acres to supply enough feed for just a single month; and a stockman may need to assemble a 10,000-acre ranch to support a herd of 200 cattle. *(BLM grazing-land users, table, this page)*

In western states, nevertheless, the range livestock industry remains the economic mainstay of many regions surrounding small towns and cities. Roughly 20,000 stockmen lease grazing rights from BLM, and the same ranchers hold many of the 15,000 grazing permits issued by the Forest Service. Some ranches are controlled by absentee owners, oilmen, and other wealthy investors who buy up ranches as tax shelters. But most ranches depending on public lands are run by longtime ranching families, and federally owned range is essential to their economic survival.

Ranching operations vary by state and region. But typically a western ranch, perhaps 10,000 acres in all, takes in federal, state, and privately owned lands laid out in the familiar checkerboard pattern of western landholdings. Even where rangelands are fenced, a single pasture could include ten 640-acre sections of land, some owned by the rancher himself, some leased from state government, and the rest controlled by BLM. Those sections cannot be economically fenced off from each other, nor are private holdings large enough to support livestock by themselves. In many areas, particularly in northern Rocky Mountain states, ranchers also depend on nearby national forests where they drive their sheep or cattle during the summer, when lower elevations are too hot and dry for livestock.

Ranchers regard those lands as their range, even though the federal government holds title to most sections. Many stockmen resent BLM and Forest Service public land regulations that effectively dictate how many animals they can graze on state and private holdings. "They recognize that federal land is federal land," Bill Bishop, a Sierra Club public lands specialist, noted in 1977. "But, by God, their granddads grazed that land, and they feel a proprietary interest." [8]

Overgrazing the Public Domain

Before white settlers moved onto the western plains, rangelands supported vast herds of bison, pronghorn antelope, deer, elk, and other large grazing animals. Spanish settlers along the Rio Grande began herding sheep across southwestern deserts and plains after New Mexico was colonized in 1598. For three centuries, until the mid-1800s, most western plains remained vast, empty grasslands, considered to lack economic value. But after the Civil War, Texans began rounding up free-roaming longhorn cattle and driving them north to transcontinental railroad lines. By the 1880s, as buffalo hunters wiped the last bison from the High Plains, the legendary "cattle kingdom" spread to the northern short-grass plains and beyond the Rocky Mountains. Cattle barons won huge fortunes by turning their herds out to fatten on "free grass" growing on public domain rangelands that lay empty for the taking. But by the mid-1880s, winter blizzards, dry summers, and undisciplined grazing on arid, fragile grasslands all but ruined the western livestock industry.

It was a classic "tragedy of the commons," noted ecologist Garret Hardin in a 1968 *Science* magazine article.[9] Each stockman, unable to buy enough lands, rushed to graze as many livestock as possible on the federally owned range before others took control of open grasslands. In the competition ranchers overgrazed the range, turning livestock out in

Livestock Grazing Fees

In the late 19th century cattlemen and sheepmen built ranching empires in the West by turning livestock out to graze "free grass" on the wide open public domain owned by the U. S. government. Despite their gradual imposition beginning in 1906, by the early 1980s federal grazing fees were far below the cost of renting private rangelands.

Ranchers who grazed livestock on federal lands in 1982 were charged $1.82 an animal unit month (AUM) — the amount of grass and other plants that one cow, one horse, or five sheep consumed during one month. At the same time private landowners in the West were charging an average of $8.83 an AUM. But efforts to lift federal fees have met with consistent livestock industry opposition.

In 1906, when the Forest Service took over administration of grazing on national forests, officials charged ranchers 20 cents to 35 cents a head of cattle for summer grazing. In 1946, as the Taylor Grazing Act went into effect, the Interior Department set grazing fees at 5 cents an AUM. Grazing fees rose only slowly, by 1966 reaching 51 cents an AUM on national forests and 33 cents on rangelands administered by Interior's Bureau of Land Management (BLM).

Since the 1960s environmental groups and the presidents' budget makers have objected that below-market grazing fees unfairly subsidized the western livestock industry. In 1969 the Nixon administration announced a plan to boost both BLM and Forest Service fees to fair market value — then $1.23 an AUM — phased in over 10 years to ease the impact on stockmen. But Congress, responding to ranchers' protests, froze fees several times in the 1970s. Then, in the Public Rangelands Improvement Act of 1978, Congress wrote into law a formula — favored by the livestock industry itself — that computed annual grazing fees through 1985 to take into account ranchers' production costs and the prices they received for cattle.

Grazing fees nonetheless reached $2.31 an AUM in 1981 but declined to $1.86 the following year to reflect falling livestock prices. BLM collected $20.8 million from grazing fees in fiscal 1982, while the Forest Service took in $12.4 million. By law, half of BLM's grazing fees goes into a range improvement fund; another 12.5 percent is turned over to western states where grazing fees are collected.

numbers that far surpassed the land's long-term capacity to support them. By the turn of the century, sheep had nibbled once-tall grasses to their roots, and cattle had trampled fragile soils into dusty, rock-strewn landscapes.

The Forest Service began regulating livestock use on national forests in 1906. Despite some resistance the service imposed fees for grazing rights and allocated livestock numbers to protect trees, watersheds, and rangeland forage. But outside the forests, range conditions continued to decline for nearly 30 years as grazing continued unregulated. By 1934, after Dust Bowl winds blew away thin western soils, stockmen themselves supported passage of the Taylor Grazing Act to regulate livestock grazing. *(Background on Taylor Grazing Act, Chapter 2, p. 32)*

But as the Taylor Grazing Act went into effect, ranchers themselves usually controlled the Interior Department decisions on allocating rights and setting fees. Advisory boards, dominated by prominent stockmen, assigned grazing rights to well-established neighbors but excluded itinerant sheepmen who had herded their flocks across public lands but owned no private ranch bases. In northern states the boards gave preference to ranchers who owned adjacent lands and relied on public range for additional grazing. In arid southwestern states stockmen who controlled nearby water holes and stream banks were assigned surrounding public range that lacked sufficient water.

Even after the Taylor Act went into effect, most stockmen continued to assume that the government eventually would sell the remaining public range. In the meantime the advisory boards usually protected ranchers' economic interests by awarding them rights to keep grazing the same number of sheep or cattle on public lands as before. Stockmen pressed Interior officials to grant 10-year grazing licenses, effectively ensuring existing ranch operations long-term tenure. District advisory boards meanwhile frequently obstructed Grazing Service, and later BLM, efforts to cut livestock grazing back to levels that government range surveys indicated the land could support continuously.

Ranching interests, still dominant in western politics, persuaded Congress to limit BLM budgets and manpower, producing minimal regulation that preserved stockmen's dominant position on public rangelands. Unsure of its authority, BLM was compelled to persuade ranchers to accept government restrictions. Employing multiple-use powers granted by the 1964 Classification and Multiple-Use Act, the bureau in the 1960s began drafting grazing allotment management plans (AMPs), specifying how many animals an individual ranch operator could turn out in different seasons of the year and proposing expensive investments — by the government — in fencing, stock watering tanks, and other facilities to control livestock movements across the public range. BLM enthusiastically embraced "rest-rotation" grazing schedules, designed to keep stock off pastures at specified times to give plants a chance to regrow. Ranchers themselves, BLM maintained, could reap economic benefits as improving conditions permitted them to expand their herds.

By 1974 BLM had put more than one thousand AMPs into effect, covering about 25 million acres of public lands.[10] The bureau sought out progressive ranchers, eager to improve the land, who were willing to work closely with officials in devising grazing plans. But most stockmen, still suspicious of government interference, refused to accept recommendations by BLM range specialists who usually never had ranched themselves.

NRDC v. Morton Decision

Despite continued battles between BLM and the livestock industry, range experts generally agreed that forage and soil conditions improved on most public rangelands after the Taylor Grazing Act regulated livestock access. Yet many BLM lands remained in poor shape, less productive than surrounding private and national forest rangelands. In a 1974 study ordered by the Senate Appropriations Committee, BLM itself found only 17 percent of public lands in good condition, with half classified as fair and one-third considered poor lands producing far less forage than their biological capacity.[11] Secretary of the Interior Thomas Kleppe, in a 1976 speech to the Society for Range Management, concluded that 87 percent of BLM rangelands were "in something less than satisfactory condition."[12]

But on Dec. 30, 1974, a landmark federal court decision set the stage for BLM to aggressively pursue grazing cutbacks, with or without ranchers' consent. U.S. District Court Judge Thomas A. Flannery, ruling on NRDC's lawsuit against Interior Secretary Rogers C. B. Morton (*NRDC v. Morton*), ordered the bureau to draft separate environmental impact statements to assess range conditions — and consider alternative grazing policies. That decision overturned BLM's plan to draft a single comprehensive EIS on all public land grazing; in effect it ordered bureau

163

officials to draft full land-use plans, including provisions for managing wildlife, recreation, and other benefits. The Interior Department declined to appeal Flannery's ruling, although ranchers intervened with their own objections. "The real losers . . . thus were the ranchers, not the BLM . . .," Interior Department economist Robert H. Nelson noted in a 1980 draft study of BLM range policies.[13]

Flannery initially ordered 212 site-specific grazing statements, but BLM and NRDC reached an agreement to scale that goal back to 144 separate EISs, to be completed by 1988. Less than two years after Flannery's decision, Congress passed the Federal Land Policy and Management Act (FLPMA) of 1976, further strengthening the bureau's authority to manage public lands for multiple uses, not just for livestock forage. "The western livestock industry must either work with BLM to get improvements on the range, or the threat of large-scale reduction of livestock use will occur," George Turcott, acting BLM director, declared in 1977.[14]

From the beginning BLM's grazing statements have been controversial. Ranchers, backed up by western state university range scientists, have protested that BLM based grazing decisions on one-time soil, water, and plant inventories — conducted by inexperienced government workers — that ignored year-to-year fluctuations in rainfall that could alter dramatically the condition of arid lands. Environmentalists, along with economists, objected that the bureau still hesitated to cut livestock numbers, proposing instead costly improvement projects to fence rangelands into pastures and pipe water to remote stock-watering tanks to disperse livestock across the land. Some wildlife groups protested that fences could obstruct animal migrations, especially by deer and pronghorn antelope, while spoiling the spacious quality of wide open public rangelands.

By the end of 1983 BLM expected to have filed 80 environmental statements, covering 112 million acres. The bureau's planning and rangeland management budgets swelled in the late 1970s as district office staffs expanded with biologists, archeologists, and other experts who worked with rangeland specialists in compiling grazing EISs. Nelson in 1982 estimated the full cost of preparing all 144 grazing statements at $300 million to $500 million.[15] One 1979 study, cited by Nelson, found that BLM was "spending millions of dollars to prepare impact statements for projects with economic impacts which can hardly be measured."[16]

Ranch Economics

Johanna H. Wald, a San Francisco-based NRDC attorney who launched the 1974 grazing lawsuit, suggested in 1983 that "conditions have gotten better" on some BLM rangelands as the bureau implemented grazing statement proposals.[17] In its initial statements BLM proposed mandatory allotment management plans that aimed to improve conditions through costly fencing and other facilities, in an effort to avoid grazing reductions. But in 1977, after President Jimmy Carter took office, Guy Martin, the assistant secretary of interior for land and water resources, shifted the focus to reducing livestock numbers and allocating whatever forage the land was producing among wildlife and wild horses as well as sheep and cattle. By 1980 BLM had completed 22 grazing EISs, many proposing to reduce some ranchers' grazing rights by 30 percent to 40 percent.[18] Under Carter administration policy, BLM moved immediately to put proposed grazing cuts into "full force and effect," even while ranchers appealed the reductions through Interior Department administrative procedures or court action.

Not all stockmen faced grazing reductions, and BLM even recommended increases on some well-managed ranches.[19] Yet the whole livestock industry, backed by small-town bankers and business executives who financed ranch operations, rallied against BLM's range policies that they felt threatened ranchers' ability to run profitable operations. BLM's grazing EISs were "just an attempt to justify a decision in Washington, D.C., to reduce livestock grazing on public lands in the West," Bud Eppers, a Roswell, N.M., cattle and sheep rancher, argued in 1979.[20]

BLM officials justified grazing cutbacks by arguing that ranchers would reap long-term economic benefits as range productivity recovered. But many ranching operations, run by men and women in their late 50s or older, faced short-term economic problems. Profits had been squeezed between fluctuating livestock prices and steadily rising costs for fencing, vaccines, pickup trucks, and other equipment.

Ranchers survive unprofitable years by borrowing against the rising value of their ranches — assets that would be undercut by BLM-imposed livestock cutbacks. Grazing reductions directly diminish ranchers' profit opportunities. But livestock cuts also reduce the financial value of BLM grazing permits. When ranches are sold, the price generally reflects not only the value of private lands and buildings but also federal permits providing access to public range at below-market grazing fees. Grazing cutbacks reduce that "permit value," thus reducing a rancher's capital assets. In Idaho's Owyhee County, BLM proposals for grazing reductions got "right down to the nuts and bolts of a federal decision on whether a third-generation ranching family will be in business," U.S. Rep. Larry E. Craig, R-Idaho, who was then a state senator, declared in 1979.[21]

Ranchers' Revolt

Other new public land policies, including BLM wilderness reviews and wild horse protection, added to ranchers' grievances. Local BLM district officials, trained in resource professions, occasionally antagonized stockmen by announcing decisions before consulting ranchers whose operations could be altered. Bureau officials often waffled on controversial issues when livestock industry leaders took their protests to western congressional delegations, sometimes demanding that district managers be fired. "Quite frankly, the bureau in some cases has been politically inept," Brant Calkin, the Sierra Club's Southwest representative, contended in 1979. "BLM people are still intimidated, if not by direct threats, at least politically." [22]

Assisted by Watt, then director of the Mountain States Legal Foundation in Denver, ranchers in northwestern New Mexico went to court to block the bureau from imposing grazing cuts proposed by a 1977 grazing EIS. BLM Director Gregg, fearing that continued litigation could only stall the bureau's entire grazing program, persuaded environmental groups to support a livestock industry proposal, called the Public Rangelands Improvement Act and passed by Congress in 1978, that authorized spending $365 million over a 20-year period on fencing, water facilities, and other range improvements. As ranchers' protests mounted over grazing EIS recommendations, Gregg tried to negotiate a compromise program with stockmen and environmental groups that would phase in livestock cuts over a five-year period — while monitoring range conditions in the meantime to determine whether reductions in fact were justified.

Even during the Carter administration, "BLM didn't have the budget to implement the projects they decided they wanted to do" through the grazing EISs, NRDC lawyer Wald recalled. "Then they didn't have the will to carry them through." [23] But some veteran bureau officials contended that the costly EIS process diverted manpower and funds from making on-the-ground decisions, while inviting ranchers' resistance to grazing cutbacks. "I don't think you can fix up the country with a shotgun," by dictating large immediate livestock reductions to reluctant ranchers, one bureau range specialist commented in 1983. "That's what the last administration was trying to do."

Watt Grazing Policy

The rapid growth of western cities beginning after World War II resulted in the West's economic diversification, reducing its reliance on the livestock industry. But in the early 1980s ranchers still held considerable political clout, far beyond their numbers. Ranchers in the Nevada Legislature led the Sagebrush Rebellion in 1979 by demanding state control over BLM lands. The effort was unsuccessful, but President Reagan's 1980 election victory brought to office an administration sympathetic to ranchers. Watt, as Interior secretary, named Garrey E. Carruthers, a former New Mexico State University official with close ties to the state's stockmen, as assistant secretary for land and water resources. Reagan appointed Robert L. Burford, a Colorado cattleman, as BLM director.

Those officials revised BLM grazing policies to reduce pressures for grazing cutbacks. They ordered the bureau to focus environmental statements on existing range conditions but barred actual livestock adjustments based on one-time range surveys. The bureau set up a five-year monitoring program to check inventory data before imposing any reductions. In a budget-cutting move BLM turned over fence and water facility maintenance on public lands to ranchers holding grazing permits. Reversing previous Interior policy, followed under a 1926 executive order that reserved for the government rights to water in stock ponds and streams crossing public lands, Interior began encouraging ranchers themselves to file under state laws for water rights.

Watt defended those policies as part of "our Good Neighbor policy of managing public lands in consultation with the people directly affected." [24] Interior in 1983 proposed making cooperative management agreements with individual ranchers who would care for federally owned range with minimal supervision by BLM. Carruthers, while acknowledging that some ranchers abuse public range, contended that "generally speaking, the livelihoods of ranchers are so dependent on their careful use and management of public resources that they're not very likely to do anything but maintain stability or attempt to enhance that resource." [25]

Environmentalists objected strenuously, and NRDC in 1983 asked Judge Flannery to review his 1974 decision on the ground that recently completed grazing statements were inadequate. Some BLM grazing experts worried that Watt's policies were creating the expectation, within the bureau as well as among ranchers, that the government no longer would pursue grazing reductions.

By encouraging ranchers to maintain government improvements and to file claims to water on public lands, administration policies strengthened ranchers' arguments for priority over other uses of federally owned lands, critics charged. By deferring grazing cuts, they added, BLM will make even larger livestock reductions necessary in future years because conditions likely will grow more serious. "We've got to find some sound ground on which to make the tough decisions," one range specialist commented. "It's not going to get any easier out there."

In the long run BLM efforts to improve range conditions may offer the western livestock industry its best chance for economic survival. Gregg, while critical of Watt's grazing policies, sees some potential for working out cooperative management programs with ranchers who take good care of public lands that would free them from detailed regulation. In the past, Gregg noted, whenever BLM or the Forest Service tried to impose grazing reductions, "the whole industry supported the lousy operator." But, if ranchers who managed rangelands well "felt they were being trusted," Gregg suggested, "the industry would put tremendous peer pressure on those people to shape up." [26]

For that to happen, however, BLM will have to overcome half a century of hostile relations with ranchers.

Notes

1. Council on Environmental Quality, *Environmental Quality — 1970* (Washington, D.C.: Government Printing Office, 1971), 182.
2. H. W. "Bud" Eppers, Roswell, N.M., April 13, 1977, interview with author.
3. "Comments of the Natural Resources Defense Council, Inc., Defenders of Wildlife, The Wilderness Society on Proposed Amendments to the Grazing Regulations," prepared by David B. Edelson and Johanna H. Wald (Natural Resources Defense Council, San Francisco, Aug. 10, 1983, Mimeographed).
4. Frank Gregg, director of University of Arizona School of Natural Resources, Sept. 8, 1983, telephone interview with author.
5. Wallace Stegner and Page Stegner, "Rocky Mountain Country," *Atlantic*, April 1978, 57.
6. U.S. Forest Service, *An Assessment of the Forest and Range Land Situation in the United States, Forest Research Report No. 22* (Washington, D.C.: Government Printing Office, 1981), 157.

7. Interior Department, Bureau of Land Management, "The Nation's Public Lands, A Briefing Package" (Washington, D.C.: Government Printing Office, 1979); Interior Department, "The New Range Wars: Environmentalists Versus Cattlemen for the Public Rangelands," prepared for the Office of Policy Analysis by Robert H. Nelson (Washington, D.C.: Government Printing Office, 1980); U.S. Forest Service, *Report of the Forest Service, Fiscal Year 1982* (Washington, D.C.: Government Printing Office, 1983), 22.

8. Bill Bishop, Sierra Club public lands specialist, Albuquerque, N.M., 1977 interview with author.

9. Garrett Hardin, "The Tragedy of the Commons," *Science* 162 (December 1968): 1244.

10. Interior Department, "The New Range Wars," 27.

11. Sabrine Kemp, "A Perspective on BLM Grazing Policy," in *Bureaucracy vs. Environment,* ed. John Baden and Richard L. Stroup (Ann Arbor: University of Michigan Press, 1981), 129.

12. Council on Environmental Quality, *Environmental Quality — 1976* (Washington, D.C.: Government Printing Office, 1977), 85.

13. Interior Department, "The New Range Wars," 51.

14. George Turcott, acting director, Bureau of Land Management, Washington, D.C., Dec. 28, 1977, interview with author.

15. Robert H. Nelson, "The Public Lands," in *Current Issues in Natural Resource Policy,* ed. Paul R. Portney (Washington, D.C.: Resources for the Future, 1982), 52.

16. Ibid.

17. Johanna H. Wald, attorney, Natural Resources Defense Council, San Francisco, Calif., Aug. 29, 1983, telephone interview with author.

18. Gregg, telephone interview with author.

19. Nelson, "The New Range Wars," 78.

20. H. W. "Bud" Eppers, Roswell, N.M., Nov. 9, 1979, interview with author.

21. Larry Craig, Idaho state senator, Midvale, Idaho, Nov. 22, 1979, telephone interview with author.

22. Brant Calkin, Sierra Club Southwest representative, Santa Fe, N.M., 1979 interview with author.

23. Wald, telephone interview with author.

24. James G. Watt, interior secretary (Remarks before the National Public Lands Council, Reno, Nev., Sept. 21, 1982).

25. Garrey E. Carruthers, assistant secretary of the interior for land and water resources, Sept. 7, 1983, interview with author, Albuquerque, N.M.

26. Gregg, telephone interview with author.

To unearth valuable copper deposits, the Anaconda Co. began mining the Berkeley Pit, at Butte, Montana, in 1957. With the ore virtually depleted and copper prices depressed, the operation was closed in 1983.

Chapter 8

HARD-ROCK TREASURE:
MINING ON PUBLIC LANDS

Most federal lands lie in mountain and desert country, on folded and crumpled terrain where complex geologic forces have pushed up volcanoes and lifted high craggy ranges. In many places the mountain-building process has laced the earth's crust with veins of gold, silver, and other minerals precious or useful to men.

Since the California gold rush began in 1848, the U.S. government has encouraged Americans to seek their fortunes by mining on the public lands. Congress as of the early 1980s had left in place a 130-year-old law that permits prospectors, without government consent, to explore national forests and rangelands and to stake private claims to valuable mineral deposits. That measure, the General Mining Law of 1872, makes mining "legally ... the most preferred intensive economic use of the public lands," George Cameron Coggins and Charles F. Wilkinson noted in their 1981 federal land and resource law casebook.[1]

Gold and silver — and other metals such as molybdenum, copper, lead, and uranium — are rare minerals concentrated in hard-to-find ores randomly distributed in the earth. Finding them requires costly, time-consuming exploration — and the promise of ample profits from expensive mining operations. But where they occur, an Interior Department task force reported in 1977, "hard-rock" minerals "generally represent the highest economic use of the land...."[2]

California's gold fields and Nevada's Comstock Lode silver veins have been largely depleted. The solitary prospector — the grizzled figure packing picks and shovels on a burro — long ago gave way to giant mining corporations employing geologists and engineers to search deep into the earth with sophisticated techniques and costly exploration equipment.

The United States produced $8.5 billion worth of metallic minerals in 1979, including $1 billion each in iron ore and copper.[3] Metals production was dwarfed economically by energy minerals output, but U.S. mines produced crucial supplies of copper, silver, lead, nickel, molybdenum, antimony, and other metals used in making steel, automobiles, household appliances, and many other common products. Mining remains a key industry in many western states, producing 92 percent of the nation's newly extracted copper, 84 percent of its silver, and virtually all its nickel — mostly from reserves that lay beneath federally owned national forests and rangelands.[4]

Hard-rock minerals lie in rare, hard-to-find formations, usually not evident on the land's surface. But new discoveries are most likely to occur in the West, on public lands near existing mining operations. In a 1979 study the congressional Office of Technology Assessment (OTA) noted that "most of the nation's known mineral resources are concentrated in federal land areas." [5] According to the study, public lands probably offered the nation's best prospects for new discoveries of key metals — including "strategic minerals" such as cobalt, manganese, chromium, titanium, and platinum that the United States imports from foreign suppliers.

As a result, the mining industry in the late 1970s and early 1980s pressured the government to open more lands for prospecting. "Much of our public land is highly mineralized, but large amounts of that land now lie off limits to exploration and development," President Ronald Reagan declared in a 1982 message to Congress outlining his administration's plans to reduce the nation's reliance on potentially unreliable foreign mineral supplies.[6] *(Strategic minerals, box, next page)*

Under Interior Secretary James G. Watt the department stepped up its review of earlier public land withdrawals that had closed, at least temporarily, as much as two-thirds of the public domain to hard-rock mineral exploration and development. These minerals generally included metals along with uranium, a metallic element used for fueling nuclear reactors that has been excluded from the federal mineral leasing laws covering coal, oil shale, and other fossil fuels.

1872 Mining Law

The General Mining Law of 1872 was a product of gold-rush days when the federal government, encouraging western economic growth, eagerly granted demands for its plentiful lands and resources. But 110 years later, as the government's role of protecting its remaining public

Strategic Minerals

The 1973 Arab oil embargo demonstrated the risks that the United States runs by relying on imported oil to fuel its economy. By the late 1970s the federal government also was debating whether the nation was growing too dependent on "strategic minerals" mined in potentially unstable foreign countries.

The United States in the 1970s imported most of all 20 critical minerals used for military and industrial purposes. That dependence expanded as U. S. industries developed lightweight, rust-resistant steel alloys using metals such as cobalt, chromium, manganese, and titanium to provide strength and durability. Those alloys are used in many products, including computers and household appliances, but also for high-technology military equipment, notably jet fighters and missiles.

Zaire, South Africa, and Gabon supply almost all of the cobalt, chromium, and manganese used in the United States. America relies heavily on imported colombium from Brazil; graphite from Mexico; bauxite from Jamaica; silver, selenium, tungsten, and nickel from Canada; and titanium from Australia. But U.S. defense strategists, along with the country's mining industry representatives, have expressed concern primarily about potential supply disruptions due to political upheavals in African nations.

Mining industry leaders have cited strategic imports in calling for federal government support for expanded mineral exploration. President Ronald Reagan in 1981 announced plans to "decrease America's minerals vulnerability" by stockpiling critical metals, expanding government research on mining technology, and opening federally owned lands for mineral exploration. Congress in the early 1980s considered legislation, offered by a Nevada congressman, providing tax incentives to the U. S. mining industry, accelerating stockpiling, and ordering the Interior Department to review mining withdrawals on federal lands that companies wanted to explore. The measure also would have required that government land-use plans treat mining as a dominant use of public lands with significant mineral deposits.

But environmentalists and other resource experts were skeptical that federally owned lands held significant strategic mineral reserves. They contended that the nation could better protect itself against import disruptions by building up stockpiles, recycling metals, and developing alternative materials.

lands and resources was in ascendance, the law still applied. It gave prospectors the right to explore federally owned lands, without government consent, and to take possession of valuable mineral veins they discovered.

In the 1872 law Congress granted miners "a system of statutory rights . . . which cannot be denied by the executive branch, the courts, or by environmental activists," Arizona lawyer and geologist Jerry Haggard noted in a 1975 legal study.[7] Congress itself, while cracking down on mining claim abuses, still has ignored environmentalists' pleas to scrap the 1872 law and replace it with a federal leasing system. Western mining interests, including small firms and part-time weekend prospectors as well as giant mineral companies, steadfastly defend the ready access to explore federal lands that the 1872 law provides.

Congress had experimented in the early 1800s with leasing federal lead deposits in Illinois, Indiana, and Missouri. But the government abandoned that system, then sold or granted most mineral lands east of the Mississippi River under disposal laws, including parts of Michigan and Minnesota with their immense iron and copper deposits. When gold was discovered in California on federally owned public domain in 1848, the government had no policy in place for administering claims.

Out of necessity the prospecting "forty-niners" themselves adopted rules to prevent and punish claim jumping. Mining codes limited claim sizes to prevent monopolies and required that miners actually work the deposits to retain control. California state law subsequently incorporated the mining code provisions.

Miners in the meantime built huge fortunes by extracting gold and silver from public lands in California, Nevada, Colorado, and Montana. Finally in 1866 California members of Congress maneuvered through legislation, called the "miners' Magna Carta," that legalized their own regulations and provided for sale of gold-bearing lands. That law retroactively validated existing claims and declared the federal mineral lands "free and open to exploration and occupation" under local customs. It allowed miners to patent — obtain legal title from the government — "lode" claims to veins of ore. In a subsequent 1870 law Congress applied a similar system to "placer" claims to unconsolidated gold nuggets that early prospectors found mixed in riverbed gravels.

The 1872 Mining Law consolidated the lode and placer claim systems. It authorized any U.S. citizen, or person intending to become a citizen, to enter the public domain without government consent to

The People's Treasures

"Except as otherwise provided, all valuable mineral deposits in land belonging to the United States, both surveyed and unsurveyed, shall be free and open to exploration and purchase, and the lands in which they are found to occupation and purchase, by citizens of the United States. . . ."

—General Mining Law of 1872

explore for mineral deposits. It allowed a prospector to establish an exclusive right to mine any "valuable mineral deposit" by driving stakes to mark off a claim. It permitted him to mine the deposit without paying any charge to the government, but it required that he perform $100 worth of development work to protect his right to the claim. It also gave a miner the option to establish ownership of the land lying above the vein by performing $500 worth of work, then paying the government $5 an acre for a patent conferring legal title.

At the time it was passed the 1872 mining law supported the government's prevailing goal of disposing of public lands and resources to encourage settlement of the West. It was a straightforward, practical measure, recognizing the arrangements that miners themselves had worked out to award rights to gold and silver veins to lucky or hard-working prospectors who found them first.

By the mid-1970s the government had issued about 54,000 patents transferring ownership of roughly 2.9 million acres under the claim-patent system. Before 1976 prospectors who staked mining claims on the public domain were not required to even notify the federal government. State laws required miners to record claims with county clerks, but they typically provided no mechanisms for determining whether mineral veins were being worked or if they had been abandoned. By 1976, when Congress finally required that mining claims be reported to BLM, individuals and companies had staked out an estimated 6 million to 10 million inactive claims on public lands, many held merely for speculation.[8]

Abandoned mine shafts, rotting claim stakes, and ramshackle ghost towns testify to the 1872 law's success in luring fortune hunters west to search the vast public domain for gold and silver. As easily discovered mineral outcrops and gold-bearing placers were exhausted, prospecting evolved into a business for well-financed corporations, usually based in the East or San Francisco, employing engineers, geologists, and expensive mining machinery to find and extract veins buried deep in the earth. Yet the 1872 law remains in effect, and the U.S. mineral industry jealously defends the predominant status the law confers to mining on public lands. As Coggins and Wilkinson observe, "It is a political symbol as well as the legal means for obtaining public hardrock minerals: as the most prominent of the free disposition laws still on the books, it is seen as the embodiment of frontier free enterprise." [9]

The 1872 mining law applies to the national forests, managed by the Agriculture Department's U.S. Forest Service, and to rangelands, managed by the Interior Department's Bureau of Land Management (BLM). This law clouds the government's title to lands where miners can stake claims to deep mineral veins and buy the surface at the 1872 price of $5 an acre. And, even where claims go unpatented, the law makes mining the preferred economic use of the public lands, one that could at any time make the land useless for other purposes — recreation, wildlife habitat, grazing, even timber harvesting — provided for by federal multiple-use policies.

Over the years mining has scarred irreversibly some federal lands, gouging highly visible open-pit mines into mountain slopes and dumping towering tailing piles into nearby valleys. Westerners in the past filed fraudulent mining claims to gain control of lands they then used to cut timber, build cabins, or establish fishing and hunting camps in the middle of national forests. The government has moved to curb such abuses, but the congressional OTA noted in 1979 that the miners' right to enter public lands, without advance notice to the government, still left the Forest Service and BLM "with no voice in the timing of mineral activities, and with little or no chance to mitigate surface impacts resulting from the initial entry." [10]

Mining Withdrawals

For the government, the White House Council on Environmental Quality noted in 1976, "The choice has been between absolutely no mining and absolutely no control." [11] Faced with that dilemma, Congress and the executive branch over the years effectively ruled out mining on millions of acres by withdrawing them from entry under the 1872 mining law. By the 1970s the U.S. mining industry was protesting that as much as two-thirds of the public lands had been "locked up" through many separate and uncoordinated government decisions. *(Withdrawals controversy, chapter 3, box, pp. 40-41)*

At first the 1872 mining law opened for mining claims the entire public domain, the vast frontier lands that the U.S. government acquired as it expanded the nation to the Pacific Coast and Alaska. But as the 19th century drew to a close, the government set large parts of the public domain aside, in national parks, forests, military posts, Indian reservations, and other reserved lands, no longer available for disposal to state or private owners. In many cases, congressional legislation or presidential proclamations also withdrew those reserved lands from entry under the 1872 law, thus forbidding mineral exploration.

Congress, in legislation creating national parks from the public domain, has closed most of them to mining. In the Mineral Leasing Act of 1920 Congress barred mining claims on lands containing fossil fuels — coal, oil shale, oil and gas — or phosphate, potash, sulfur, or sodium deposits for fertilizer or chemical production. The 1920 law instead set up a system for leasing those minerals, but it left the hard-rock metals still available under the 1872 mining claim system. As the government began to buy up private lands to extend national parks and establish eastern national forests, however, Congress directed that the Interior Department lease all minerals, including hard-rock varieties, beneath those acquired holdings.

In theory, at least, the remainder of the public domain, including national forests in the West, are available for mining exploration. Even on those lands, however, the Interior Department, Forest Service, and other agencies that manage the surface have barred or restricted prospecting. By administrative action, the Interior and Agriculture secretaries withdrew millions of acres in separate decisions over many years to protect wildlife refuges, recreation sites, petroleum and oil shale reserves, utility corridors, and other sites against disruptive mineral exploration by private companies. Similarly, the Defense Department closed military bases and testing ranges to prospecting to safeguard security and keep prospectors out of dangerous areas.

In the Wilderness Act of 1964 Congress itself barred mineral claims in federal wilderness areas, effective Jan. 1, 1984. Even though the law allowed 20 years for exploration, mining industry spokesmen complained that the Forest Service sharply restricted access to wilderness lands during those years, making sophisticated exploration impossible.

In some areas officials withdrew lands to protect other values on areas with known mineral-deposit potential. In other places, lands were withdrawn with little consideration of whether or not minerals might lie beneath them.

In 1975 the *American Mining Congress Journal*, an industry publication, printed a study by two BLM employees who concluded that two-thirds of the public lands were unavailable for hard-rock mining. "What is perhaps even more alarming," they added, "is that the cumulative effect of this situation has occurred without the knowledge of the government." [12]

In 1977 a task force appointed by Thomas S. Kleppe, President Gerald R. Ford's secretary of the interior, reported that "the amount of federal lands on which mineral exploration and development have been prohibited, limited, or restricted, either formally or informally, has increased substantially over the past 10 years." [13]

But the Carter administration, taking control that year, disowned the task force report. Environmentalists contested industry assertions that the lands being protected held significant mineral reserves. The 1979 OTA report found 271.4 million acres of federal lands formally closed to hard-rock mining, one-third of the government's total holdings. It also reported that another 48.4 million acres, 6.1 percent of federal lands, were "highly restricted" to mineral entry.[14] *(Mineral leasing restrictions on public lands, table, next page)*

In the Federal Land Policy and Management Act of 1976, Congress directed the Interior Department to review existing withdrawals on BLM lands in the 11 western states by 1991. The law also required congressional review of future Interior withdrawals of more than 5,000 acres. Both the Carter and Reagan administrations in following years began revoking earlier withdrawals and restrictive land regulations to reopen lands for mining. In addition Congress in 1980 cleared the way for ending withdrawals on millions of Alaskan acres when it passed legislation settling the status of that state's federal lands. BLM reopened lands to mining entry as it whittled down roadless areas being considered for wilderness status. In approving legislation establishing new wilderness

Degree of Mining, Mineral Leasing Restrictions on Public Lands*

Percent of Total Federal Lands

Law	Closed		Highly Restricted		Moderately Restricted		Slight or No Restriction		Total	
	DOI Study	OTA Study	DOI Study	OTA Study	DOI Study	OTA Study	DOI Study	OTA Study	DOI Study	OTA Study
Mining Law:[1]										
Non-ANCSA	14.7	13.1	2.3	5.3	10.4	12.8	30.0	32.6	57.4	63.8
ANCSA[2]	27.2	26.8	13.9	1.2	—	6.8	1.8	1.4	42.9	36.2
Total	41.9	39.9	16.2	6.5	10.4	19.6	31.8	34.0	100.0	100.0
Mineral Leasing Laws:[3]										
Non-ANCSA	8.2	10.9	15.8	9.3	5.0	12.7	32.1	36.6	61.1	69.5
ANSCA	30.4	27.4	6.9	1.0	1.6	1.0	—	1.2	38.9	30.6
Total	38.6	38.3	22.7	10.3	6.6	13.7	32.1	37.8	100.0	100.0

* The U.S. Department of the Interior (DOI) and the Office of Technology Assessment (OTA) both prepared studies on mining and mineral leasing restrictions on federal lands, from which these figures were taken.

[1] OTA study included acquired lands in the closed category and Indian reservations in the no restriction category. DOI study did not include these lands.

[2] Federal lands affected by Alaska Native Claims Settlement Act.

[3] OTA study included Indian reservations with federal lands. DOI study considered them private lands.

Source: U.S. Department of the Interior, *Report on the Issues Identified in the Nonfuel Minerals Policy Review* (Draft for public review and comment, August 1979), table c-5.

179

regions within the national forests, Congress in some cases carefully adjusted boundaries to exclude existing mines or previously mapped mineral deposits. Former Assistant Interior Secretary Guy Martin noted in a 1981 television interview that "the trend now is toward opening up those lands. . . ." As a result, Martin insisted, the mining industry was finding "an adequate and growing supply of land for exploration." [15]

Mining Claim Regulation

The 1872 mining law in effect denies federal land agencies authority to regulate hard-rock mineral deposits on public lands. Yet those agencies are responsible for protecting the surface resources, including wildlife habitat, timber, range forage, watersheds, and natural scenery. In the 1970s the government drew on its authority to regulate the surface impacts from mining claims on forests and rangelands.

Congress, in the Surface Resources Act of 1955, restricted land use within mining claims to prevent timber-cutting, hunting and fishing camps, and other non-mining activities. In the Federal Land Policy and Management Act of 1976 Congress also attempted to clear up the status of millions of acres of public lands under old, often abandoned mining claims. For the first time the 1976 law required that persons holding existing mining claims report them to BLM within three years. After that 1979 deadline, the law declared, unreported claims no longer would be considered valid.

Federal land agencies, attempting to strengthen multiple-use policies, meanwhile sought more control over mining's environmental impacts. The Forest Service, drawing on authority from its 1897 organic law, adopted regulations in 1974 that required mining claim holders to file plans, subject to agency approval, describing their operations and reclamation plans for surrounding surface lands. Congress in 1976 barred new claims in six national park units — Death Valley National Monument in California; Mount Denali National Park and Glacier Bay National Monument in Alaska; Coronado National Memorial and Organ Pipe Cactus National Monument in Arizona; and Crater Lake National Park in Oregon — and authorized the Interior Department to regulate mining operations on previously established claims that remained valid in those areas. BLM, following the Forest Service lead, drew up regulations for claims on its lands.

But environmentalists maintain that the only way to adequately control mining on public lands is to repeal the 1872 law. They advocate making hard-rock minerals subject to leasing by government agencies, keeping the land itself in government ownership, while collecting royalties on mineral production. The Carter administration in 1977 endorsed a leasing proposal that would have allowed prospecting to continue on public lands but would have required government exploration licenses before prospectors could disturb the surface. To maintain exploration incentives, the proposal also would have allowed the Interior Department to grant leases without competitive bidding to companies that made discoveries.

The American Mining Congress, a trade group representing major mining corporations, agreed that revision of the mining law was inevitable. The group offered alternative legislation with provisions to protect miners' right to hold and develop minerals they discovered on federally owned lands. "At stake is the ability of our domestic mining industry to discover, develop, and produce the minerals required to supply the needs of our economy," Howard L. Edwards, associate general counsel to the Anaconda Corp., a major mining corporation, contended in 1977 congressional testimony on the mining group's behalf.[16]

But small mining companies opposed any change in the 1872 law, contending that a leasing system would freeze out prospectors who lacked large financial resources. Environmentalists disputed whether individual prospectors were likely to make major mineral discoveries. But as opposition mounted in the West, House Interior and Insular Affairs Committee Chairman Morris K. Udall, an Arizona Democrat who offered the administration-backed leasing bill, shifted position by endorsing the American Mining Congress legislation.

Congressional divisions continued to block mining law revision in the early 1980s. Meanwhile the Reagan administration took office determined to encourage exploration on public lands. Interior Secretary Watt pressed reviews of existing public land withdrawals and strengthened the mineral assessment capabilities of the Bureau of Mines, an Interior agency. Rather than change the 1872 law, the administration vowed to open more lands for mineral entry and to consider mineral potential before approving new withdrawals. Reagan, in announcing his 1982 minerals policy, contended that it would recognize "the vast, unknown, and untapped mineral wealth of America and the need to keep the public's land open to appropriate mineral exploration and development." [17]

Notes

1. George Cameron Coggins and Charles F. Wilkinson, *Federal Public Land and Resources Law* (Mineola, N.Y.: Foundation Press, 1981), 334.
2. Interior Department, *Task Force on the Availability of Federally Owned Mineral Lands, Final Report* (Washington, D.C.: Government Printing Office, 1977), 16.
3. Hans H. Landsbert and John E. Tilton, with Ruth B. Haas, "Nonfuel Minerals," in *Current Issues in Natural Resource Policy*, ed. Paul R. Portney (Washington, D.C.: Resources for the Future, 1982), 76.
4. Office of Technology Assessment, *Management of Fuel and Nonfuel Minerals in Federal Lands* (Washington, D.C.: Government Printing Office, 1979), 43.
5. Ibid.
6. President Ronald Reagan, "National Materials and Minerals Program Plan and Report to Congress," White House, Office of the Press Secretary, April 5, 1982.
7. Jerry Haggard, "Regulation of Mining Law Activities on Federal Lands," Rocky Mountain Mineral Law Institute, 1975. Reprinted in Coggins and Wilkinson, *Federal Public Land and Resources Law*, 378.
8. Coggins and Wilkinson, *Federal Public Land and Resources Law*, 357, 370.
9. Ibid., 334.
10. Office of Technology Assessment, *Management of Fuel and Nonfuel Minerals*, 205.
11. Council on Environmental Quality, *Environmental Quality — 1976* (Washington, D.C.: Government Printing Office, 1977), 85.
12. Gary Bennethum and L. Courtland Lee, "Is Our Account Overdrawn?" American Mining Congress Journal, 1975. Reprinted in April 8, 1976, *Congressional Record*, 94th Cong., 2d sess., S10012-S10019.
13. Interior Department, *Task Force Final Report*, 5.
14. Office of Technology Assessment, *Management of Fuel and Nonfuel Minerals*, 337.
15. Guy Martin, former assistant secretary of the interior for land and water resources, "MacNeil-Lehrer Report" interview, June 17, 1981.
16. Howard L. Edwards, associate general counsel, Anaconda Co., and chairman, American Mining Congress Public Land Committee, statement before the House Interior and Insular Affairs Committee Subcommittee on Mines and Mining, Oct. 14, 1977, 95th Cong., 1st sess.
17. Reagan, "National Materials and Minerals Program."

The first of the government's huge, multi-purpose dams used for generating electric power as well as for storing irrigation water, the Hoover Dam was authorized in 1928 and, over the following decade, was built on the Colorado River near Las Vegas, Nevada.

Chapter 9

NATURAL RESOURCE POLICIES
AND REGIONAL TENSIONS

Federally owned lands belong to all Americans, 235 million people in all, in every part of the United States. But public lands are not distributed evenly across the country. Nor do the federal government's decisions to preserve or develop those lands and their resources carry equal consequences for every part of the country.

These imbalances have contributed to regional tensions over natural resource policies that have been building since the early 1970s. In the East, Midwest, and South, states with declining industries and dwindling resources have begun insisting that the U.S. government manage the timber, coal, and other raw materials that it owns in the West for the entire nation's benefit. Meanwhile, in Alaska and 11 western states, governors, local officials, ranchers, miners, and loggers have demanded control over how the national government develops public lands that will determine the region's destiny.

Those conflicts can only intensify as the nation's population expands and shifts west to states where federal lands are concentrated. Resources for the Future writer Kent A. Price has noted that ". . . land and its attributes and services may be the oldest sources of social contention. . . . It is all but guaranteed by the sheer size and diversity of the United States." [1]

Regional feelings currently run deepest in Alaska, the Rocky Mountain states and other parts of the West. The Interior Department and the Agriculture Department's U.S. Forest Service control most of the public land and resources, and national pressures to develop federally owned timber, coal, oil shale, and other raw materials could alter the balance between steady economic growth and destructive boom-town development. The federally owned forests and rangelands also produce 60 percent of the West's water, and the government has built and operates the federally subsidized dams and reservoirs that irrigate the desert and supply fast-growing western Sun Belt cities. As a result Colorado Gov. Richard D. Lamm, a Democrat, told fellow western governors in 1980, "In many respects, the West is seen as a federal region." [2]

But as the West tries to cope with rapid growth, longer-settled regions must struggle to overcome economic stagnation, declining industrial bases, and decaying cities and public facilities. They have responded, often through large congressional delegations in the U.S. House of Representatives, by challenging federal programs that provide most of their benefits to western and southern states already well-endowed with natural resources. Most notably, eastern and midwestern representatives have allied with environmental groups to curtail federally subsidized western dam-building projects. Joined by some southern states, they also have attacked severance taxes that Montana and Wyoming now levy on federally owned coal production. Those severance taxes are "going to create something closely akin to an energy war," possibly leaving the nation "as divided as it was after the Civil War," cautioned U.S. Sen. Dale Bumpers, an Arkansas Democrat.[3] As resources become more precious the United States will grow more deeply divided between the energy-producing West and the energy-consuming East, and between the humid coastal and prairie regions and the dry desert and mountainous West. Federal land management agencies increasingly will be buffeted by conflicting regional pressures as well as by continued deep philosophical differences, cutting across regional lines, between environmental protection and economic development.

"Regionalism is the name of the game in the 1980s," Utah Gov. Scott Matheson, a Democrat, noted in 1980. "Regionalism is the way that the competitive nature of the democratic system is going to operate." [4]

Controversies Over Water

Water is the nation's most common natural resource. But it also is the most essential, for agriculture, industry, and Americans' daily lives. Since 1824 the U.S. government has played a major role in building dams and other structures to develop the country's water resources.

Three major federal agencies have spent billions of taxpayers' dollars on government-financed irrigation, flood control, power generation, and navigation projects along the nation's rivers and streams. Their programs have opened many areas, notably in the West and South, for settlement and economic growth. Yet by the late 1970s the United States faced potential water problems that some observers warned could be more serious than the nation's energy shortages. In the same period, economic and environmental concerns prompted a broad national debate over whether federal dam-building programs produced more costs than benefits.

In the early 1980s nobody was predicting that the United States was about to run out of water. "The U.S. as a whole can count on at least 50 years without serious shortages...," Harvard University environmental engineering professor Peter Rogers suggested in 1983. "Extremely difficult choices will have to be made soon in some regions, however, and almost everywhere methods of allocating present supplies and developing new ones need to be more conservative." [5]

Water always has been precious in the West, a land where barren deserts and treeless plains surround snow-tipped mountain ranges. Fed by melting snows, the region's few river systems — the Missouri, Colorado, Rio Grande, Snake, and Columbia — provide most of the renewable supplies of surface water. But runoff varies from year to year, and the region's economic prospects depend heavily on damming the rivers, thereby storing wet-year flows to tide farmers and cities through the droughts that inevitably follow.

Blessed with more dependable summer rains and winter snows, the East, South, Midwest, and Pacific Coast have fewer water problems. But droughts sometimes hit, and municipal water systems built as long as a century ago have been decaying rapidly. Eastern and midwestern congressional delegations, dismayed by the wealth and power shift to the South and West, have been questioning federal dam-building programs that supply cheap water for Sun Belt growth. They also are demanding federal support to renovate and expand crumbling water supply systems in cities such as Boston and Philadelphia that still contain century-old wooden pipelines.

Even where it is scarcest, water remains a relatively cheap commodity, priced well below its true economic value. Federal dam-building programs have encouraged profligate uses by providing water for irrigating farmlands and sprinkling lawns in the desert West at government-subsidized rates. Western state water laws, by awarding water rights to the first person to divert it for "beneficial" use, encouraged wasteful competition and ignored the hard-to-quantify value of free-flowing streams for recreation and wildlife habitat. *(Federal water rights, box, pp. 188-189)*

Controversy Developing ...

The U.S. government owns nearly half the land in 11 western states, including high mountain ranges and forested ridges that catch winter snows providing valuable water. Ownership gives the national government potentially large claims to that water.

National parks, forests, Indian reservations, and other federally reserved lands produce an average of more than 60 percent of the surface water that flows through surrounding lands in Montana, Wyoming, Colorado, New Mexico, Nevada, Idaho, Utah, Arizona, Washington, Oregon, and California. Federal lands produce 96 percent of the water in the Upper Colorado River Basin and 77 percent of average runoff from watersheds that feed the Rio Grande. Downstream, federally financed dams impound the runoff in reservoirs to generate electric power and to supply water to farmlands and faraway cities.

Since gold rush days, Congress generally has acquiesced to territorial and state laws developed to assign rights to the West's limited water resources. Eastern states, with ample water supplies, adapted English common law tradition to grant the owners of riparian lands along riverbanks and lakeshores rights to use the water flowing through them. But in the West, where early prospectors had to divert water from scattered streams, laws generally followed a "prior appropriation" doctrine, awarding rights to the first persons who put water to a beneficial economic use. Congress, in an 1866 law that confirmed prospectors' right to stake mining claims on the public domain, also sanctioned private appropriations of water flowing through federal lands under western customs and laws.

So long as the federal government was trying to dispose of its western lands, the question of whether the national government itself held rights to water flowing across those lands never arose. But in the late 19th century Congress and the executive branch reserved vast areas for continued

By the late 1970s the government already had dammed most of the nation's rivers at the best sites. Federal budget restraints, combined with environmental concerns, signaled that the dam-building era was closing. Yet Congress in 1977 fiercely contested President Jimmy Carter's attempt

... Over Federal Water Rights

government control in national parks, forests, Indian reservations, and military reservations. Then in a 1908 decision (*Winters v. United States*), the U.S. Supreme Court ruled that the government, when it established the Fort Belknap Indian Reservation on Montana's Milk River, also had reserved implicitly part of the river's water for the Indians' use.

Federal courts have ruled that the government, when it established a national forest, park, or Indian reservation, at the same time established an implied right to an unspecified amount of water for those lands. As a result, those federal rights have priority over subsequent claims to the water under uses begun in years after the federal reservation was made.

The Supreme Court, ruling on a 1963 case (*Arizona v. California*), assigned nearly 1 million acre feet of Colorado River water to five Indian reservations. The court accepted an allocation based on the amount of reservation land that could be practically irrigated. Indian tribes throughout the West since then have been pressing large reservation water claims that threaten the rights of farmers and other downstream users who began diverting water after reservations were established. The Navajo nation, whose reservation lies adjacent to the Colorado River and straddles its major San Juan River tributary, is pressing a claim to most of the river's water.

In its 1963 *Arizona v. California* decision, the Supreme Court also confirmed federal reserved water rights for national forests, wildlife refuges, and recreation areas set aside from the public domain. Western state governments, concerned by potentially broad federal water claims, have pressed court cases attempting to quantify those rights. The Carter administration, in a 1979 opinion by the Interior Department's solicitor, asserted priority "non-reserved" federal rights to water on Interior Department lands that had not been reserved for specific purposes. But in 1981 the Reagan administration repudiated that opinion.

to halt some controversial projects, and western state water interests resisted Carter's efforts to rethink national water policies.

In the early 1980s Congress still was trying to forge a political consensus behind a water development package that would complete western dam projects while improving eastern municipal water delivery systems. But debate continued over President Ronald Reagan's "cost-sharing" plan that would require states and communities benefiting from federal water development construction to pay a much larger share of the costs.

National Water Supplies

Water — or its lack — always has been the major geographic characteristic separating one part of the United States from another. Rainfall averaging 40 or even 50 inches a year gives New England, the Mid-Atlantic states, the South, and most of the Midwest humid climates where forests and crops grow readily. The Pacific Coast from Washington to northern California also benefits from dependable moisture from ocean storms that wash over fertile valleys and mountain forests. But in most of the West — from the Dakotas and Texas on westward to Pacific Coast mountains — treeless plains, barren basins, skeletal mountain ridges, and rivers that trickle or run dry most of the year testify to a meager flow of water.

The U.S. Water Resources Council, assessing water supplies and uses in 18 river basins across the country, found that total water use exceeded streamflow in four western areas, including the Rio Grande, Lower Colorado River, and Great Basin water regions.[6] But even the Northeast, generally well watered, has experienced periodic if rarely severe shortages. Ground-water pollution, sometimes from toxic chemicals, has endangered supplies for drinking and other uses all across the country. In 1980 the federal Council on Environmental Quality calculated that at least 34 states, including virtually every state east of the Mississippi River, had found drinking water supplies contaminated by underground pollution.[7]

"A natural resource more precious than oil is in increasingly short supply in many parts of America," *U.S. News & World Report* warned in 1976. "Water, if present trends continue, seems likely to provoke the next crisis with nationwide impact."[8] The concerns were amplified by drought conditions that threatened crop production from the Midwest to California during some years of the late 1970s and early 1980s. A study by the U.S. Army Corps of Engineers warned that the highly populated northeastern states — particularly the Boston, New York, and Washington, D.C., metropolitan areas — were growing more vulnerable to droughts that could bring drinking-water shortages.[9]

Leo F. Laporte, of the University of California at Santa Cruz, in a 1975 natural resource assessment, concluded: "For most of the country, water demand in the year 2000 will significantly exceed supply. Of the major drainage basins within the 48 states only three — regions in the Northeast, Southeast, and Ohio Valley — will have an assured supply of water in the year 2000 if current trends of water use and consumption continue. In other regions — Mid-Atlantic, Midwest and Northwest — supply will be greater than consumption, but in-channel water [that used in streams and returned] will be in short supply unless we change certain laws and encourage multiple use of water. In the remainder — mostly the West — projected future demand grossly exceeds the total supply." [10]

West's Water Shortages

Nineteenth century mapmakers described the West as the "Great American Desert." Since 1902 the U.S. government has been building and operating huge dams across the Colorado, Columbia, and Missouri rivers and their tributaries, supplying water and electric power for the irrigated farms and sprawling cities. But desert conditions persist, and limited water supplies threaten to cut short the West's economic growth.

Historians have identified the beginning of the West as the 100th meridian, running north-south through the heart of the Great Plains. Beyond the 100th meridian, annual rainfall dwindles progressively to below 20 inches a year, except along the narrow Pacific Coast slope and on the high Sierra Nevada and Rocky Mountain ranges. Between those mountains, which catch most of the moisture rolling in off the Pacific or from the Gulf of Mexico, rain in many arid basins averages less than 10 inches a year.

Homesteaders passed up those driest lands, leaving them part of the public domain. The well-watered mountain forests, too steep and rocky for farming, also remained under federal control in national parks and forests. The Rocky Mountain West as a result has developed an "oasis civilization," with cities, towns, and ranches clustered around the region's few rivers and natural water holes. That fundamental dryness has shaped western economic development, social customs, and resource laws. Despite federally financed water projects, "the overriding influence that shapes the West is the desert," University of Texas historian Walter Prescott Webb wrote in 1957. "That is its one unifying force." [11]

In some western regions water demand by the 1980s already had surpassed dependable natural supply from rivers whose flow fluctuates widely with year-to-year changes in Rocky Mountain snows that feed their tributaries. In other places, ground-water pumping for agricultural irrigation on the High Plains of west Texas, eastern New Mexico, Colorado, Kansas, and Nebraska and in Arizona's citrus-growing valleys was rapidly drawing down water that had been stored up in underground aquifers over thousands of years. Many western cities were outgrowing rapidly sustainable water supplies. The once-mighty Colorado River, the lifeline for half the western population, could be fully committed to human consumption by 1990 or earlier. "We've been so concerned with the idea that we must get our share," Sierra Club President Brant Calkin said in an interview, that western dam-building and well-drilling "have gone beyond the point of diminishing return." [12]

The population and economic power shift to the Southwest Sun Belt and Rocky Mountain states can only reinforce the trend. The expected drive to develop the West's vast energy resources adds yet another potential claim to dwindling water reserves. Native American Indian tribes are laying claim to ancestral water rights, while environmentalists are fighting to preserve many rivers and lakes in a natural state.

Without massive efforts to enlarge supplies — by diverting faraway rivers or by augmenting natural precipitation — or to conserve supplies, the West most likely will face more bitter struggles over water. Expanding cities and booming industries, wielding great economic power, already have begun taking over water rights from irrigated farms. The shift of water away from agriculture, as suburban developments and industrial parks spread onto neighboring fields, threatens the region with painful political, social, and economic adjustments.

Federal Water Development Programs

The U.S. government, with broad constitutional powers to regulate interstate commerce on navigable waters, has been developing the nation's water for economic use since 1824. River and harbor improvements were the government's first natural resource development program. In the 20th century federal water programs expanded to finance and build huge dams, supplying water and hydroelectric power for economic development of vast regions, notably in the West and the South.

Four federal agencies build, maintain, and operate water projects. The Army Corps of Engineers, part of the Defense Department, constructs flood control dams and clears navigation hazards on rivers

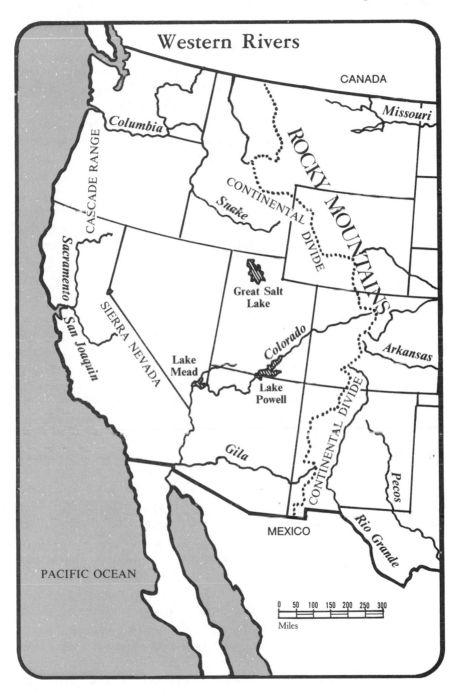

Western Rivers

CANADA

Missouri

Columbia

ROCKY MOUNTAINS

CASCADE RANGE

CONTINENTAL DIVIDE

Snake

Sacramento

Great Salt Lake

SIERRA NEVADA

Colorado

Arkansas

San Joaquin

Lake Mead

Lake Powell

CONTINENTAL DIVIDE

Gila

Pecos

MEXICO

Rio Grande

PACIFIC OCEAN

0 50 100 150 200 250 300
Miles

and harbors in all 50 states. The Tennessee Valley Authority (TVA), a semi-autonomous New Deal agency, maintains dams and runs electric power plants to promote economic development in a previously impoverished region of the South. The U.S. Bureau of Reclamation, an Interior Department agency, builds and operates dams that distribute water and electric power across a 17-state region in the West. The Soil Conservation Service, part of the Agriculture Department, since 1954 has provided technical and financial assistance for small upstream dams and erosion-control projects to retard watershed runoff.[13]

In an 1824 decision *(Gibbons v. Ogden)*, the U.S. Supreme Court confirmed Congress' power to regulate navigation on interstate streams, clearing the way for the government to build canals and dredge rivers promoting barge and steamboat trade. That year Congress promptly passed legislation approving navigation improvements on the Ohio River. With no other agency possessing engineering experience, the government assigned the task to the Army Corps of Engineers. By the end of the 19th century the government had given the corps responsibility for keeping rivers and harbors cleared throughout the land.

Federal water development objectives expanded in the 20th century as the government assumed a more direct role in the nation's economic growth. Under various 19th century laws Congress had encouraged state and privately financed irrigation projects to bring water to western homesteads. But after the turn of the century, with backing from President Theodore Roosevelt, Congress approved the Reclamation Act of 1902 to authorize the Interior Department to take on these responsibilities.

The 1902 law attempted to reinforce the government's efforts to dispose of its western public domain by supplying water to irrigate undesirable arid lands. It financed initial projects with receipts from public land sales, while assessing farmers receiving water a share of the cost, to be repaid within 10 years. It allowed an individual to receive federally provided water for up to 160 acres, the conventional homestead size.

The Bureau of Reclamation's mission was enlarged to include generating electric power and transporting water to distant water-short cities. Congress, in the Boulder Canyon Project Act of 1928, authorized the bureau to build Hoover Dam on the Colorado River near Las Vegas, Nev., the first of the government's huge, multi-purpose dams used for generating electric power as well as for storing irrigation water. During the 1930s the bureau also built Grand Coulee Dam on the Columbia River, other Colorado River dams, and started work on California's massive Central Valley water project.

The bureau's construction program continued with completion in 1964 of Glen Canyon Dam on the Colorado just above the Grand Canyon and with work on Arizona's ambitious Central Arizona Project and Upper Colorado River Basin storage projects in Colorado, Wyoming, Utah, and New Mexico.

In the meantime, President Franklin D. Roosevelt created the TVA in 1933 to promote southern economic recovery through flood control, navigation, and power generation programs. Beginning in 1936 a series of federal flood control measures directed the Corps of Engineers to develop flood control dams that also provided irrigation water, hydroelectric power, and recreation lakes on river basins all over the country. In 1944, trying to head off Roosevelt's proposal to set up a Missouri Valley Authority patterned on TVA, the corps and Reclamation Bureau agreed on the Pick-Sloan Plan for both agencies to build major irrigation and flood control dams along the flood-prone Missouri River.

By the 1980s the four federal water development agencies had built about a thousand dams, along with many canals, locks, reservoirs, and other facilities. Between 1965 and 1980 the government spent $52 billion on all water projects, and the Reclamation Bureau and Army Corps of Engineers still had 289 projects authorized by Congress under construction. Congress had approved more than 600 projects but had yet to provide appropriations.[14]

Reclamation Bureau projects provided irrigation water for about 11,000 acres in the West, roughly a sixth of the nation's irrigated crop land. Federal projects supplied water and power to some of the country's largest and fastest-growing regions, including Los Angeles, Denver, and other western cities. Despite those accomplishments, a study sponsored by consumer advocate Ralph Nader, environmental groups, resource economists, and a National Water Commission in recent years all have sharply criticized the bureau's record, along with other federal water development agencies.[15]

Over the years Congress has used federal water development projects to practice "pork barrel" politics, distributing government-financed construction among members' districts to improve their re-election prospects. State and local community leaders, especially in the water-poor West, have formed regional alliances to mutually support federal dam-building projects enabling different states to develop rivers flowing through their borders. Seven western states along the Colorado River system, for instance, reached an interstate compact allocating its waters for use within their borders. Then, led by powerful congressional leaders such as former House Interior and Insular Affairs Committee Chairman Wayne N. Aspinall, a Colorado Democrat, and former U.S. Sen. Carl Hayden, an Arizona Democrat, the Colorado River states won congressional approval for a system of massive dams along the river and its tributaries to allow each state to use its share.

In making political tradeoffs, Congress approved water developments with little economic justification, critics charged. "Since political considerations often preempt economic criteria in the selection of projects. . . , enormous sums of public funds have been spent on projects of questionable merit," Kenneth D. Frederick, director of Resources for the Future's Renewable Resources Division, concluded in 1982. "Furthermore, some of these projects, especially irrigation projects, contribute to the inefficient use of the nation's water resources." [16]

Federal irrigation projects have provided farmers with irrigation water at heavily subsidized rates. In the 1902 Reclamation Act, Congress initially required that farmers repay the government for their share of capital construction costs — but not interest — within 10 years. From the outset, the law provided a considerable subsidy by not charging irrigation recipients a share of the interest the government paid to borrow funds for dam construction. But irrigation project costs escalated beyond expected levels, and homesteaders were unable to repay even capital costs. Congress extended the 10-year repayment period in stages, eventually to 50 years, with a 10-year grace period. In 1939, after the government wrote off part of the costs of 21 western projects, Congress limited farmers' repayment obligations to their ability to pay. In addition federal law fixed repayment rates without providing for adjustments for inflation throughout repayment periods that run as long as 60 years.

The amount of subsidy granted for irrigation water varied from project to project. Resources for the Future's Kenneth Frederick noted a 1980 Interior Department study that calculated an average $792 per-acre subsidy in 18 irrigation districts supplied by federal water projects.[17] Another study cited by Frederick estimated that farmers would repay only 3.3 percent of $3.6 billion that the Reclamation Bureau had spent to build irrigation projects.[18] Partly as a result of those subsidies, U.S.

irrigation water prices range between less than 1 cent to 9 cents per thousand gallons, far below economic value.

Federally subsidized irrigation projects also supply low-cost water for municipal and industrial use in western cities. Economists and environmentalists contend that cheap water encourages farmers to grow crops that require large amounts of water and to use inefficient irrigation methods even where long-term supplies are dwindling. Using inexpensive water, migrants to Sun Belt cities such as Phoenix, Tucson, and Albuquerque plant trees and lawns instead of landscaping with cactus and other native desert plants. Federal water projects made it possible for western cities to grow into sprawling metropolitan areas with air-conditioned shopping malls, manicured golf courses, and car washes. "It is almost forgotten," ecologist George Borgstrom noted in a 1969 book, "that the 19th century West of North America was won largely through a harsh adjustment to the strongly felt limitations of locally available water. There is a shrill contrast between these prime settlers and the excessively wasteful dwellers of our days." [19]

Water Project Slowdown

But building dams has grown more expensive as construction costs have skyrocketed. Since the 1960s, moreover, with the emergence of a politically influential environmental movement, Congress has grown skeptical about whether the economic benefits from water development projects outweigh the damage they cause to natural scenery and wildlife habitat. Along the Colorado, Missouri, and Columbia river systems, as well as in the Tennessee Valley, massive federally built dams have flooded productive farmlands, destroyed archeological sites, and drowned beautiful valleys and haunting canyons. Downstream from dams, water releases timed to control floods or generate power for peak electrical consumption have disrupted the rhythm of riverbed and riverbank wildlife by altering the natural water flow.

By the late 1970s mounting environmental concerns combined with the federal government's growing budget deficits to slow construction of new water projects. In 1976 Congress approved an omnibus water projects bill authorizing $742 million for planning, design, and construction work in 36 states. But over the following seven years Congress approved few new water project starts and slowed appropriations for ongoing construction to a fraction of levels in previous decades.[20]

President Carter, a former Georgia governor, attempted a thorough overhaul of federal water policy during his four-year term in the White House between 1977 and 1981. But Carter's administration, heavily staffed with former environmental activists, got off on the wrong foot when the Interior Department in February 1977 announced a "hit list" of 19 partly built water projects that the president wanted to cancel. Congress eventually agreed to terminate funding for nine of the projects and to modify plans for four others, including the Reclamation Bureau's Central Arizona Project.

But Carter's plan infuriated members of Congress from states where the proposed projects were located, contributing to a lasting impression that the administration was insensitive to the West's particular concerns with federal water and other resource policies. The following year Carter proposed a new national water policy that would have curtailed new projects not justified on economic or environmental grounds, required states to share costs on federally built projects within their borders, and promoted water conservation. But western water interests resisted Carter's program, and Congress paid little attention.[21]

The 1980 election victory of President Reagan, a one-time Republican governor of California, encouraged Westerners' hopes for more rapid completion of water projects. James G. Watt, Reagan's interior secretary, in 1981 told the National Water Resources Association that Reagan administration officials "reject the contention that all water projects worth building have been built." But Watt cautioned that increased water development funding would depend on national economic recovery — along with reduced federal budget deficits — and on "a new cost-sharing policy which will bring the states more positively into the financing of projects." [22] *(Public land sales proposed to help balance federal budget, box, pp. 200-201)*

Cost-Sharing Debate

In its fiscal 1984 budget the Reagan administration proposed funding for 14 new water projects for which state and local sponsors had agreed to pay a larger share of up-front construction costs than previously required. But House and Senate Appropriations committees, perhaps wary of the cost-sharing precedent, were reluctant to provide appropriations for those projects.[23] In the meantime, the administration itself appeared still uncertain about how large a share of up-front costs the federal government should demand from water-project beneficiaries.

In 1982 Reagan's Cabinet Council on Natural Resources and Environment, headed by Watt, proposed a uniform cost-sharing formula to require farmers, industry, and state and local governments in regions where federal water projects were built to pay larger shares of construction costs. As proposed, that policy specified the percentage of costs that beneficiaries would have to repay the federal government for multiple-purpose projects that generated electric power, stored irrigation water, controlled floods, and supplied water for use by factories and households in urban areas.

It required that power companies and states or local governments pick up 100 percent of the costs of the hydroelectric-generating capacity of projects. It also required 100 percent repayment of costs attributed to municipal and industrial water supplies. Yet the proposal also recognized that farmers, sportsmen, and local governments would be unable to assume full financial responsibility for irrigation, flood control, or recreation facilities. It thus required beneficiaries to repay only 50 percent of recreation costs and 35 percent of irrigation and flood control costs. The U.S. government would continue to subsidize the remaining costs for those projects.

By requiring beneficiaries to pay those shares of project costs — up front, while construction was under way — the administration proposal was designed to test the merits of federal water developments by ending the hidden subsidy in previous local repayment calculations.

William R. Gianelli, the assistant secretary of the army in charge of the Corps of Engineers, in mid-1983 told the Senate Environment and Public Works Subcommittee on Water Resources that the administration had accepted the proposed cost-sharing formula. But Interior Department officials, concerned by western objections, continued to insist that cost-sharing was still under study. In a 1983 letter to the president, 15 senators from western states warned that the lack of action on new water projects could cost Republicans support in 1984 presidential and congressional elections. "We have yet to initiate construction on any new western projects in the past two years, and we are now contemplating an up-front financing scheme even more draconian than that proposed by Jimmy Carter," the senators complained.[24]

Watt, in a 1982 letter to James Abdnor, R-S.D., chairman of the Senate Water Resources Subcommittee, stated that Interior would apply cost-sharing arrangements to new water project starts on a case-by-case

Reagan Proposes Public Land Sales...

The U.S. government has been selling off public lands ever since the public domain was created nearly 200 years ago. The Taylor Grazing Act of 1934 closed most western public lands to homesteading, and since that time federal land disposals have been limited. But in 1982 the Reagan administration's "asset management" program set off a furor over possible large-scale land sales.

By executive order on Feb. 25, 1982, President Ronald Reagan established a federal Property Review Board to expedite government sale of surplus lands and buildings — including lighthouses, abandoned military bases, and warehouses — no longer needed by federal agencies. The administration goal was to reduce the national debt by selling surplus property worth $17 billion over five years. In 1983 the Interior Department identified 2.5 million acres in scattered tracts for possible sale.

In the Federal Land Policy and Management Act (FLPMA) of 1976, Congress gave Interior's Bureau of Land Management (BLM) authority to sell public lands for fair market value after determining that they would better serve the public interest if no longer owned by the government. Using that power, the bureau offers isolated tracts — often mixed in a checkerboard pattern with state or private lands — that are impossible for the government to manage effectively. Interior also has been negotiating land exchanges with western state governments to "block up" lands in consolidated federal and state holdings.

The Agriculture Department's Forest Service also exchanges lands to consolidate its holdings and eliminate private lands within national forests. The Forest Service has only limited power to sell national forest lands to communities, school districts, and private persons to permit cities and towns to expand their boundaries. In 1983 the Forest Service identified roughly 6 million acres of national forest land, including tracts in eastern national forests, for further study for possible sales under the asset

basis. "It's the view of the Department of the Interior that, particularly 100 percent, up-front financing in some cases is not a realistic expectation," Garrey E. Carruthers, Watt's assistant secretary for land and water resources, commented in 1983. "... You have to treat these on a case-by-case basis.... You have to look at the project itself, the

. . . To Help Balance the Federal Budget

management program. John B. Crowell Jr., assistant secretary of agriculture in charge of the Forest Service, was considering asking Congress to give the service more general authority to sell lands to the public.

From the beginning of his stormy tenure, which ended in October 1983, Interior Secretary James G. Watt insisted that the government had no plans to sell national park, wildlife refuge, or wilderness lands. But during the uproar that followed Watt's appointment in 1981, conservationists warned that Watt might put large tracts of valuable recreation land up for sale. Arizona Gov. Bruce Babbitt, a Democrat, objected that, under the asset management program, land sales would preclude trades between the state and federal government to consolidate western land holdings into more easily managed patterns.

Western ranchers long had assumed that the Interior Department eventually would make public rangelands available for private ownership. But as asset management planning continued, it became clear that most stockmen never could afford to pay the government fair market value for public lands lying in the middle of their ranches. In Idaho's Owyhee County, for instance, a 40-acre parcel might be worth $100 an acre as grazing land, U.S. Rep. Larry Craig, R-Idaho, pointed out in 1983, but "a Californian is willing to pay $400 an acre for a 40-acre ranchette" right in the middle of a rancher's rangelands.

"We're experiencing a kind of Sagebrush Rebellion in reverse," among ranchers who concluded they never could afford to buy rangelands the government was offering, Craig commented. As Westerners' protests mounted Watt wrote governors in the region to announce that Interior land disposals no longer would be conducted under the Property Review Board. BLM continued to identify some lands for sale through its normal land-use planning process, but the department discarded the asset management program objective of reducing the federal debt.

lay of the land, economic situation within the project area, the kinds of commitments that one can expect from the state and/or county or city, the interests in the private sector." [25] Interior officials agreed with the Defense Department that private companies, along with state and local governments, should pay 100 percent of the costs attributed to hydropower and municipal and industrial water, Carruthers added.

Cost-sharing proposals, along with continued uncertainty about funding to start or complete planned water projets, struck sensitive nerves in the West. Funding cutbacks, and pronouncements such as Carter's on his ill-advised hit list, raised doubts about the government's commitment to follow through with construction of long-planned projects such as the Central Arizona Project to pipe Colorado River water across the desert to Phoenix and Tucson to relieve the state's reliance on rapidly declining underground aquifers. They also threatened Upper Colorado River Basin projects that would permit Utah, Colorado, New Mexico, and Wyoming to start making full use of their water entitlements under the 1922 Colorado River Compact with downstream states of California, Arizona, and Nevada.

In authorizing the Central Arizona and Upper Colorado projects in 1968 Congress "accommodated the interests of all seven of those states after years of controversy, litigation, and negotiation," New Mexico State Engineer Steve Reynolds contended in 1977 testimony on Carter's water policy proposals. "To renege on some of those commitments while fulfilling others would compound the inequity" of cancelling projects on which western states and communities had been counting.[26]

Federally financed dams and reservoirs were not expected to solve all the West's water problems. In dividing up the Colorado, for instance, western state negotiators relied on overly optimistic forecasts of the river's flow. The 1922 compact allocated rights to 15 million acre feet of water a year among the seven states, but the river's annual flow since then has averaged well below that level. As a result, California farmers likely will be forced to cut back irrigation with Colorado River water as the Central Arizona Project comes on line and Upper Basin states begin using more water. (An acre-foot is the volume of water needed to cover one acre of land to a depth of one foot, equal to 43,560 cubic feet or 325,851 gallons.)

With its limited water, the West probably cannot provide for all competing uses. Already, as Phoenix, Denver, and other cities have spread onto surrounding farmlands, water once used for irrigation has been converted to municipal and industrial purposes. In Colorado, Wyoming, Utah, Montana, New Mexico, and other states, rapid development of coal, oil shale, and other federally owned energy reserves could command huge amounts of water now being used for farming.

Plans to transport coal mixed with water through lengthy "slurry" pipelines to southern states could require large amounts of water. With vast financial resources, energy companies can easily afford to buy up rights to irrigation water, paying far more for them than farmers or ranchers could earn from crops or livestock. While providing a windfall to individual farming or ranching families, water right sales could damage the West's agricultural industry and leave some regions without a permanent economic base after energy reserves have been depleted. "It's hard to see energy water withdrawals not just eclipsing agricultural water," Colorado Gov. Lamm remarked in 1979. "One of the problems of having energy come on is that it's a one-time harvest." [27]

Completing western water projects to provide dependable supplies for energy, agricultural, industrial, and municipal demands requires balancing in Congress between eastern and western interests. In 1983 the House Committee on Public Works and Transportation Subcommittee on Water Resources considered omnibus water development legislation providing for 150 new projects or major changes in existing projects, at a cost of between $10 billion and $20 billion over seven to 10 years. Put together by Rep. Robert A. Roe, a New Jersey Democrat who headed the panel, the measure included an $800 million loan fund to be administered by the Corps of Engineers to improve municipal water supplies. "One thing that's essential to the nation is to establish a fair and equitable system, not pitting one section of the country against the other," Roe contended, suggesting that House approval of the omnibus bill was impossible without regional equity.[28]

State Resource Policies

Congress holds pre-eminent power to manage public lands. But state governments, partners in the U.S. federal system, are not without authority to influence federally owned resource development within their borders. Ever since the 1973 Arab oil embargo, Rocky Mountain governors and legislatures have been putting policies in place to control long-expected coal, oil shale, and oil and gas booms — and turn them to their region's long-term advantage.

Rocky Mountain state governors, including aggressive young Democrats, in 1977 organized the Western Governors' Policy Office (WESTPO), to develop a united regional response to federal government pressures for resource development. State legislatures updated plant-siting, pollution, and other resource rules devised to control social and environmental impacts in boom-town areas. Most controversial of all, western states began reaping fast-rising revenues from taxes, state royalties, and shared federal mineral leasing receipts — and investing those funds both to improve public facilities and to promote future economic expansion in the nation's fastest-growing region.

The West's objective, Utah Gov. Matheson told fellow WESTPO governors in 1980, was "to be participants and not mere bystanders in the shaping of our region during the next decade." [29] But outside the West rising energy prices in the 1970s produced hardship for homeowners and industries in regions already pressed hard by economic decline and the flight of business and population to warmer Sun Belt climates. The Rocky Mountain states' energy policies raised hackles among industries, electric utilities, consumer groups, and politicians in areas that were growing more dependent on western coal to supply their energy requirements. Through those policies, Arkansas Sen. Bumpers complained, western states were "trying to make themselves blue-eyed Arabs." [30]

Severance Tax Protests

Those resentments broke into the open in the late 1970s and early 1980s in protests against the severance taxes that western states levied on coal production. Concerned by rapid strip-mining expansion in the Powder River Basin, Montana and Wyoming in the mid-1970s sharply boosted the tax rates they levied on the value of coal that mining companies "severed" from deposits within their borders. Montana lifted its tax to 30 percent in 1975, then began pouring half the revenue into a trust fund to finance economic diversification to prepare for the time when the state's coal reserves were exhausted. *(State severance tax rates, table, next page)*

Wyoming followed suit, imposing a 17 percent severance tax, including local government levies. Colorado, New Mexico, and North Dakota by 1980 also charged coal severance taxes — Colorado's tax was 95 cents per ton — but Utah imposed none. With congressional consent, granted by the Mineral Leasing Act of 1920, the states collected those taxes from companies mining federally owned coal as well as state and private deposits.

State governments have imposed severance taxes on natural resources since 1846. By 1981, 33 states enforced severance taxes on depletable resources, including timber, coal, oil and gas, and other raw

State Severance Tax Rates, 1980

(percent)

	Oil	Gas	Coal
Alaska	12.25%(a)	10.0 %	0
Arizona	2.5	0	0
California	(b)	0	0
Colorado	4.5	0	(f)
Idaho	0	0	0
Louisiana	12.25	(e)	0
Montana	2.65	3.1	30.0
Nevada	(c)	0	0
New Mexico	7.75	(d)	(g)
North Dakota	5.0	5.0	(h)
Oregon	0	0	0
Texas	4.6	7.5	0
Utah	2.0	1.95	0
Washington	0	0	0
Wyoming	4.0	4.0	10.5 (i)

(a) Nominal tax, average tax is about 11 percent with the application of economic-decline factors.
(b) Variable tax set to cover state regulatory agency administrative costs.
(c) Tax rate is 0.50 cents per barrel.
(d) Tax rate is 6.40 cents per million cubic feet.
(e) Tax rate is 6.88 cents per million cubic feet.
(f) Tax rate is 44 cents per ton for underground coal, 95 cents per ton for surface mined coal.
(g) Tax rate was 72.80 cents per ton in 1979, is adjusted for inflation.
(h) Tax rate is 85 cents per ton plus a price index adjustment.
(i) Excludes 6.5 percent local tax collected by state.

Source: Treasury Department, *The Outlook for Severance Tax Collections and the Interstate Allocation of Revenue Sharing* (Washington, D.C.: Government Printing Office, 1981).

materials. State severance tax revenues in 1981 reached $6.4 billion — including $5.1 billion that Texas, Alaska, Louisiana, Oklahoma, and New Mexico collected primarily from taxes on oil and gas production as oil prices were soaring.[31]

Texas' and Louisiana's oil and gas severance taxes in 1980 brought those states $1.5 billion and $509 million respectively. Those receipts dwarfed Montana's $75 million and Wyoming's $42.9 million in coal severance taxes. Among them, eight western states — Alaska, California, Colorado, New Mexico, North Dakota, and Utah as well as Montana and Wyoming — took in $812.3 million in 1980 from severance taxes on oil and gas. That far exceeded the $143.3 million in coal severance tax revenues collected by Colorado, Montana, Wyoming, and North Dakota — the four western states that imposed coal severance taxes that year. New Mexico's coal severance tax took effect later.[32] *(State severance tax revenues, table, next page)*

Oil and gas production has been falling off since the early 1970s, and, as oil prices retreated from the late-1970s peak, state petroleum revenues also declined. Coal remains one of the nation's best future energy bets, and federally owned reserves in six western states likely will supply much of the fuel to help the nation meet electric power needs until the 21st century. To the rest of the country, Montana's stiff 30 percent severance tax, and Wyoming's 17 percent levy as well, appeared as an attempt by energy-rich states to fill their own coffers at the expense of energy consumers in less well-endowed areas.

The controversy produced warnings about an energy "civil war" and charges that the West was creating a domestic coal cartel to take advantage of the need for energy. In Congress the Northeast-Midwest Congressional Coalition, made up of more than 200 members from industrial states, worried that "the creation of a kind of 'United American Emirates,' a group of 'superstates' with unprecedented power to beggar their neighbors in the federal system . . . will accelerate the decline of energy-poor regions and thwart efforts to revitalize the troubled economic structure of the older industrial states." [33]

Even senators and representatives from Texas, with its large oil revenues, joined to protest the Montana and Wyoming coal taxes. Critics contended that severance taxes of that magnitude discouraged badly needed coal production while raising energy costs. As coal mining increased and prices rose, they added, western states would benefit from climbing severance tax revenues — paid by residents in other states — while keeping other state taxes down to draw business and industry away from other regions. The results, New Jersey Gov. Brendan Byrne, a Democrat, charged in 1981, could be "potentially the largest transfer of wealth in the history of this country." [34]

State Severance Tax Revenues*

(millions of dollars)

	1970	1975	1980	1983**	1985**
Alaska	$10.8	$29.3	$506.5	$2,116.9	$2,744.0
Arizona	0	0	0	0.3	0.3
California	1.6	2.3	25.9	36.8	50.8
Colorado	1.1	2.4	31.1	104.9	132.2
Idaho	0.3	0.5	1.9	4.4	7.6
Montana	4.7	14.7	94.6	193.9	252.1
Nevada	0.1	0.2	0	0	0
New Mexico	35.4	71.6	213.6	362.1	428.6
North Dakota	3.2	6.9	43.9	104.9	135.2
Oregon	1.9	3.1	50.6	60.6	68.3
Utah	4.3	6.2	10.6	35.3	47.8
Washington	0	23.2	49.9	78.9	107.1
Wyoming	4.3	18.2	105.7	550.0	772.3
Total	67.7	178.6	1,134.3	3,649.0	4,746.3
Louisiana	251.0	548.5	525.3	1,036.6	1,060.5
Texas	273.2	666.9	1,525.1	3,180.1	3,811.2

* Includes revenues from production of energy and other natural resources, both federal and
nonfederal.
** Projected.

Source: Interior Department, *Past and Projected State Revenues from Energy and Other Natural
Resources in 13 Western States, September 1981* (Washington, D.C.: Government Printing Office).

Energy-consuming regions in the early 1980s mounted legal and
political attacks on the Montana and Wyoming taxes. The U.S. Supreme
Court, ruling on a lawsuit brought by a giant Illinois electric utility
(*Commonwealth Edison v. Montana*), in 1981 found that Montana's 30
percent tax, applied equally to coal burned in Montana and shipped out
of state, was a constitutional measure that did not unfairly restrict
interstate commerce. But the court suggested that Congress held power

207

to limit state severance tax levels, and members offered legislation to cap tax rates at 12.5 percent, which would have forced reductions by Montana and Wyoming.

House members in 1981 offered a bill to limit severance taxes to 12.5 percent on all coal, while Bumpers and Sen. David Durenberger, R-Minn., chairman of the Senate Governmental Affairs Subcommittee on Intergovernmental Relations, proposed a cap limited to coal produced from federal lands and Indian reservations. But Congress took no action, as WESTPO governors rallied opposition to what they viewed would amount to federal interference in state governments' sovereign taxing powers.

Montana and Wyoming officials, joined by other western state governors, defended the taxes as reasonable levies that add little to energy costs in other regions and have little effect on production. The West has a long history of mining booms that collapsed when ore veins played out, leaving ghost towns and ruined local economies. Coal-tax revenues provide funds to pay for highways, hospitals, and other facilities for fast-growing populations, governors contend, and to invest in long-term economic development that states can rely on when coal mining has run its course. Through severance taxes, said Montana Gov. Ted Schwinden, a Democrat, western states can prevent "the mistakes of the past, cover the costs of today, and leave us something when all the coal is gone." [35]

Studies have suggested that coal severance taxes contributed little to the overall surge in energy costs during the 1970s compared with oil price increases and railroad coal-hauling rates. But the concept remains controversial, especially where state taxes are applied to federally owned coal, a national resource. State severance taxes "are an irritant even at their present level," Hans H. Landsberg noted in a 1982 Resources for the Future analysis entitled "Energy 'Haves' and 'Have-Nots'." ". . . In time the revenue-raising power of the major oil, gas, and to a lesser degree, coal states indeed could become large enough to constitute a real threat to the energy-deficient states." [36]

Federal Mineral Revenue Sharing

While severance taxes have drawn most attention, western states have been collecting even larger financial benefits from energy development. State governments themselves own important energy resources beneath lands that the U.S. government granted them when they entered the Union. Congress, in the 1920 Mineral Leasing Act and later legislation, granted the states 50 percent of the federal government's revenues from coal, oil and gas, and other mineral production from public lands within their borders.

In 1980, 13 western state governments, including Alaska and North Dakota, collected $3.5 billion from natural resource production. Those receipts included $1.1 billion from state severance taxes — $812.3 million on oil and gas — and $1.7 billion in royalties and rents from state-owned resource production. Revenues from both those sources multiplied 10-fold in the 1970s as western coal production climbed and world petroleum prices skyrocketed.[37]

In the same period, western state governments' share of federal mineral leasing revenues also climbed spectacularly. The 1920 mineral leasing law required the federal government to return 90 percent of the revenues it collected to states where resources were extracted. The 1920 law assigned 37.5 percent to state governments for use to support education or road construction and maintenance, and dedicated another 52.5 percent to finance Reclamation Bureau water projects in a 17-state western area.

Congress, in 1976 coal leasing amendments, reduced the reclamation fund contribution to 40 percent. The measure increased the share contributed directly to state governments to 50 percent and allowed state governments to use those funds to provide public services and construct various facilities to help booming areas cope with population growth. In Alaska, where the 1902 Reclamation Act does not apply, the state continued receiving its full 90 percent share.

In separate 1976 legislation Congress authorized the federal government to make "payments in lieu of taxes" directly to local governments, compensating for property tax loss on large federally owned lands immune from state and local levies. In 1977 strip-mining legislation Congress also allocated the states 50 percent of abandoned-mine reclamation funds collected from coal-mining companies.

The U.S. Forest Service pays 25 percent of its timber revenues to local counties. The Interior Department's Bureau of Land Management (BLM) turns half of timber receipts from its Oregon & California railroad-grant forests over to Oregon counties where those lands are located. BLM also pays states 12.5 percent of its grazing fees, and another 50 percent goes into the bureau's range improvement fund to finance fencing, stock watering tanks, and other facilities for livestock grazing.

By 1980 BLM and Forest Service payments to states for mineral, timber, grazing, and payments in lieu of taxes amounted to $747.3 million, up from $154.6 million 10 years earlier. By agency projections, those contributions were expected to double to $1.5 billion by 1985; but those estimates anticipated oil revenue increases that since have been undercut by declining world petroleum prices. Even so, combined with state severance taxes on federal coal, oil, and gas, those contributions handsomely reward western states for public land development.[38]

Western state governments, especially in Wyoming, New Mexico, Montana, Colorado, Utah, and North Dakota, can expect energy revenues to swell as coal and possibly oil-shale development accelerates. Yet state officials note that most receipts begin coming in only after mining has begun, too late to help counties and municipal governments build hospitals, parks, schools, and expanded police forces to serve growing populations. Congress, nevertheless, has been reluctant to approve western states' requests for energy "impact assistance" providing up-front grants to prepare for the social and economic strains. As Jim Monaghan, Gov. Lamm's energy adviser put it: "Congress as a body really feels the West is getting rich off energy development."[39]

Federal-State Tensions

The West always has been uneasy with the federal government as its major landlord. Since frontier days, Westerners have awaited eagerly the economic benefits of resource extraction. But they also have objected vehemently to control by outsiders — the railroads, the mining and timber corporations based in New York, Chicago, and San Francisco — that profited from the region's great natural wealth. "Since the 1890s, westerners have loudly protested their colonial status," University of Wyoming historian Gene M. Gressley has noted.[40]

Since the early 1970s that resentment more and more has been directed at the U.S. government, particularly the Forest Service and BLM. Alarmed by continuing federal plans, through both Democratic and Republican administrations, to accelerate energy development on public lands, western governors and other spokesmen repeatedly have declared the region unwilling to serve as an "energy colony" for the rest of the country. To back up those words, governors from 13 states — Alaska, Arizona, Colorado, Wyoming, New Mexico, Montana, Nebraska, North and South Dakota, Utah, Nevada, Washington, and Idaho — formed WESTPO to articulate common concerns and form a unified position for negotiations with Congress and federal resource management agencies. "We're not trying to cartelize western energy," Gov. Lamm insisted in 1979. "But when Washington makes energy decisions, we want to make sure we have a place at the table, that our citizens don't subsidize the energy needs of the East." [41]

Lamm, Babbitt, Matheson, and other governors have spoken forcefully for the region's interests in Washington, D.C. They have pushed for a role in making federal resource policies, generally urging a go-slow approach to give western states and communities time to adjust to economic growth and preserve clean air, scenic vistas, and rural agricultural economies. During the Carter administration, Interior Secretary Cecil D. Andrus approved a federal coal-leasing program establishing regional teams including state governors' representatives to recommend leasing targets to department officials.

State governments themselves have adopted plant-siting laws and mining-permit systems to control development on federally owned lands. Some states, under agreements with the Interior Department, enforce federal strip-mining regulations on federal lands as well as state and private holdings. Western state water laws governing diversion of scarce surface waters give states potential control over water transfers from agriculture to energy. "If we had exclusive authority on water, nobody could do anything to us," Matheson commented. [42]

But the federal government's control over western dam projects reduces state authority over major rivers. Potentially large federal water rights concern some western officials who worry that the U.S. government could take water from existing users for its own purposes. Even if the federal government applies for water under state laws, "you can't turn the federal government down, because they're federal," Babbitt pointed out. "And they always have the option of eminent domain" to condemn water for public purposes. [43]

In addition to coal and oil-shale projects, western states have been alarmed by federal plans to devote their public lands to toxic dumps, nuclear waste disposal sites, and controversial MX missile storage. Recent court decisions also have strengthened federal authority to manage public lands over state objections. Ruling in 1976 that federal law protecting wild horses and burros on public lands pre-empted state authority over wildlife (*Kleppe v. New Mexico*), the U.S. Supreme Court expanded earlier decisions that "the power over the public land thus entrusted to Congress is without limitations." [44] In 1980 the Supreme Court upheld a 1979 U.S. Court of Appeals decision (*Ventura County v. Gulf Oil Corp.*) that exempted oil company drilling on federal lands from a California county's zoning ordinance.

Congress in the 1970s directed the Forest Service and BLM to consult western leaders in drawing up comprehensive land-use plans for managing federal resources. The National Forest Management Act (NFMA) and Federal Land Policy and Management Act (FLPMA), both passed in 1976, carried extensive requirements for involving state and local officials at different stages of the planning process. WESTPO governors, notably Babbitt, have called for stronger legislation requiring federal decisions to be consistent with state land-use policies.

"The current language is sufficiently vague that I think any judge would probably be satisfied by a phone call" from federal to state officials, Babbitt commented. Babbitt suggested that Congress could pass legislation writing into law requirements for joint federal-state decision making — for instance, by Interior's regional coal-leasing teams. "You want to try to structure a process which does not put a given decision into endless litigation or back into the United States Congress," the governor added.[45]

Interior officials maintained that existing law and department regulations gave western states and local governments a sufficient role in shaping national land policies. "What the governors would really like is to run BLM in their states," Carruthers remarked in 1983. Watt's policies "appropriately addressed state and local concerns, but we still have to consider the national interest."[46]

Continuing Public Land Issues

This struggle to balance national with regional interests will continue to challenge the federal government. As the nation's population kept growing — and shifting to western states — the government also will be faced with difficult choices between developing the nation's resources for economic use and preserving public lands for future generations. Watt's stormy two-and-one-half year tenure as interior secretary focused national attention on those tensions resulting from federal resource policy.

Watt resigned the Interior post on Oct. 9, 1983. Three weeks earlier, calls for his dismissal had mounted after the secretary told a Washington,

D.C., audience that the department's advisory commission on coal-leasing policy had "every kind of mixture. . . . I have a black. I have a woman, two Jews, and a cripple." Similar off-the-cuff remarks had offended other groups, including American Indians, environmentalists, and even rock-music fans, making Watt a political liability for Republicans, even in the West.

Watt, in his letter of resignation, insisted that his campaign to speed federal resource development had left behind "a legacy that will aid Americans in the decades ahead." Conservative Republicans, especially in the West, concurred that Watt's determined, if abrasive, management of the Interior Department had brought a necessary shift away from the Carter administration's environmental protection emphasis back to the department's traditional resource development mission.

President Reagan on Oct. 13, 1983, nominated William P. Clark, previously his national security advisor, to replace Watt as interior secretary. The nomination of Clark, a long-time Reagan friend and political advisor, underscored the growing importance that the administration placed on federal land resource issues. Environmentalists initially criticized the appointment because Clark had no previous experience in managing natural resources, but Western conservatives endorsed the selection of a California native from a fourth-generation ranching family. Observers expected Clark to continue Watt's general policies but to take a more conciliatory stance toward Congress and environmental groups as the 1984 elections approached.

But further controversies were expected to arise as Interior and Forest Service officials made day-to-day decisions on producing public resources or protecting public lands. Environmental groups, stung by Watt's frequent attacks on their motives, have taken harder stances as public opposition mounted to the Reagan administration's coal leasing, offshore oil and gas, and wilderness development policies. "I'm concerned about what Reagan and Watt are going to do to the tenor of government resource management debates in the next 10 or 15 years," Brant Calkin, then the Sierra Club's Southwest director, had said in 1981. "The provocation of this kind of administration may not go away."[47] In 1983 Calkin was appointed secretary of the New Mexico Department of Natural Resources.

Many observers cautioned that a backlash against Watt's policies could carry federal resource management too far in the other direction. Even among energy company officials who supported accelerated federal coal leasing, "certainly there are thoughtful people who are agreed that what the secretary is doing is just setting up another wild policy swing," Frank Gregg, the Carter administration's BLM director, suggested during 1983 controversies over Watt's leasing program. After Watt departs, Gregg went on, "the new secretary will be under immense pressure to put in a very rigid system" for leasing federally owned resources.[48]

The reaction against Watt's programs, in addition to strengthening environmental groups' political power, could confirm the American people's commitment to keeping public land and resources under federal government control. Whatever the consequences, Watt's tenure at least forced Congress and the nation to address some fundamental questions about what the country should do with its vast and rich heritage of federal lands.

Notes

1. Kent A. Price, "Introduction and Overview," *Regional Conflict and National Policy,* ed. Kent A. Price (Washington, D.C.: Resources for the Future, 1982), 4-5.
2. Colorado Gov. Richard D. Lamm, *Energy Activities in the West* (Address to Western Governors' Policy Office annual meeting, Sept. 3-6, 1980, Park City, Utah).
3. Andy Plattner, "Severance Taxes on Energy Seen Widening Gap Between Rich, Poorer Areas of Nation," *Congressional Quarterly Weekly Report,* Feb. 20, 1982, 317.
4. Utah Gov. Scott Matheson, D, 1980 telephone interview with author.
5. Peter Rogers, "The Future of Water," *Atlantic Monthly,* July 1983, 86.
6. Kenneth D. Frederick, "Water Supplies," in *Current Issues in Natural Resource Policy,* ed. Paul R. Portney (Washington, D.C.: Resources for the Future, 1982), 222.
7. Rogers, "The Future of Water," 83.
8. "Coast to Coast — Water Becomes a Big Worry," *U.S. News & World Report,* Sept. 6, 1976, 27.
9. John Hamer, "World Weather Trends," in *Editorial Research Reports, Vol. II, 1974* (Washington, D.C.: Congressional Quarterly, 1975), 517-588.
10. Leo F. LaPorte, *Encounter With the Earth: Resources* (San Francisco: Canfield Press, 1975), 83.
11. Walter Prescott Webb, "The American West — Perpetual Mirage," *Harper's,* May 1957, 25.
12. Brant Calkin, Sierra Club national president, 1976 interview with author.
13. *Congress and the Nation,* 5 vols., *Congress and the Nation: 1945-64,* vol. 1 (Washington, D.C.: Congressional Quarterly, 1965), 771.
14. Rogers, "The Future of Water,", 87-88.
15. Richard C. Berkman and W. Kip Viscusi, *Damming the West, Ralph Nader Study Group Report on the Bureau of Reclamation* (New York: Grossman Publishers, 1973); National Water Commission, *Water Policies for the Future — Final Report to the President and to the Congress, June 14, 1973* (Washington, D.C.: Government Printing Office).

16. Frederick, "Water Supplies," 243.
17. Ibid., 244.
18. Ibid.
19. Georg Borgstrom, *Too Many: An Ecological Overview of the Earth's Limitations* (New York: Macmillan, 1969), 169.
20. Joseph A. Davis, "Water Projects Await Funding As Debate Over Cost Sharing Stalls Action on Capitol Hill," *Congressional Quarterly Weekly Report,* July 30, 1983, 1551.
21. *Congress and the Nation, 1977-80,* vol. 5 (Washington, D.C.: Congressional Quarterly, 1981), 534, 541.
22. James G. Watt, secretary of the interior (Remarks before the National Water Resources Association meeting, Albuquerque, N.M., Nov. 2, 1981).
23. Davis, "Water Projects," 1553-54.
24. Ibid., 1553.
25. Garrey E. Carruthers, assistant secretary of the interior for land and water resources, Sept. 7, 1983, interview with author.
26. S. E. Reynolds, New Mexico state engineer (Statement presented before President Jimmy Carter's Water Policy Study hearing, Denver, Colo., July 28-29, 1977).
27. Colorado Gov. Richard D. Lamm, D, Dec. 23, 1979, telephone interview with author.
28. Davis, "Water Projects," 1550.
29. Utah Gov. Scott Matheson, "The West and the Eighties," (Address to Western Governors' Policy Office, annual meeting, Park City, Utah, Sept. 3-6, 1980).
30. "How the West Is One," *Republic Scene,* February 1981, 46.
31. Plattner, "Severance Taxes on Energy," 319.
32. U.S. Department of the Interior, Office of Policy Analysis, *Past and Projected State Revenues from Energy and Other Natural Resources in 13 Western States, Background Report* (Washington, D.C.: Government Printing Office, 1981).
33. Plattner, "Severance Taxes on Energy," 318.
34. "War Between the States," *Time,* Aug. 24, 1981, 19.
35. Ibid., 19.
36. Hans H. Landsberg, "Energy 'Haves' and 'Have-Nots,'" in *Regional Conflict and National Policy,* ed. Kent A. Price, 44.
37. U.S. Interior Department, *Past and Projected State Revenues from Energy.*
38. Ibid.
39. Jim Monaghan, aide to Colorado Gov. Richard D. Lamm, D, 1980 interview with author.
40. Gene M. Gressley, "Regionalism and the Twentieth Century West," in *The American West, New Perspectives, New Dimensions,* ed. Jerome O. Steffen (Norman, Okla.: University of Oklahoma Press, 1979), 197.
41. Neal R. Peirce and Jerry Hagstrom, "Western Governors Seek Stronger Voice Over Energy Policy for their Region," *National Journal,* Oct. 13, 1979, 1692.
42. Matheson, 1979 telephone interview with author.
43. Arizona Gov. Bruce Babbitt, D, March 19, 1983, interview with author.
44. *Kleppe v. New Mexico.*
45. Babbitt, March 19, 1983, interview with author.

46. Carruthers, July 6, 1983, telephone interview with author.
47. Brant Calkin, Sierra Club Southwest director, July 31, 1981, interview with author.
48. Frank Gregg, former Bureau of Land Management director, July 8, 1983, telephone interview with author.

SELECTED BIBLIOGRAPHY

Articles

Baden, John A. "The Environmental Impact of Government Policies." *Policy Report*, February 1982, 1.

"Battle Over the Wilderness." *Newsweek*, July 25, 1983, 25.

Brammer, Dana B. "Water Resource Management: A Challenge for the States." *Public Administration Survey*, Autumn 1982, 1-4.

Burroughs, R. H. "OCS Oil and Gas: Relationships Between Resource Management and Environmental Research." *Coastal Zone Management Journal*, 1 (1981): 77-88.

Carruthers, Ian, and Ray Stoner. "A Legal Framework in the Public Interest (Equitable Allocation of Irrigation Water From Large Ground Water Projects)." *Ceres*, September/October 1982, 15-20.

Clawson, Marion. "The National Forests." *Science*, Feb. 20, 1976, 762-767.

"Controversy Over Wilderness Areas Minerals Policy: Pro and Con." *Congressional Digest*, December 1982, 289-314.

Cortner, Hanna J., and Dennis L. Schweitzer. "Institutional Limits to National Public Planning for Forest Resources: The Resources Planning Act." *National Pressures Journal*, April 1981, 204.

Crow, Patrick. "Interior Secretary Watt Defends OCS Leasing Plan in Courts, Congress." *Oil and Gas Journal*, June 20, 1983, 57.

Davis, Joseph A. "Wilderness Issues Erupting Again in Congress." *Congressional Quarterly Weekly Report*, Feb. 12, 1983, 355.

Dobra, John L., and George A. Unimchuck. "Property Rights, Legal Efficiency and the Political Economy of the Sagebrush Rebellion." *Nevada Review of Business and Economics*, Winter 1981/1982, 2-12.

Drew, Elizabeth. "Secretary Watt." *New Yorker*, May 4, 1981, 104.

Ferrett, Robert L., and Robert Ward. "Agricultural Land Use Planning and Ground Water Quality (Effects of Various Chemicals on Water Quality Includes a Summary of Federal and State Legislative Actions Directed Toward Protecting Groundwater Resources)." *Growth and Change*, January 1983, 32-39.

Frederick, Kenneth D. "The Future of Western Irrigation." *Southwestern Resource Management and Economics,* Spring 1981, 19-33.

Hamer, John. "Forest Policy." In *Editorial Research Reports,* vol. 2, 1975. Washington, D.C.: Congressional Quarterly, 1976.

Helford, Gloria E., and Peter M. Emerson. "Timber Supply, Community Stability and the Wilderness Scapegoat." *Western Wildlands,* Winter 1983, 14.

"How Interior Plans to 'Unlock' Public Lands." *Business Week,* March 23, 1981, 84.

Jaroslovsky, Rich. "Reagan's Drive to Open More Public Lands to Energy Firms May Spark Major Battles." *Wall Street Journal,* April 1, 1981.

Lenard, Thomas M. "Wasting Our National Forests: How to Get Less Timber and Less Wilderness at the Same Time." *Regulation,* July/August 1981, 29-36.

Leshy, John D. "Wilderness and Its Discontents — Wilderness Review Comes to the Public Lands." *Arizona State Law Journal,* 2 (1981): 361-446.

McGreggor, Cawley R. "Changes in Federal-State Relations: The Sagebrush Rebellion (Issues Underlying Recent Claims by Nevada, Arizona, New Mexico, Utah, and Wyoming to Federal Public Lands Within Their Boundaries, Particularly Increasing Environmental Protection Values in Federal Land Management Decisions)." *Southwestern Resource Management and Economics,* Summer 1982, 1-12.

Mollison, Richard M. "The Sagebrush Rebellion: Its Causes and Effects." *Environmental Comment,* June 1981, 411.

Mosher, Lawrence. "Wilderness System Is Under Siege by Oil, Gas, Mineral, and Timber Interests." *National Journal,* Nov. 21, 1981, 2076-2080.

Nelson, Gaylord. "Oil and Gas in Wilderness: Not Necessary." *National Journal,* Feb. 13, 1982, 309.

Noble, Heather. "Oil and Gas Leasing on Public Lands: NEPA (National Environmental Policy Act) Gets Lost in the Shuffle." *Harvard Environmental Law Review,* 1 (1982): 117-158.

Novak, Eva. "Mining and the National Park System." *Journal of Energy Law and Policy,* 2 (1983), 165-179.

Parry, Thomas B., Henry J. Vauz, and Nicholas Dennis. "Changing Conceptions of Sustained-Yield Policy on the National Forests." *Journal of Forestry,* March 1983, 150.

Rasnik, Carol D. "The Conflict Between the Environmentalists and the Surface Mining Industry: Federal Legislation and Litigation." *Northern Kentucky Law Review*, 3 (1982): 427-444.

Riggs, Cynthia. "Petroleum in the U.S. Energy Future." *Antioch Review*, Spring 1982, 219-224.

Sander, William. "Federal Water Resources Policy and Decision Making: Their Formulation Is Essentially a Political Process Conditioned by Government Structure and Needs." *American Journal of Economics and Sociology*, January 1983, 1-12.

Schroth, Peter W. "The Impact of Environmentalism on Land-Use Control." *American Journal of Comparative Law*, 30 (1982): 491-513.

Shanks, Bernard. "BLM Back in the Spotlight After Years of Neglect." *High Country News* (Lander, Wyo.), Jan. 26, 1979.

Stegner, Wallace. "Land: America's History Teacher." *Living Wilderness*, Summer 1981, 5.

Stewart, Richard B. "Interstate Resource Conflicts: The Role of the Federal Courts." *Harvard Environmental Law Review*, 2 (1982): 241-264.

Thompson, James G., and Audie L. Blevins. "Attitudes Toward Energy Development in the Northern Great Plains." *Rural Sociology*, Spring 1983, 148-158.

"Water and Energy." *State Government*, 4 (1982): 111-138.

"Western Coal: The New Energy Frontier." *Journal of Commerce*, Sept. 16, 1981, 1c-4c.

Books

Alston, Richard M. *The Individual vs. the Public Interest: Political Ideology and National Forest Policy*. Boulder, Colo.: Westview Press, 1983.

Arrandale, Tom. "Access to Federal Lands." In *Editorial Research Reports*, vol. 2, 1981. Washington, D.C.: Congressional Quarterly, 1982.

Arrandale, Tom. "Western Oil Boom." In *Editorial Research Reports*, vol. 1, 1981. Washington, D.C.: Congressional Quarterly, 1981.

Baden, John A. *The Environmental Impact of Government Policies, Policy Report*. Washington, D.C.: Cato Institute, 1982.

Barlow, Thomas J., Gloria E. Helfand, Trent W. Orr, and Thomas B. Stoel, Jr. *Giving Away the National Forests, An Analysis of U.S. Forest Service Timber Sales Below Cost*. Washington, D.C.: Natural Resources Defense Council, 1980.

Boorstin, Daniel K. *The Americans, the Democratic Experience.* New York: Vintage Books, 1965.

Boschken, Herman L. *Land Use Conflicts: Organizational Design and Resource Management.* Urbana: University of Illinois Press, 1982.

Church, Arthur M. *Conflicts Over Resource Ownership: The Use of Public Policy By Private Interests.* Lexington, Mass.: Lexington Books, 1982.

Clawson, Marion. *Forests For Whom and For What?* Washington, D.C.: Resources for the Future, 1975.

Coggins, George Cameron, and Charles F. Wilkinson. *Federal Public Land and Resources Law.* Mineola, N.Y.: Foundation Press, 1981.

Congress and the Nation. Vol. 1, *Congress and the Nation, 1945-1964.* Washington, D.C.: Congressional Quarterly, 1965.

Culhane, Paul J. *Public Land Politics: Interest Group Influences on the Forest Service and the Bureau of Land Management.* Washington, D.C.: Resources for the Future, 1981.

Dana, Samuel T., and Sally K. Fairfax. *Forest and Range Management.* New York: McGraw-Hill, 1980.

Dowdle, Barney. "An Institutional Dinosaur With an Ace: Or, How to Piddle Away Public Timber Wealth and Foul the Environment in the Process." In *Bureaucracy vs. Environment.* Edited by John Baden and Richard L. Stroup. Ann Arbor: University of Michigan Press, 1981.

Everhart, William C. *The National Park Service.* Boulder, Colo.: Westview Press, 1983.

Fisher, Anthony C. *Resource and Environmental Economics.* New York: Cambridge University Press, 1981.

Gordon, Richard L. *Federal Coal Leasing Policy: Competition in the Energy Industries.* Washington, D.C.: American Enterprise Institute, 1981.

Hyde, William F. "Compounding Clear-Cuts: The Social Failures of Public Timber Management in the Rockies." In *Bureaucracy vs. Environment.* Edited by John Baden and Richard L. Stroup. Ann Arbor: University of Michigan Press, 1981.

———. *Timber Supply, Land Allocation, and Economic Efficiency.* Washington, D.C.: Resources for the Future, 1980.

Lake, Laura M. *Environmental Regulation: The Political Effect of Implementation.* New York: Praeger Publishing, 1982.

Lamm, Richard D., and Michael McCarthy. *The Angry West: A Vulnerable Land and Its Future.* Boston: Houghton Mifflin, 1982.

Little, Dennis L., ed. *Renewable Natural Resources: A Management Handbook for the Eighties.* Boulder, Colo.: Westview Press, 1982.

Meyers, Robert A., ed. *Handbook of Technology and Economics.* New York: John Wiley & Sons, 1983.

Nash, Roderick. *Wilderness and the American Mind,* 3d ed. New Haven, Conn.: Yale University Press, 1982.

Nelson, Robert H. "The Public Lands." In *Current Issues in Natural Resource Policy.* Edited by Paul R. Portney. Washington, D.C.: Resources for the Future, 1982.

Perelman, L. J., ed. "Ascent of Oil: The Transition from Coal to Oil in Early Twentieth-Century America." In *Energy Transitions: Long Term Perspectives.* Boulder, Colo.: Westview Press, 1981.

Perelman, L. J., A. W. Giebelhaus and M. D. Yokell, eds. *Energy Transitions: Long-Term Perspectives.* Boulder, Colo.: Westview Press, 1981.

Portney, Paul R., ed. *Current Issues in Natural Resource Policy.* Washington, D.C.: Resources for the Future, 1982.

Price, Kent A. *Regional Conflict and National Policy.* Washington, D.C.: Resources for the Future, 1982.

Regens, James L., ed. *Energy and the Western United States: Politics and Development.* New York: Praeger Publishers, 1982.

Shands, William E., and Robert G. Healy. *The Lands Nobody Wanted.* Washington, D.C.: The Conservation Foundation, 1977.

Smith, V. Kerry, and John V. Krutilla, eds. *Explorations in Natural Resource Economics.* Baltimore: Johns Hopkins University Press, 1982.

Stephenson, Richard M. *Living With Tomorrow: A Factual Look at America's Resources.* New York: John Wiley & Sons, 1981.

Tiratsoo, E. N. *Oilfields of the World.* Beaconsfield, England: Scientific Press, 1973.

Udall, Stewart L. *The Quiet Crisis.* New York: Holt, Rinehart & Winston, 1963.

Watt, Kenneth E. F. *Understanding the Environment.* Rockleigh, N.J.: Allyn & Bacon, 1982.

Webb, Walter Prescott. *The Great Plains.* New York: Grosset & Dunlap, 1981.

Weimer, David Leo. *The Strategic Petroleum Reserve: Planning Implementation and Analysis.* Westport, Conn.: Greenwood Press, 1982.

Young, Oran R. *Natural Resources and the State: The Political Economy of Resource Management.* Berkeley: University of California Press, 1982.

Government Documents

Information Resources in the U.S.A. on New and Renewable Energy; A Description and Directory. Oak Ridge, Tenn.: U.S. Energy Department, Technical Information Center, 1981.

Public Land Law Review Commission. *One Third of the Nation's Land, A Report to the President and the Congress by the Public Land Law Review Commission.* Washington, D.C.: Government Printing Office, 1970.

U.S. Agriculture Department. Economics Research Service. *Northern Great Plains Coal Mining: Regional Impacts.* Washington, D.C.: Government Printing Office, 1982.

———. *Coal Development in Rural America: The Resources at Risk. (Rural Development Research Report, no. 29).* Washington, D.C.: Government Printing Office, 1981.

U.S. Agriculture Department. Forest Service. *Alternative Goals: 1985 Resources Planning Act Program. December 1981.* Washington, D.C.: Government Printing Office, 1982.

———. *An Analysis of the Timber Situation in the United States 1952-2030.* Washington, D.C.: Government Printing Office, 1982.

———. *An Assessment of the Forest and Rangeland Situation in the United States. October 1981.* Washington, D.C.: Government Printing Office, 1981.

———. *Draft Environmental Impact Statement, Deschutes National Forest.* Washington, D.C.: Government Printing Office.

———. *Draft Environmental Impact Statement, Klamath National Forest.* Washington, D.C.: Government Printing Office.

———. *Principles of Land and Resource Management Planning.* Washington, D.C.: Government Printing Office, 1982.

———. *A Recommended Renewable Resources Program — 1980.* Washington, D.C.: Government Printing Office.

———. *Report of the Forest Service, Fiscal Year 1982.* Washington, D.C.: Government Printing Office, 1983.

U.S. Army Corps of Engineers. Office of the Chief of Engineers. *Shaping Environmental Awareness: The United States Army Corps of Engineers Environmental Advisory Board, 1970-1980.* Washington, D.C.: Government Printing Office, 1983.

U.S. Congress. Joint Economic Committee. *Coal as a Catalyst in America's Revitalization. Hearing, Jan. 13, 1982.* 97th Cong., 2d sess.

———. Subcommittee on International Trade, Finance, and Security Economics. *Natural Gas Deregulation. Hearing, Feb. 18, 1982.*

U.S. Congress. General Accounting Office. *Actions Needed to Increase Federal Onshore Oil and Gas Exploration and Development.* Washington, D.C.: Government Printing Office, 1981.

———. *Analysis of the Powder River Basin Federal Coal Lease Sale: Economic Valuation Improvements and Legislative Changes Needed.* Washington, D.C.: Government Printing Office, 1983.

U.S. Congress. House. Committee on Agriculture. Subcommittee on Department Operations, Research and Foreign Agriculture. *Natural Resources Data Bases. Hearing, June 2, 1981.* 97th Cong., 1st sess.

U.S. Congress. House. Committee on Science and Technology. Subcommittee on Energy Development and Applications. *Coal Research. Hearings, May 18-Sept. 16, 1982.* 97th Cong., 2d. sess.

U.S. Congress. Office of Technology Assessment. *An Assessment of Development and Production of Federal Coal Leases: Summary. November 1981.* 97th Cong., 1st sess.

———. *Impacts of Technology on U.S. Cropland and Rangeland Productivity.* 98th Cong., 1st sess.

———. *Management of Fuel and Nonfuel Minerals in Federal Land.* 96th Cong., 1st sess.

U.S. Energy Department. *The Use of Federal Lands for Energy Development.* Prepared by Edward Porter as Vol. 8 of Energy Policy Study. Washington, D.C.: Government Printing Office, 1980.

U.S. Interior Department. Bureau of Land Management. *Final Environmental Statement, Federal Coal Management Program.* Washington, D.C.: Government Printing Office, 1979.

———. *Managing the Nation's Public Lands.* Washington, D.C.: Government Printing Office, 1983.

———. *Public Land Statistics, 1981.* Washington, D.C.: Government Printing Office, 1982.

———. *Public Land Statistics, 1982.* Washington, D.C.: Government Printing Office, 1983.

———. *Wyoming Land Use Decisions, Seven Lakes Area.* Washington, D.C.: Government Printing Office, 1978.

U.S. Interior Department. Fish and Wildlife Service. *Annual Report of Lands Under Control of the U.S. Fish and Wildlife Service as of Sept. 30. 1982.* Washington, D.C.: Government Printing Office.

U.S. Interior Department. Office of Policy Analysis. *Past and Projected State Revenues from Energy and Other Natural Resources in 13 Western States.* Washington, D.C.: Government Printing Office, 1981.

———. *Timber Harvest Policy Issues on the O & C Lands.* Washington, D.C.: Government Printing Office, 1977.

U.S. Senate. Committee on Energy and Natural Resources. Subcommittee on Energy and Minerals Resources. *Implementation of the Surface Mining Control and Reclamation Act of 1977. Hearing, Sept. 2, 1981.* 97th Cong., 1st sess.

———. *The President's National Materials and Minerals Program and Report to Congress. Hearing, June 29, 1982.* 97th Cong., 2d sess.

INDEX

A

Agriculture Department. (*See also* Forest Service, U.S.)
History - 29, 31, 32
Soil Conservation Service - 194
Alaskan public land
Federal land ownership - 35, 39, 42, 43 (map), 47 (chart)
Offshore resources - 106, 111, 112, 114
Oil/gas exploration - 120
Wilderness areas - 41, 44
Allotment Management Plans (AMPs) - 69, 163
American Mining Congress - 181
Andrus, Cecil D.
Energy resource leasing - 80, 87, 92, 108, 111-112, 211
Environmentalism - 72
Arizona v. California - 189
Army Corps of Engineers - 192, 194, 195
Aspinall, Wayne N, (D-Colo.)
Colorado River dams - 52, 53, 196
Election defeat, 1972 - 54
Public Land Law Review Commission - 54, 68
Wilderness uses - 60

B

Babbitt, Bruce - 2, 5, 201, 211, 212
Behan, R. W. - 64
Bitterroot National Forest - 61
Bob Marshall Wilderness - 125
Brown, Edmund G. "Jerry" Jr. - 112
Bumpers, Dale (D-Ark.) - 186, 204, 208
Bureau of Land Management (BLM)
Authority - 38, 65, 68-69, 71
Coal leasing - 91-92, 96
Grazing reduction - 155-156, 162-168

Grazing regulation - 68-71, 158-161
History - 65-66, 72-75
Holdings - 42, 158
Image - 48, 65
Multiple-use decisions - 51, 54-58, 68, 71
Offshore leasing - 109-110
Oil/gas leasing - 115, 118-120
Payments to states - 209-210
Public land sales, exchanges (box) - 200-201
Revenues - 67 (chart)
Timber management - 132, 139
Bureau of Reclamation - 40-41, 49, 194-197
Burford, Robert L. - 74, 167
Burgess, Philip M. - 86
Burros, wild - 157 (box), 211
Byrne, Brendan - 206

C

California
Offshore oil leasing - 108-114
Roadless area development - 149
Santa Maria Basin - 108-114
Calkin, Brant - 116, 126, 166, 213
Capitan Wilderness - 124
Carruthers, Garrey E.
Coal policies - 80, 88, 93, 96
Grazing policies - 167
Water projects - 200-202
Watt's achievements - 10-11
Western interests - 212
Wilderness exploration - 125
Carter, Jimmy
Environmentalism - 72
RARE II - 149
Synthetic fuel - 95
Timber harvests - 139
Water projects - 9, 72, 188-189
Cascade Mountains - 132, 148

225